PIETY

CANADA'S TOMORROW

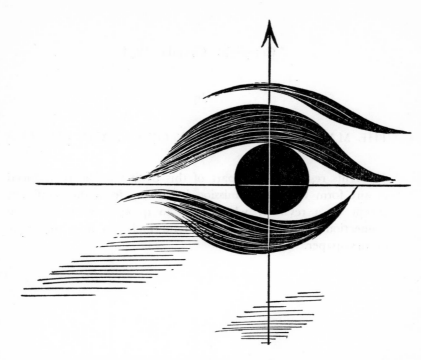

CANADA'S TOMORROW

PAPERS AND DISCUSSION
CANADA'S TOMORROW CONFERENCE
QUEBEC CITY, NOVEMBER 1953

Edited by G. P. GILMOUR
Illustrations by Eric Aldwinckle

TORONTO · MACMILLAN · 1954

PREFACE

This book grows out of a Conference on "Canada's Tomorrow", held in Quebec on November 13 and 14, 1953. That stimulating gathering, attended by nearly three hundred representative Canadians, was an experiment in national self-examination and in sober prophecy. If forecast was in the end subordinated to analysis, there was substantial gain, since insubstantial prophecy might be dismissed as visionary, whereas objective appraisal provides a solid foundation for advance. The resultant volume contains the papers prepared for the meetings, plus a digest of the discussion, which, although severely limited as to time, indicated disagreement as to some facts and inferences, and showed that the last word has certainly not been said. It is hoped that the discussion thus modestly begun will continue as the papers are more widely read.

The Conference and the book, in turn, grew out of an idea born many months ago in the minds of officials of The Canadian Westinghouse Company, Limited, in Hamilton, Ontario, who

wished the Company's 1953 observance of the Golden Jubilee
of its formation in Canada in 1903 to include a survey and
an anticipation of the life of the nation in which the Company
continues to be a leading factor. If the Canada of 2003 could
be envisaged in broad terms, the result, it was thought, would
be stimulating, and the Company would do something to advance
and to safeguard the interests of the entire country. This idea,
new in Canada, was put forward also as a token of the increasing
sense of social responsibility felt by a great industry.

The idea was handed over, for translation into tangible
expression, to a Committee, composed of the following: G. P.
Gilmour (Chairman), President and Vice-Chancellor, McMaster
University; Leonard G. Gillett, Vice-President and General
Manager, The Bank of Toronto; F. C. A. Jeanneret, Princi-
pal of University College, University of Toronto; Maurice
Lamontagne, Chairman, Department of Economics, Laval
University; D. A. MacGibbon, Professor of Political Economy,
McMaster University; C. J. Mackenzie, President, Atomic
Energy of Canada, Limited; W. A. Mackintosh, Principal
and Vice-Chancellor, Queen's University; H. H. Rogge, Presi-
dent, Canadian Westinghouse Company Limited; B. K. Sand-
well, journalist; E. W. R. Steacie, President, National Research
Council; R. K. Stratford, Scientific Adviser, Imperial Oil
Limited, President of the Research Council of Ontario; R. C.
Wallace, former Principal of Queen's University.

To this Committee were added its efficient and hard-working
Secretary, D. G. Seldon, of the Westinghouse Company; G. E.
Pendray, of New York; Eric M. Coles, a Westinghouse Vice-
President; Hunter MacBain, Assistant to the President; and
C. W. Hale, Manager of Public Relations for the Company.
My own secretary, Miss Jean Montgomery, has been close to
the project throughout.

On behalf of the Committee, I express appreciation of the
generous interest of the Company, and particularly of the con-

fidence shown by Dr. Herbert H. Rogge, its President, who insisted that the Committee must have a free hand. To him for his constant and intelligent interest, despite the self-denying ordinance by which he bound himself, everyone is deeply indebted; and to his provision of expert help from Company officers much of the success of the Conference was due.

G. P. GILMOUR

Hamilton, Ontario
November, 1953

CONTENTS

PREFACE

INTRODUCTION
      GEORGE PEEL GILMOUR   1

THE CANADIAN PEOPLE
      BERNARD KEBLE SANDWELL   11

CANADA'S NATURAL RESOURCES
      MAXWELL WEIR MACKENZIE   35

THE CHALLENGE TO SCIENCE
      REGINALD KILLMASTER STRATFORD   65

THE CONTRIBUTION OF INDUSTRY
      DOUGLAS WHITE AMBRIDGE   93

THE ROLE OF GOVERNMENT
      MAURICE LAMONTAGNE   117

THE CHALLENGE TO EDUCATION
      NORMAN A. M. MACKENZIE   153

CULTURAL EVOLUTION
      HILDA NEATBY   185

CANADA IN THE WORLD
      DONALD GRANT CREIGHTON   225

AN OUTSIDER LOOKING IN
      DENIS WILLIAM BROGAN   255

DIGEST OF DISCUSSION   287

CANADA'S TOMORROW

INTRODUCTION

George Peel Gilmour

M.A., D.D., D.C.L., LL.D.
Chairman, "Canada's Tomorrow" Conference, 1953; President and Vice-Chancellor, McMaster University; President, Canadian Council of Churches, 1946-48; President, National Conference of Canadian Universities, 1951-52.

INTRODUCTION

No man can say what shall be, and none would choose to know beforehand exactly what the future holds for him or for his country: but serious men must ponder on what may be and should be, since we must prepare for the future, and go out to meet it armed with physical and moral resources. To many nations, the next fifty years will present problems of survival and of unity, of needed changes in institutions or traditions: but to Canada the next half-century presents a happier prospect, of a people greatly blessed with goods and resources, as yet unspoiled by power or riches, with a record of representative government remarkably free from corruption, and with habits of honesty and decency of inestimable value. If it is not given to us to map the future, we can at least get a running start into it by discovering where we are and by what stages we have come thus far, and by gaining a sense of direction and an awareness of possible dangers.

We are not yet a reading people in the best sense, a thoughtful

3

people who have contributed richly to the world's philosophy, theology and political theories. But we are a people mature enough to indulge in self-examination; we are more self-conscious as a nation than we would have thought possible in 1903, and other people no longer take us for granted. But when they want to know more about us, they find us busy learning more about ourselves. The essays in this book represent one attempt at self-knowledge, self-discipline and self-direction.

Much is said here, but more is left unsaid. It is unsaid in some cases because there is neither time nor need to present such things as catalogues of quantities and percentages, man-hours and relative rewards, investment figures and legal respon-sibilities not yet clear or not yet assumed. There is nothing here about the British North America Act or the fact that labour unions have scarcely begun to take or accept full legal and corporate form. But much is unsaid also because the serious-ness and profundity of certain themes make them baffling, and unprofitable except they be clarified by a prophetic voice. On some of these the silence is scarcely broken, not because they are not vital but because they are all-embracing. One can easily defend the omission of references to the exact future of agriculture or to the changing status of women, because these are subdivisions of topics that are explored in broad principle, and eight or nine topics must be somewhat arbitrarily chosen: but one cannot so easily defend a presentation that takes too little notice of the chief asset and the chief danger of a people, their spiritual resources, their faith, their charity.

Let it be said at once, then, that those who participated in making this book are conscious that, beyond the problems set by the physical framework and the political and economic institutions of this nation, there is the problem of man himself. We are not believers in inevitable progress, or in the power of education and ease to subdue the evil that has tainted all men and all societies. We know that there are hazards and limitations inherent in human nature, and that the problem is not that man is not strong enough or clever enough, but that he is not good enough. Beyond the Canadian land is the Canadian soul. The land is before us, the soul within us; and the latter gives us more furiously to think.

We have a promising future. Ernest Watkins recently expressed it over the BBC thus: "Canada grew into freedom naturally, as a child grows up. Canada is the one country in the Americas of European stock which has become a nation without fear of Europe, without resentment against Europe. I think she may carry the torch lit by Europe further than any other country."

James Thomson, writing his part of the *Masque of Alfred* in 1740, could declaim about Britannia, with deistic confidence and considerable self-congratulation,

> "The nations, not so blest as thee,
>   Must in their turns to tyrants fall;
>   While thou shalt flourish great and free,
>   The dread and envy of them all."

That was two centuries ago, and we no longer sing it. It has become too clear that a nation that arouses dread and envy circulates deadly poisons in the veins of the world. And as for rejoicing that others will fall prey to tyrants, we now know that no nation can flourish if tyrants rule its neighbours. Napoleon, Hitler and the rest have come and gone since 1740, but their rise and fall has not left the free world flourishing and secure. Yet circumstances are now such that one might adapt Thomson's words, if not his metre, to say of Canada,

> "Great and free, thou hast just begun,
>   The envy of all, but the dread of none."

We are envied, yet we do not appear dreadful to anyone. It is an unprecedented combination, the more so because the envy

is without sting as yet. Other people look on us with friendly
rather than malicious eyes as a most favoured nation whose
history, circumstances and temperament are still without hint
of aggression or dangerous design. They seem to be actually
pleased that things are at last going well with us, and to hope
that we will not spoil our future or worsen theirs by repeating
the mistakes of older nations or misusing our heritage. We
are no powder-keg that men eye askance lest it touch off a
world explosion. We sing of ourselves as "the true north
strong and free", and no man is offended or afraid.

Yet we ourselves are not free from dread. It is not dread
of invasion or destruction, since we all take for granted that
Canada will have a tomorrow, will exist fifty years from now,
neither flying apart because of internal stresses nor being reduced from its national status; nor can we bring ourselves to
believe that secrets wrested from the atom will blot us out.
It is rather the dread that is born of the dangers and inade-
quacies we feel within ourselves, when we consider our physical
immensity (one might call us geographically a monstrosity),
our peculiar population distribution that greater numbers will
not basically alter, the high overhead expense of running a nation
whose history is at war with its geography, cleavages between
our various parts and cultures that time and mutual sympathy
have not yet closed, our vulnerability because of inevitable dependence on foreign trade, our proximity to a great neighbour
whose very friendliness and resemblances pose problems, whether
of cultural and economic colonialism, of internationally uniform
wage-scales or of divergent political habits and tariff policies.
If we are the envy of the world, we have no overweening
self-confidence; and we indulge in no Utopian dreams, knowing that Utopias are usually dreadful and unreal, whether they
be built on the pessimism of a Wells, a Huxley or a Foster,
dominated by scheming aristocracies or a soulless Machine, or
on the materialistic determinism and amoral egalitarianism

of a Marxist dream that has so far produced more tears than
joy. We are not in these papers, therefore, treated to dreams
or nightmares, but to a sober examination of our strength and
weakness, the assumption being that our institutions are intrinsically sound and that our bitterness can be relieved by mutual
forbearance and by enlightened self-interest, plus considerations
more evangelical.

We know enough about ourselves to realize that there are
obstacles to our progress, geographical, cultural, economic and
international: too much space and too few people, and those
people now in a national adolescence that makes us feel
awkward and unsure of ourselves, not too confident of our
standards, eager to laugh at ourselves lest others smile. Yet
we know that we are free from most of the obstacles that hinder
others: we have no insoluble problems of race and colour, no
long memories of high-handed injustice, no spectre of want, no
scars from social revolutions. We are not Ireland, or France, or
South Africa, or India-Pakistan. True, we can conjure up spectres
of a Riel and a Family Compact and Maritime Rights and
the Plains of Abraham: but our national cupboard is relatively
free of skeletons. Most nations would be glad to have only
skeletons as little forbidding as ours to rattle.

But there is, as was stated earlier, one danger that is more
to be dreaded than all others, that of man's history of lack
of self-control, his imperfect and unwilling awareness of and
obedience to a Will beyond his own. We do not talk of this
skeleton often, because it is omnipresent. It cannot be rattled
when we want to goad ourselves into indignation over what
other people did to our ancestors: it can arouse in us no tension
against our neighbours by making us feel put upon or mis-
understood. It can only goad us into a remembrance of what
we all are, men beset by what theologians have called, with
better reason than they have usually been able to make plain,
Original Sin, by what novelists now write about, sardonically

or desperately or with salacious pleasure, the radical evil that couches at the door of every man's heart. The difference is that the theologians and prophets call us sinners in need of grace, which grace gives us grounds for faith and hope, while the others are chiefly anxious to show that we are rotten, and should either enjoy it or despair of it.

Because this is so, men who talk of their nation's future must give thought not only to the outward forms of religion, its institutions, its creed, its moral codes, its forms of worship; but to the inward forms of it, wherein the soul abases itself before its Creator, and thinks of itself as dependent upon His Will, answerable to His Authority. We must remember, as Professor Herbert Butterfield has reminded us in *Christianity and History,* that every generation is equidistant from eternity and is not simply a stepping-stone for its successors, and that "The truth is that if men were good enough neither the ancient city-state, nor the medieval order of things nor modern nationalism would collapse. Neither humanism, nor liberalism nor democracy would be faced with intellectual bankruptcy." Man still cannot be trusted with power or ease; he can still make a garden a wilderness, a palace a prison, a home a cage, an education a polished veneer to hide an emptiness within or a bag of tricks to keep him usefully untroubled by thought. Thoughtlessness and selfishness do not die with prosperity, men at ease are not men at rest, and the pursuit of life, liberty and happiness may turn into a pursuit, not a possession. It is mysteriously true to say,

> "How oft the sight of means to do ill deeds
> Makes ill deeds done,"

and equally true that the converse situation does not make good deeds done.

We are a people religiously well-born. It is not simply that our forefathers, in the main, did not come here to escape

religious persecution, carrying with them hot memories of
ecclesiastical injustice that would have made all formal belief
questionable. It is not simply that we have not bred fanatics
or strange and antinomian sects to the extent our great neighbour has. It is rather that we have been bred from a stock
of people who were earnest in their Christian faith, and who
lived so close to the edge of civilization that they could never
quite lose touch with the Infinite. In only one province is the
religious life overwhelmingly of one pattern; but in all it is
a power to be reckoned with, and however lightly we may
regard the census evidence that most Canadians profess to be
part of one Christian body or another, it is not evidence to be
taken lightly. It is a condition for which many a nation would
envy us, and we should accept it with hope and with a determination that we will not forget our Creator in the days of our
national youth, when the evil days come not nor the years draw
nigh when we shall say we have no pleasure in them. We
have little outspoken opposition to Christian faith, because
most of us, however we may feel about the awkwardness
of some expressions of piety, realize that we are neither animals
nor machines, but children of God. We may not be fully mature
or articulate, but at least we are inclined to be patient and
penitent, realizing with Thornton Wilder that "of all the forms
of genius, goodness has the longest awkward age", and that
things would be a lot more awkward without that form of
genius.

Those who listened to these papers and discussed them were
an important cross-section of the Canadian people. They, along
with those who study them in book form, represent many prejudices, many hopes, many wounds, many mistakes. All will
find themselves taking for granted a host of things that other
nations and other times could not take for granted. But all
should come to feel that if we are stupid and wasteful, if
we underestimate the complexity of the things we must do,

if we are self-confident and self-indulgent, if we fail to read
well the lessons of history, of geography and of the spirit of
man, we can spoil what is probably the greatest opportunity
that God has given to any people. What we now highly
resolve will affect our descendants in 2003 A.D.

THE CANADIAN PEOPLE

Bernard Keble Sandwell

D.C.L., LL.D., D.Lit.,
F.R.S.C. Feature writer, *Financial Post*;
Editor Emeritus, *Saturday Night*, 1951,
formerly editor-in-chief; Assistant Pro-
fessor of Economics, McGill, 1919-23;
Head of English Department, Queen's,
1923-25; a Founder and first Secretary,
Canadian Authors Association; author,
The Privacity Agent, 1928; *The Cana-
dian Peoples*, 1942, etc.

THE CANADIAN PEOPLE

THE population of North America is so extremely mobile, and the freedom of movement between Canada and the United States, in both directions, is so great, that the two countries should properly be regarded, if not as a single reservoir of population, at least as two reservoirs so closely connected that the same natural economic forces will operate upon both of them at the same time.

This does not mean that these natural economic forces will operate always upon both of them in the same degree, and that their populations will therefore remain in a more or less constant ratio. If we examine the record of the last hundred years we shall see that there have been times when they operated much more strongly in favour of the United States and other times when they operated more in favour of Canada. Both countries are in the expansion stage, the stage of constantly taking economic possession of new natural resources, made available by transportation improvements and by discovery. For long periods the supply of these newly available resources has been greater in the United States; for other periods it has been relatively greater, in proportion to existing population, in Canada. In the former periods the American population has increased faster, in the latter periods the Canadian. If we examine the conditions existing in these various periods, we shall find that natural economic forces, not political forces, have been almost wholly responsible for the differences.

There is one exception. North America is geographically a unit, separated by several thousand miles of ocean from the rest of the world, and provided as to its interior with the most perfect system of cheap water transportation in the world. The fact that that water system had its natural outlet in the St. Lawrence gave Canada for a long time a substantial advantage. But the St. Lawrence is ice-bound in winter; and the rise of the railways, and even of the Erie Canal for a short time before them, transferred the command of the continent's economy to the ice-free ports of the Atlantic States. Canada became thus, in regard to many of its products, an outlying area of the economy, contributing raw materials to the more advanced part of the economy in the Eastern States. The fact that it was possible to erect a tariff barrier between the States and Canada enabled the Americans to insist upon taking Canadian products in the rawest possible state, and they have so insisted for the best part of a hundred years. Much processing which could advantageously be done at the site of the raw material production has thereby been prevented in Canada and transferred to American points, keeping the Canadian area in a relatively pioneering condition. In cases where the political influence of the American consumer of the finished product was strong, as with newsprint in 1911, this policy was in a few instances abandoned, with immense advantage to the Canadian economy; but broadly speaking it has remained a consistently effective policy and has strongly influenced the distribution of population between the two countries.

There have been nine censuses of the United States and of Canada since the latter country became a single political entity. If we add together the population recorded in each of these censuses (the Canadian census is taken a year later than the American, but we can ignore that slight difference), we find that on the average the population of Canada has been 7.75 per cent of that of the entire continent north of Mexico. But if we examine the variations from this average we shall find them highly significant.

Canada's share in 1870-71 was much above the average, and if we could trace it back into the preceding decades we should find it higher still. In the first census after Confederation it was 8.7 per cent of the population of the entire continent; from that time it declined steadily, to 7.9, to 7.1, and finally in 1900-01 to 6.6 per cent, or one-fifteenth of the whole as against better than one-twelfth in 1870-71. This was the low point; and from then on the Canadian share of the total rose slowly but steadily, to 7.3, to 7.6, to 7.7 (in 1931 after several years of extreme agricultural depression) to 8.0, and finally in 1951 to 8.4 per cent, back to the one-twelfth ratio, and almost up to the point where it stood at Confederation. Estimates for both countries for March 1953, indicate slightly under 8.5 per cent.

Now both of these progressions, the downward one of the first three decades and the upward one of the succeeding five decades, can be amply accounted for by natural economic forces, plus the power of the United States to insist upon taking imports in the raw state. In 1871 the United States had had forty years of railway development, had already completed one transcontinental railway, and was pushing its lines into the immensely fertile prairie area at a very rapid rate. The

outflow of population from Europe, caused by the reaction from
the liberal movements of the mid-century and by famine conditions in certain countries, was thus attracted far more heavily
to the United States than to Canada. At the same time this
rapid growth of population was itself giving a great stimulus
to industrialization, which in those pre-hydro-electric days was
based chiefly on the coal of Pennsylvania and the water-power
of the New England States. Such was the fluidity of population
movement across the border that even the language difference
did not prevent an immense migration of French-speaking people
from Quebec into the New England States, Ohio and Michigan.
(The truth is that neither race, language nor constitutional
polity has had much influence on the distribution of population
between the two countries. The emigration of the French
was a case of economics triumphing over language and religious privilege, for there were no Separate Schools in the
states to which they moved; and the large share that Canada
obtained of the immigration from Ireland was a case of
economics, and perhaps religion, triumphing over political prejudice, for the Irish emigrants started out with small affection
for either the British flag or the monarchical system. Yet in
1871 they were the largest single racial element in Canada after
the French.)

Canada at the time of which we are speaking had a railway
network confined to the Maritimes, the St. Lawrence Valley
and the peninsula of Southern Ontario. The Canadian Shield
area of rock and muskeg, extending from Hudson Bay to the
Great Lakes, was a powerful barrier against any westward
population movement along the north shore of the lakes, and
to get to the Canadian West by the south shore it was necessary to pass through hundreds of miles of American territory.
Even when the Canadian Pacific Railway was opened to Winnipeg in 1881 the development of the Canadian prairies was
still held back, for until the end of the century there was a

lingering distrust of these areas because of their high latitude and short ripening season. It was actually not until the Americans reached the point where their hunger for land could no longer be satisfied at home, and began coming to Canada for it, that the Canadian prairies really came into their own. In *The American Born in Canada* by R. H. Coats (1943, a volume in the Carnegie Endowment Series on "The Relations of Canada and the United States") it is estimated that in 1891 there were only 11,000 Americans living in Canada who had come in during the previous decade; but the new-comers in the following decade to 1901 rose to 55,000, and in the decade ending 1911 to 189,000. The prairie provinces, which had been too remote for easy settlement up to 1891, had become accessible, but what was still more important was that the American prairies had been filled up.

Canada in 1878 did endeavour to follow the American lead and equally insist upon the processing in her own territory of at least a large part of the products destined for consumption by her own people. But, in a period of constantly extending mass production in industry, the effectiveness of a tariff covering a population of only 4.3 million is not great as compared with that of one covering 50 million, in addition to which capital for industrial investment in Canada was diffident until after 1896, when the rival political party came into power and showed that it would not seriously impair the protective advantage enjoyed by the manufacturers. And by that time other factors were developing in the Canadian economy, which were destined to be quite as potent as free land and much more so than any artificial stimulus to industry.

The decade of the nineties saw the discovery of the three great factors which, along with agricultural development in the West, were to reverse the direction of the movement of Canada's population ratio to that of the rest of North America.

These were the suitability of the Canadian Shield timber for newsprint, the transmissibility of hydro-electric power, and the mineral resources of the Shield and other areas. In 1891, 85 per cent of Canada's exports were agricultural products, animal products or forest products, the last-named being chiefly sawn lumber. By 1901 non-ferrous metals, previously negligible, had jumped to 33 million, and agricultural and animal exports had almost doubled. Newsprint did not rise sharply until after 1911 and the U.S. tariff change. In twenty-five years the total of domestic exports rose from 88 million in 1891, scarcely higher than in 1881, to 742 million in 1916; the 1921 figures are misleading because of inflated prices. The outlying areas, which had been almost valueless until the turn of the century, had become hugely productive.

The Great Depression, everywhere striking earliest and hardest at the primary producers, administered a severe check to this progress between 1926 and 1931. As noted, the population ratio of Canada to the continent was practically unchanged during the decade in 1931. The population-bringing capacity of new wheatlands has of course long since been exhausted; increased mechanization, and the elimination of some parts of the new area by drought, have actually reduced the population of one wheat-growing province, while the other two have continued their expansion by developing new economic resources and some manufacturing. The newsprint industry has stabilized itself temporarily, but other types of industry based on water-power continue to expand, and the oil discoveries of the prairies and the iron ore discoveries of Labrador have laid the foundations for a much enlarged population in future decades. It will be the task of subsequent participants in this Conference to assess the economic possibilities of these most recent additions to the known and available resources; but it belongs to this paper to point out that the type of new worker who is invited by the present opportunities of Canada is very different from that which was invited in the nineteenth century and during most of the first quarter of the twentieth.

In practically every class of employment there has been in the second quarter of this century a pronounced increase in mechanization, so that mere muscle unaccompanied by any technical skill or native intelligence will henceforth be of very little value. The old immigration was largely of the navvy type, capable of hard manual labour of the simplest kind under skilled direction, but not of much beyond that. In the United States mechanization has been almost a generation ahead of Canada, creating a demand for the services of skilled and educated persons which has drawn across the border a great many Canadians. In certain professions, notably certain kinds of engineering, Canada has had to make an organized national effort to replenish the supply. Unfortunately the merely muscular type of labour is much the most mobile part of any population. It has no ties with its old habitat when employment is lacking, and no new techniques to learn in its new habitat. In the nineteenth century the population of North America was largely built up by this sort of migrant from Western Europe. The skilled worker and the professional man are much less easily movable, especially between countries which have not the same language.

In this view, Canada's population at any time is largely determined by two factors: first, the total population of the continent, and second, the relation of Canada's economic capacity at the time to the total and immediately available economic capacity of the continent. If this view is sound it is useless to attempt to forecast the population of Canada at any future date without first considering the population of the United States at that date. On the subject of future trends of population in the United States there is plenty of divergence among the forecasters, but the more extreme of them on either side need not engage much of our attention.

The Bulletin of the Population Reference Bureau for June of this year reports that two U.S. government statisticians recently estimated the 1975 population of that country upon three different sets of assumptions regarding fertility, mortality and migration, and came up with these three possibilities: "low 165.6 million; medium 190.1 million; and high 225.3 million". Similarly two special commissions on different economic problems have made estimates which coincide closely with the "medium" one of these statisticians—the Water Resources Policy Commission 190 million, and the Materials Policy Commission 193 million. On the other hand Dr. Raymond Pearl of Johns Hopkins, who in 1925 made a good guess at the actual 1950 population, sees only 173 million for 1975.

These more conservative estimates—Dr. Pearl's and the "low" of the statisticians—are considerably influenced by the rate at which the natural resources of the United States are diminishing, and appear to include the assumption that population will cease to increase, or slow down its rate, if the standard of living is in any degree impaired. Considering how enormously high that standard at present is, compared both with past American standards and with the present standards of almost every other country in the world except Canada, this seems a rash assumption. But in any event, the more allowance is made for this factor, the better becomes Canada's outlook in comparison with that of the United States, because we are still discovering new natural resources, have every expectation of going on doing so for some generations, and have not yet approached the American rate of diminution even with our oldest ones.

If therefore the United States is destined to have only 173 million people in 1975 because its natural resources are wearing out, then Canada should be able to maintain a considerably higher proportion of the continent's total population than the

9 per cent which we are already rapidly approaching. Even that 9 per cent of the total would give us practically 10 per cent of the American share, which means a Canadian population of 17.3 million in 1975 on the worst American calculations. And this is conceding us hardly any advantage from our well-maintained resources as compared with the depleted resources of the United States. If we can raise our ratio to 10 per cent of the whole—and we have already raised it from 6.6 to 8.4 per cent in half a century—we should have 19.2 million by 1975.

Taking the medium estimate of about 190 million for the U.S., we should have 17.3 million even if we did not increase our ratio at all from its present figure, and if we should continue to increase it at the average rate of the past fifty years, which would bring it to about 9.5 per cent by 1975, we should have about 20 million. This seems to be a reasonably conservative forecast. I do not think we need bother with the "high" U.S. estimate of 225 million, except to say that all the economic factors on which it could be based exist in a much higher degree in Canada, and if they operate to that extent in the U.S. we should expect them to operate somewhat more strongly in Canada, and thus to give us a better rate of population increase than the American one. Even if they did no more than to raise Canada's share of the continental population to 10 per cent instead of 9, we should have 25 million to the U.S. 225 million.

This figure of 25 million is that which the Bank of Nova Scotia recently forecast for 1975 on the assumption that there would be no change in the recent pattern of immigration, emigration and natural increase, though it preferred to postpone the achievement of the figure to 1980 so as to allow for a moderate decline in the natural increase rate, which has lately been exceptionally high. But we do not yet know how much of that high natural increase rate is due to several years of full employment and a great degree of economic security, factors which make for early marriage and diminish the reluctance to have children. These conditions have been studiously maintained and stimulated by governments, and it is safe to assume that they will continue to be maintained and stimulated, though there is the possibility that government efforts in that direction may not always be so successful.

By the time the population of this continent, north of Mexico, has reached the figure of 250 million, it seems possible that the forces which govern the distribution of population over the surface of the world may have changed. If, for example, the numbers of a nation's available fighting forces should become a more important factor in war than the nation's wealth and ability to pay for fighting equipment, a 250-million North America might find itself in a difficult position against a possible 400-million India or 500-million China. Moreover, the Soviet Union, which is not an overcrowded or impoverished country, is quite likely to reach the 250-million mark about the same time as North America does. On the other hand, the economic effects of the development of atomic power are quite unpredictable, and we can obviously assume that it will be even more transportable, even less restricted to the area of its origin, than the hydro-electric power which has already so greatly changed our lives. The utility of speculating on these matters much beyond the year 1980 thus seems very questionable.

One thing, however, does seem reasonably clear. It is that the possibilities of sustaining an expanded population, without any serious reduction of the standard of living, are immensely greater in Canada than in the United States, where the authorities are already viewing with deep concern the inroads already made, and those which will continue to be made for some years more, upon the natural resources of the area. The very inaccessibility of vast areas of Canada has preserved until now their mineral and forest contents, the two forms of resources which it is easiest to exhaust by excessive exploitation, whereas no part of the United States has been difficult of access for at least fifty years. The new means of transport and of surveying and research by air have suddenly opened the whole of Canada to exploration, and it is impossible to doubt that we shall continue to discover new and exploitable resources on a very large scale for several generations.

As for agriculture, the increasing density of the population itself will compel a higher rate of utilization of land surface. The specialized wheat economy, with its heavy mechanization, will be partially replaced by a much more diversified cultivation, producing not for the export of a single staple product but for the complex needs of a large population with a very high standard of living. The specialized wheat economy is natural to a new and thinly populated area at a great distance from any populous market. The prairie regions could not have been opened up with anything like the same speed without that specialization. But as the populous market approaches nearer, the pressure towards the single crop diminishes, labour becomes more obtainable, land rises in value and must be more efficiently used. (Political attitudes are of course unpredictable, but it seems almost inevitable that the increasing density of population in the United States will lead that country to a greater and more continuous readiness to accept the higher and more finished products of Canadian agriculture, especially animal products. The uncertainty about this highly contiguous but at times prohibited market has been a strong factor in keeping Canadian agriculture specialized on products which can readily be transported to any part of the world.)

It is not in the matter of migration alone that the continent of North America (north of the Mexican border) constitutes practically a single economy, broken only by the boundary line with its persistent possibility of governmental interference.

The same considerations apply to the movement of goods as to those of persons. Much of the traffic across the border which appears in the statistics of both countries as international is really traffic within a natural economic unit. The only effect of the boundary in such cases is to render it necessary for each country to acquire currency of the other country with which to pay for its purchases. In the days before the First World War, when sterling was an international currency and Canada was kept well supplied with it by her exports to Great Britain, this presented no difficulty. When the sterling ceased to be available in sufficient quantities, and ceased also to be acceptable as a means of payment in the United States, the situation was radically changed, and the monetary relations between Canada and the United States have since been kept in balance, sometimes by a heavy discount on the Canadian dollar, sometimes by heavy movements of capital from the United States to Canada. The historical position of Canada in this respect has been concisely described by J. D. Gibson in *Canada's Economy in a Changing World*: "The European market is the natural outlet for many of her primary products. At the same time, Canada's methods of production and habits of consumption are American and her natural source of supply for the majority of her imports the United States."

Canada's exports are still so largely primary or nearly so, and in the case of foodstuffs they are still so largely of a kind not acceptable to the United States for protectionist reasons, that the problem raised by the necessity of finding purchasers who can pay in dollars is and will continue to be a serious one. It is part of a world-wide problem resulting from the indisposition of the United States, in spite of having become the world's chief creditor country, to accept settlement of its claims in the goods of the debtor countries. It is the intention of this paper, however, to suggest that the seriousness of this problem for Canada will be diminished because the increasing density of the population on the whole continent will inevitably lead to the consumption on the continent of a greatly increased proportion of its primary products, and because the expansion in the output of those products will occur mainly in Canada rather than in the United States. In the volume just quoted, for example, Wynne Plumptre, an economic expert of the Department of External Affairs, cites the case of fish as an article of which "the United States market, at least at its present level of prosperity, needs substantial supplies from outside" and is therefore receptive as regards the raw product, though the tariff "is still designed to let in the raw product but to keep out the processed". And J. D. Gibson in the same books says: "As Mr. Plumptre points out, the long-range tendencies favor a relative expansion in Canadian exports to the United States. Depletion of United States resources and the growth in their economy will in future as in the past turn American attention towards alternative sources of supply in Canada. Canadian insistence on processing Canadian basic materials will increase the value of exports. But the process is likely to be gradual. . . . The process is also likely to be uneven, since a number of the things we supply to the United States are marginal supplies, needed in good times but much less required when general conditions are unfavorable." Against this last consideration we should remember that government policy now has powerful means of preventing general conditions from becoming too unfavourable.

This last reflection brings us straight to the question of the variations which we may expect in the economic health of both Canada as a unit, and the whole North American economy of which it is the smaller part. If the thesis of this paper is correct, it obviously follows that the more serious variations, indeed any variations which can deserve to be called serious at all, will be in the economic health of the whole continent and not in that of Canada separately. We shall not see Canada suffering even a minor depression, for even so much as the larger part of a year, while the United States is enjoying prosperity, nor vice versa.

Both countries have now for several years enjoyed a condition which can properly be described as one of full employment, and this without it being necessary for either government to adopt any special policies for bringing full employment about. Obviously the natural operation of economic laws cannot always be relied upon to maintain a condition of full employment, even though it may be true that the worst instances of depression are due rather to human (and usually governmental) disregard of economic laws than to their natural and unimpeded operation. But in any event full employment is now so predominant, and so politically necessary, an objective of governments, that for the next generation or two any errors that may occur are more likely to be the result of excessive concern about full employment than of disregard for it. We do not accurately know yet what price may have to be paid for maintaining full employment at a juncture when economic law would operate naturally to diminish it.

It must be admitted that the maintenance of full employment in Canada would become extraordinarily difficult if the United States, apart from or in reaction to a degree of depression in its own business, should adopt a definitely more exclusive tariff policy against imports from Canada. A nation which sells more than half of its total exports to a single customer is obviously in an extremely exposed position, even if a large part of those exports are essential to the customer's ordinary economic life. The trouble is that to a great extent the goods which we can export to the United States, the goods for continental trade, are different from the goods that we can export to the rest of the world, the goods for ocean trade. To quote J. D. Gibson again, they even come from different parts of the country: "Our chief exports to England and

Europe come from the farm lands spread all across Canada; our chief exports to the rest of the Commonwealth and other overseas markets come from the industries of central Canada; but our chief exports to the United States have come and will continue to come from the Laurentian Shield." We cannot at short notice switch from one type of production to another. Changes due to long-term movements in the tides of international trade we cannot complain of; but we have rather often had ground to complain of changes made abruptly and with no regard for Canadian interests, and frequently reversed a few years later, in the terms of admission of important Canadian exports to the United States.

Mr. Gibson, however, sees a considerable ray of light in the change which has taken place in recent years in the national interest of the United States. To quote again: "In the early days the national interest of the United States may still have lain in the direction of protection. Now it surely lies in the direction of free trade. . . . The time has come when the United States must, in large measure, go forward on her own if there is to be any further general reduction in tariff levels." It is surely not too much to hope that in this matter, as in so many others, time works on our side.

Continuance of full employment in the two countries means the maintenance of the highest general standard of living that any part of the human race has ever achieved. With that goes the consumption, at a rate increasing with population and probably increasing faster than population; of natural resources, many of which are beginning to fall short in the United States but are far from doing so in Canada. It means the maintenance of a high consumption rate for all foodstuffs but especially the best ones, for iron ore, for newsprint, for nickel, uranium, copper, titanium, asbestos, lead, zinc and many other commodities for which the United States has become or must shortly become dependent on outside sources.

Assuming that something which can justifiably be described
as full employment can be maintained steadily for an indefinite
future, we can next consider the kind of society which, in
Canada, may be expected to develop in these conditions. It
will be, for one thing, a society in which the national income
will be much more evenly distributed than has ever been the
case in the past. Full employment is one name for something
which viewed from another angle is often called shortage of
labour. John T. Bryden, general manager of the North American
Life Assurance Company, one of the participants in the 1953
Town Hall (New York) lecture series on Canada, since published as *Canada: Nation on the March,* says that "Business
subscribes to the view that over the last several years there
has been a significant shortage of labor, despite the growth
in the labor force; and that trade unionism has not been
backward in advancing its claims at every opportunity, against
an inflationary background built to order for the purpose." It
is still to be demonstrated whether full employment can be
maintained without some measure of this inflationary background. If it cannot we shall probably tolerate the inflationary
background rather than do without the full employment.

The real average weekly earnings of the Canadian worker
in manufacturing industry—his earnings in terms not of the
dollar but of the actual commodities which he buys for the
living of himself and his family—have risen from an index
number of 98.1 during 1945 to an index of 118.5 for May
of this year, or more than 20 per cent, and during the same
interval his actual weekly working hours have diminished from
44.3 to 41.9. This of course would not have been possible
without a great increase in his per capita production per hour,
the result of technological progress and also of near-capacity
operation in the factories. Presumably technological progress
will continue during the next few decades, though not necessarily always at the same rate. The association between wage

increases and technological progress is strongly suggested by the fact that the increases have been less in the durable goods industries, in which technological change has been somewhat slower, than in the non-durable goods industries.

But there has also been another cause of increase in the total income of the average income-earning family, in the shape of a great increase in the number of females working for wage or salary. Women now constitute 22 per cent of the gainfully employed population of Canada, as against 15.4 per cent in 1921 and 13.3 per cent in 1901. Since most of the widows and other women without males to support them and with no other source of income must always have been included in this class, and are indeed now under less compulsion to work because of various social welfare payments by the State, it follows that the majority of the new recruits to the labour force must be women in families where there is also a male earner. The nature of their employment has also changed; whereas a great number of them used to be employed in private domestic service, the number in that occupation, far from increasing, has greatly diminished, though the reduction is not visible in the statistics because these make no distinction between private and restaurant or hotel service.

The social effects of this revolution are very difficult to estimate. It has not in recent years impaired either the marriage rate or the birth rate, but that may be due to the counter-vailing effects of post-war conditions and of full employment, which latter is probably a powerful aid both to early marriage and to fertility. So large an amount of female gainful employ-ment would not have been possible without the present generous supply of mechanical devices for reducing labour in the home; and for those home tasks for which no mechanical device is avail-able it has brought about a new type of employment—which perhaps does not show much in the census—in the shape of the "baby-sitter". It has obviously greatly reduced the economic dependence of women upon men, a consideration which has probably much to do with the willingness of women to accept such employment when not absolutely necessary. It is one of the factors tending to diminish the importance of the home in urban society.

Since this increase in the paid employment of women has continued long after the cessation of major hostilities, it is clearly not a result of any exceptional drain upon man-power for military service and munitions industry, although it was undoubtedly expedited during both the world wars. But in the present state of international relations it seems almost inevitable that an increasing amount of effort will have to be devoted by Canada as by the rest of the Western countries to purposes of defence, and hence that if the supply of goods and services for civilian consumption is to be maintained there will have to be a continued expansion of the total labour force, which will have to come from the female part of the population. Moreover, every time an operation which used to be performed in the home household without cash consideration is transferred to the cash-payment field, there results a business transaction which involves buying, selling and accounting, all of which increases the amount of service and "paper-work" required by the community, and usually performed by women. The largest single classes of women workers are, in order of size, clerks, stenographers, and sales clerks. Increasing mechanization also adds to the number of tasks which can be as well performed by women as by men.

Both increased mechanization and expansion of population mean a large and constant supply of new capital. The movement of that capital across the U.S.-Canada border is so extremely fluid that the problem of the source from which it is to be obtained is far more a North American than a purely Canadian problem. If the United States continues to have such capital in adequate supply, an adequate proportion of it will come to Canada. However, the effects of the redistribution of the national income which is now in progress in both countries on the operation of saving capital are not yet clear. It is obviously much easier for a wealthy class to save capital voluntarily than for a somewhat egalitarian society no portion of which is greatly richer than other portions. Both full employment and the extensive redistribution of income are phenomena too recent for us to tell much about their consequences in this respect. A large part of the new capital supply at present available is secured by withholding part of the profits of corporations from the shareholders and reinvesting them, a treatment to which present tax systems are fairly favourable. And the extent to which the fiscal power of the State can be used to manipulate the flow of the national income as between saving and consumption is much greater today than when *laissez-faire* theories held sway.

One element in the new world situation which has been little discussed is the necessity which the Western countries are now under of having one or more economically powerful nations of the Far East on their side in the international line-up. This makes the economic strength of Japan and in lesser degree of South Korea a thing to be encouraged in every possible way. These are over-populated countries whose chief need is increased supplies of foodstuffs, and it will apparently be necessary for Western countries to learn to accept greater quantities of their manufactured exports, at any rate in the case of Japan, to enable them to pay for imported food. Canada, as the Western country with the greatest potentialities for expanding food output, should be the chief beneficiary of any such a change. A generation ago Canada was looking forward optimistically to a great expansion of its exports to China as a result of the modernization of that country's economy. That is scarcely likely to occur now that China has passed into the Communist orbit, but precisely the same considerations apply now to Japan, which we then left out of consideration on the assumption that she would continue to be ill-disposed towards both the United States and Canada. The truth is that for the next decade or two considerations of international politics will enter so largely into the picture of international trade that a country so dependent on that trade as Canada is can do little but strive for the maximum liberality in the trade policies of all the non-Communist nations towards one another.

In conclusion, while I have been reluctant to push these calculations beyond the next twenty-five years, which is only one-half of the period assigned for examination in this Conference, I should add that the possible changes in international relations which cause this reluctance appear to me far more likely to operate in the direction of increasing population movements towards North America, and especially towards Canada, than they are to operate in the opposite manner. We cannot overlook the fact that if population were free to move without political interference on the part of both the country left and the country entered, there would be a vastly greater movement into Canada than there is today. Within the non-Communist world, migration is at present hampered chiefly by restrictions imposed by the receiving countries. These restrictions are of various kinds, and are aimed at various different objectives. One of these objectives, the purpose of limiting the population of the receiving country to what are considered to be assimilable races, is under vigorous attack and seems likely to be, if not abandoned, at least much less extensively pursued than it has been in the recent past. The doctrine that racial differences carry with them important differences in cultural capacity, for example, is under heavy attack. Canada has already receded from her former position concerning the racial unsuitability of Oriental peoples for admission to Canada, by conceding the admission of a "token" number of

Indians, Pakistanians and Ceylonese. The token principle is at present limited to the peoples of Commonwealth countries, but it seems likely to be extended to other Oriental countries in proportion as their friendship becomes increasingly important to the cause of the free world. The numbers involved are extremely limited, but they are much more likely to be expanded than to be decreased. The resistance to such immigration is, moreover, almost entirely based on its supposed effect on the labour market; and the longer we can maintain a condition of reasonably full employment the more this resistance will diminish. (The theory of non-assimilability is nowadays little more than a rationalization of an emotional attitude towards "cheap labour".)

Restrictions on movement of population into Canada seem likely, therefore, to be gradually but progressively diminished except in so far as they aim at maintenance of the national health (of body and mind) and keeping the *rate* of inflow from exceeding what can be readily absorbed with regard to housing and employment. This could easily mean a return to the rate of immigration which prevailed between 1900 and 1915, or an average of well over 200,000 a year. Such a rate, which caused some strains at the time because it was disproportionate to the size of the existing population, 5½ millions at the beginning of the period, would produce no difficulty with a population of 20 millions, which I have suggested as a reasonably conservative estimate for 1975, provided only that new natural resources continue to become available.

Assuming some relaxation, after 1975, of the restrictions on entry of immigrants, and the maintenance of a domestic rate of natural increase favoured by a continuance of full employment and a general sense of economic security, I shall suggest that percentage rate of growth of the population of Canada from 1975 to 2000 ought to exceed the percentage rate which we have predicted from now to 1975. This would bring us to something like 30 million by the end of the century. It would involve a more intensive use of our food-producing areas, but this we can expect from the progress of science and from the increased supply of labour. It would materially reduce our need for imported manufactured goods, by increasing the opportunity for mass production at home. And if some of the 30 million found themselves over-crowded, it would be hard for them to discover a less crowded country to which to remove themselves.

CANADA'S NATURAL RESOURCES

Maxwell Weir Mackenzie

C.M.G., B.Com., C.A.
Executive Vice-President, Canadian
Chemical and Cellulose Co. Ltd.; Deputy
Minister of Defence Production, 1951-
52; Deputy Minister of Trade and Com-
merce, 1945-51; Foreign Exchange Con-
trol Board, 1939-42; Deputy Chairman,
W.P.T.B., 1943-44; member, Royal Com-
mission on Taxation of Annuities and
Family Corporations, 1944.

CANADA'S NATURAL RESOURCES

IT IS generally agreed that natural resources are a Good Thing, that we in Canada have quite a lot of them, that we should make good use of what we have, and that we should search for more. These are generalizations on the subject with which few will argue, and I am inclined to think that they are about the only ones on the broad subject of "Canada's Natural Resources" that are universally accepted.

These generalizations, of course, can be expanded at great length. Indeed, that is the temptation, because of the ease of doing so in well-rounded phrases. It is easy to say that as we have been endowed with great resources we should process these through to the final product, and should not, in that worn-out phrase, be hewers of wood and drawers of water. Apart from the fact that the great bulk of our resources are, in fact, now processed in Canada, there is no easy way, by simple decree, of accomplishing this further processing, involving as it does persuading someone to buy the finished product at a satisfactory

37

price in a currency we can use. Again, it is easy to quote estimates of the amount of damage done each year to our forests by fire and insects and to say that something should be done about it. It is another matter to finance and carry out remedial measures in areas that are virtually without population. It is easy to point to areas in Canada where early settlement was badly located, or to those where all the ground cover has been removed and serious damage has been done to the soil. At the same time one knows that in the pioneering of any new venture or the opening up of new areas there is bound to be waste and error, or at least what, with the benefit of hindsight and using standards of an entirely different generation, we sometimes call waste and error.

We do know, however, that Canada's record to date, particularly in resource development, is a matter of world-wide interest—and the basis of a good deal of envy—and we also know that we are not alone in having great undeveloped resources. Indeed, one of the matters that must continually be kept in mind is that, just as we are employing new techniques and learning to live and work in the colder and more rigorous climates of the north, similar progress is being made in production under tropical and sub-tropical conditions. If a spur be needed for our resource development programme, it is the existence and development of resources in other countries—wood as a base for cellulose in countries that enjoy an annual growth of double or treble what is possible in Canada; a mountain of high-grade iron ore in Venezuela and major reserves in Brazil only serve to illustrate some of the world potentials of a mineral much in the news in Canada because of Labrador, but which after all is one of the most abundant of metals. Nickel, of which we produced over 90% of the free world's supply in 1950, is known to exist in Cuba, in Brazil, in Indonesia, and New Caledonia. Our copper production, which ranked second only to gold in our mineral production values of 1950, was exceeded not only by that of the United States, but by that of Chile and Northern Rhodesia as well. South America has about twice and Africa about six or seven times our water-power potential. As the Red Queen said to Alice, "It takes all the running you can do to keep in the same place—and if you want to get somewhere else you must run at least twice that fast."

But irrespective of whether or not our progress in the past might have been better, the fact remains that great progress has been made in developing the country. Our concern now need not be so much what might have been done differently in the past, but what we must do in the future to achieve the developments of which we are capable and which can easily dwarf the record accomplishments of the past few years. This paper, therefore, will not attempt to catalogue our national heritage, to summarize the volumes that have been written by experts on the technical problems of conservation in all its ramifications, nor attempt any statistical calculations about how long our resources will last.

Rather the purpose is to look at the situation as it exists today and to provoke some thought and discussion about future developments in the utilization of our resources. To do this natural resources can be considered under the two headings of Energy and Materials, both of which can be further divided into Renewable and Non-renewable. In the energy classification water-power, which has been of such importance in Canada's development, should be classed as renewable and could be dealt with separately from thermal power. But for the purposes of this paper the two sources of energy can be bracketed together, partially because of their interchangeability, but perhaps more important, because as time goes on we in Canada will be increasingly dependent on thermal power. Under the three headings, then, of Sources of Energy, Renewable Material Resources, and Non-renewable Material Resources, the follow-

ing questions can be examined: What is the outlook for the
future demand for our resources, with which is bound up the
problem of substitution; and should we deny current use of our
resources against the possibility of a more profitable use later
on? Then in more general terms consideration can be given
to Incentives for Risk-Taking, Tariff Policy, and finally, Opportunities for the Individual.

SOURCES OF ENERGY

Throughout the whole history of Canada's resource development runs the dominant factor of low cost hydro-electric power,
the use of which has more than doubled about every ten years.
Without this all-important source of energy Canada's development would have been a very different story. We would still
have had our important position as a producer of wheat, feed
grains, livestock, fish, lumber and some other products. But
cheap power is one of the very foundations of our biggest
single industry, pulp and paper. It is virtually the only thing
we have to contribute to the manufacture of aluminum, and
it is, of course, the basis of the whole of our electro-metallurgical
and electro-chemical industries. In the same way that the
industrial growth of England and Germany was based on coal
so hydro-electric power has been fundamental to Canada's
development.

Of the various sources from which electrical energy can be
derived, that created by falling water has been the cheapest.
It has been Canada's good fortune to have that form of
energy strategically placed and in abundance. We have about
eleven million kilowatts of installed capacity, with a con-
servatively estimated additional potential of four times that
amount.

Coal, too, we have in quantity, although it is not as widely
distributed throughout the country. And recently to water-

power and coal have been added oil and natural gas in amounts which, while they are still undetermined, are known to be of great magnitude.

These are the resources that have provided our sources of energy, but no one in this day and age can look to the future without taking into account energy derived from atomic power. With the pace at which developments are being made, it is reasonable to assume that well before this century is out we will see, at competitive cost, the commercial use of power based on atomic energy. We in Canada have the resources and are acquiring the knowledge to take advantage of this form of energy.

Sources of energy are the basic framework on which a highly industrialized nation is built, and it is worth noting that to date no country has been able to achieve that objective on the basis of imported power. Hence the importance of our water-power, coal, oil, gas, and eventually our uranium. It is true, of course, that each of these has its special uses, but to an important degree they are already interchangeable and greater flexibility in their use is promised for the future. Consequently, we need not be too concerned about the exact extent of our reserves of each singly. The question is, then, not "How much have we got and how long will it last?" but rather, "How will we use these sources of energy to the best advantage in terms of our growth and development?"

At first examination, our total reserve of energy is probably greater than we shall ourselves ever need. Yet it is a fact that we rely upon foreign sources of supply for about 60% of our coal and that, despite our great strides in oil development since the war, our net imports last year were larger than they were in 1945. The reasons for this superficial paradox are obvious and result from the location of our resources and the economics of their distribution.

The facts are that we do not have available at the present

time a large reserve of economically accessible energy. Southern Ontario, for example, has almost exhausted its water-power potential and keeps abreast of mounting industrial demands by steam-turbine generation, using mainly imported coal.[1] Under present conditions, it means nothing to Southern Ontario industry that, say, the Moose River which drains into James Bay some 600 miles away has an undeveloped power potential. This is the situation today, but it need not continue to be so for all time. Great strides are being made in the technology of moving energy in its various forms, which will make for a greater degree of interchangeability in the use of the various sources of energy—but more important, it will make for a more unified and developed Canada.

The early development of Canada as a political entity depended in large measure on the building of the trans-continental railroad, which provided a means of transporting people and goods throughout the whole country. Railways, canals, highways, and air routes have been and will continue to be basic to our development. Looking to our future development, a network throughout the country by which energy can be transported, whether by the interconnection of electrical systems, pipelines, or any other form, will work in the same direction. It will build a more unified Canada, allow a better utilization of our other resources, and make for a more even distribution of our prosperity. It is not necessary to debate with the experts the relative costs, for example, of moving natural gas east by an all-Canadian route as against the alternative of a route partially through the United States, or again, of the proposal to export energy in one part of the country against imports in other parts. It may be that short-term benefits could be derived by taking the latter, and easier, courses; but longer-term issues are at stake. To take the example of the

[1] St. Lawrence Seaway power, when it comes, will improve Ontario's power supply but will not meet anticipated demand.

proposed all-Canadian east-west gas line, as against a system designed to exchange gas with the United States, the total difference in cost between the two is negligible when considered in terms of the long-range values to the country as a whole and of other measures that we have financed in the past and that are now basic to our structure.

The building of the trans-continental railroad was no doubt considered by many at the time as an uneconomic venture, but without the increased accessibility to areas of our country that it brought, we would not have Canada as we know it today. That project was made possible by the use of special incentives and inducements—and we should not be afraid of repeating the principle, though probably in a different pattern, to increase the area of accessibility of our energy resources.

There can be little doubt that a demand will always exist in the United States for any low-cost energy that we can supply in the form of the diversion of water or hydro-electric power; already there is a growing demand for natural gas, and, no doubt, as time goes on there will be a substantial demand for our oil. Coal, however, will probably always have to depend on the domestic market. In general there should be an increasing demand in the United States for our resources that provide energy, but export commitments of energy raise different problems from exports of our other resources. An important difference is the almost inevitable permanence of any arrangements for the export of water, hydro-electric power, gas, and to a lesser extent of oil when transported by pipeline. Industries and whole communities become established on the basis of such energy—and then, if a domestic demand arises later, it would be very difficult if not impossible to terminate the commitment.

Under all these circumstances, it seems advisable that we should not at present take on export commitments of low-cost energy. In the light of rapidly growing demands for power and the non-renewable nature of oil, gas and coal, the benefits to be derived from such exports do not appear to balance the hazard of possible future reliance on increased imports of thermal energy. That is not to say that we should never consider such arrangements. But the important thing is that we should first achieve greater development and flexibility on a nation-wide basis in the availability of our presently usable energy sources. Export commitments entered into now would probably slow those developments, and in certain cases might easily prejudice individual projects that are probable for the future even though not yet planned.

It may be, of course, that the development of atomic energy will in time change our whole approach to this problem, for the energy that can be obtained from one pound of fissile material is the equivalent of that in 1,200 tons of coal. It is interesting to speculate on the possibility of exporting energy in that form to the densely populated but power-poor areas of the world and what it would mean to world trade and stability. However, even though this may well turn out to be the most significant contribution of atomic energy, it cannot yet be a factor in determining our policies.

RENEWABLE MATERIAL RESOURCES

Under the general heading of Renewable Material Resources come the forests, farmland, and fishing- and hunting-grounds. These can be described as renewable because they are all capable of being utilized on a perpetual yield basis. As noted earlier, mistakes were inevitable in the early stages of our history, and these mistakes are now particularly evident in the excessive harvesting of some of our natural resources and in the failure to provide for their regrowth.

But again there is little purpose in reviewing what has happened in the past. The fact is that these resources are and for years have been making a tremendous contribution to our well-being, particularly through their part in our all-important export trade. It is worth noting that in 1951 exports of newsprint, pulp, and lumber aggregated almost a billion and a quarter dollars, representing 31% of our total exports. In the same year, wheat, oats and barley accounted for another 14%. What is important and what suggests confidence for the future is the extent to which improved conservation techniques are coming into more common use in forestry, logging, farming and fishing. For example, nearly all pulp and paper companies are today practising sustained-yield logging, and the development of new strains and improved cultural methods have materially increased wheat yields.

Though some of our past mistakes are irreparable, others can with patience, care, and the expenditure of a good deal of money, be repaired. Lands that have suffered from bad lumbering practice or that have been burnt over can be reforested; overworked farmland can be rehabilitated; fishing-grounds restocked; and the wild-life population rebuilt. Much is already being done to achieve these results in all these fields.

An examination of any of these fields would no doubt point up many desirable things that still remain to be done, but it is beyond the scope of this paper to discuss the methods by which proper conservation can be practised. Similarly, we need not examine the actual amount of research that is being done through experimental farms and other research organizations. Our purpose is to consider and examine the policies most likely to ensure that good judgment will be brought to bear on these highly technical problems.

Because farming, fishing and hunting are occupations that are particularly suitable for the small operator who usually can afford little for experimenting with new and improved production methods, it is of great importance that collective research be carried on and that the results be made freely available to all who want them. This can probably be done best at public expense. A good research programme, private ownership of land, a measure of economic stability through price support programmes, and a system that recognizes the need for profits and incentives will combine to give strong encouragement to the adoption of good conservation practices.

A rather different situation exists where a longer growth cycle is involved, as in the forests. A merchantable crop may involve 30, 40 or 50 years or more of growth. In this case it seems reasonable to assume that the desired results are more apt to flow if the management of the forest is the responsibility of those having a large capital investment, such as a modern pulp or paper mill, the continuing value of which depends on the success of the conservation measures.

What about the future demand for Canada's renewable resources? Taking foodstuffs first, one could start with the basic assumption that there never has been a true surplus of food in the world, in the sense that there have always been hungry people. That, however, is too much of a generalization. The question involved is not only whether people want and need the food that we can produce, but whether or not they can pay for it in some form that we can use. This raises the broad questions of national policies, standards of living, and fiscal policies of other countries, which find expression in tariffs, quotas, bulk buying, and support prices. One of the major problems in building dependable export markets for foodstuffs is the comparative ease with which most countries can either do without or, alternatively, increase domestic production of any foodstuff. It is undoubtedly true that it makes good economic sense for Canada to produce large quantities of a variety of foods to supply the United Kingdom, but other considerations of national importance to the United Kingdom may prevent them from buying. For a variety of reasons, some good, some bad, economic considerations do not have the same practical effect on the international trade of foodstuffs as they do on the trade in other materials. We must, of course, keep working towards the objective of freer movement in international trade, but a Utopian system seems to be a long way off. All this makes difficult the long-range forecasting of the export demand for our foodstuffs. The prospects for wheat are clearer than for most other products, because it is such a basic foodstuff and because we have such very real economic advantages in its production. The outlook for feed grains should be good, but in the last few months we have seen a clear example of the instability of the United States market for feed grains.

Taking the long view, and with all the qualifications that go with any generalization, it would appear wise to plan that, with the exception of wheat and possibly one or two other basic items, the output of foodstuffs in this country should be based on the probable demand in the domestic market. There is every reason to expect that over the years to come the population of Canada will materially increase, which of itself will provide dependable markets for an increasing production of foodstuffs.

As to the forests, while our resources are not fast-growing judged by the standards of some other countries, we have the compensation that there are in Canada vast areas of land, eminently suitable for the growing of trees, which are un-likely ever to support crops of higher economic value. We have fast-moving rivers which provide a means of transporta-tion and a source of power. Of the management of our forests we have already learned much: utilization on a sustain-ed yield basis is no longer merely a paper concept but is an operational reality in an ever-increasing number of cases. More-over, our growing knowledge of silvicultural techniques per-mits us to speak with certainty of much higher tree-crop yields without impairment of our forest capital. On the requirements side, there is a growing domestic market, and with an increasing world population, higher literacy and growing industrialization, there can be little doubt of future needs for forest products of all kinds. We, in Canada, will have the opportunity to meet these needs, provided—and this is a most important proviso— that we are in the forefront of world developments in the technique of growing trees, as well as in the utilization of cellulose in an industry which is rapidly becoming a chemical industry. Even the elemental and basic use of the forest—the production of sawn lumber—is fast changing. Modern techniques have demonstrated that it is more economical not to have to rely on the shape and form in which a tree grows, but by various processes, some mechanical and some chemical, to form a product of a size, shape, and dimensional stability suitable for the end purpose for which it is to be used. Before long one would expect to see much greater advances in this direction.

If we can look forward to a growing demand for our forest products, the question is how shall we meet this demand? At the present time the great bulk of timber cut in this country that is finally exported does receive a fair measure of processing in Canada, but there is none the less still some export in primary form or after having been subject only to a small degree of processing. Should we insist that the processing be done in Canada? Any answer immediately involves questions of tariff and trading policies.

For example, the United States tariff is such that while we have access to that market for ordinary sawn lumber, we are denied access in the more highly processed products such as plywood and composition boards. At the same time, there is some export of big logs, many of them three and four hundred years old, which are suitable for plywood manufacture. This raises the question whether we should deny the export of these logs, which are to all intents and purposes irreplaceable, in the hope that we would thereby save them for our own future use, or alternatively persuade the United States to modify their tariff arrangements. Supporting the argument for denying raw material exports, it is claimed that prohibition of the export of pulpwood from some parts of the country has resulted in the building of pulp mills, with attendant benefits to our national welfare. However, so many factors have a bearing on the decisions lying behind major plant investments in Canada that it is probably impossible to prove categorically the truth of this claim. In any case, even if such prohibitions may have had some bearing on particular situations in the past, they are not desirable as a general policy. Policies like that work two ways—and it must not be forgotten that many of our important industries depend on the purchase from others of materials in the raw state: cotton and wool for the textile industry, to cite only two. Moreover, it is probable that if a prohibition were placed on the export of our big "peeler logs", it would not bring about the manufacture in Canada and supply to the United States of plywood, but rather would accelerate the development of different types of composition board in the United States.

The further industrialization of Canada and the ability to give further processing to our raw materials rest on matters which are much more fundamental—stability of government and government institutions, the system of justice, the reputation for fair treatment of foreign capital, a dependable labour supply, coupled with basic economic factors such as means of transportation and the all-important question of cheap sources of energy. As has already been said, it is difficult to generalize on these matters—an exception in the case of sources of energy has already been noted—but in so far as it is possible to generalize, I believe that we should not deny access by other countries to our material resources, though pressing all the while for reduction of tariffs and other trade barriers that shelter uneconomic processing of those resources in friendly countries.

NON-RENEWABLE MATERIAL RESOURCES

The first impression of a visitor travelling westward and assessing the Canadian scene must be of the importance of the St. Lawrence River and the Great Lakes, which provide a unique waterway to the heart of the continent. The next impression is probably of our developed and potential water-power exemplified by the St. Lawrence River and Niagara Falls—then of the vast expanse of the prairie, the grandeur of the Rockies, and finally of the lush growth of the West Coast. Yet our greatest single asset, the Canadian Shield, is one that few visitors ever see, and indeed, is far from familiar to the average Canadian. This area, accounting for more than two-thirds of our total land area, is one of the world's great storehouses of the minerals on which our present machine age is based. It also provides natural reservoirs and turbulent rivers as the basis of great hydro-electric power developments with which the minerals can be processed. Because of these things, or more accurately, the combination of them, and because of the undoubted demand that there will be for our minerals, it is the pre-Cambrian shield that can provide the most spectacular developments in Canada over the next fifty years.

If proof be needed of the increasing demand for our minerals, one has only to look at the comprehensive study of U.S. resources prepared by the Paley Commission.[2] This analysis of the resources of the U.S., the present and projected demand for key materials over the next twenty-five years, and the sources to which the U.S. will have to look to fill its anticipated

[2] The President's Materials Policy Commission, *Resources for Freedom*, Washington, D.C., 1952.

deficiency is clear evidence that in the long term we will not lack demand for the minerals that we can produce—copper, lead, zinc, nickel, cobalt, tungsten, iron ore, and titanium, as well as many of the lesser known but increasingly important alloying metals. As the Paley Report says, "The United States has crossed the great industrial divide and from being a nation with a surplus of raw materials has become a deficit nation."

The implication of this seems obvious—a growing market for what we undoubtedly have in quantity—but as in the case of other types of resources, what others have too. What then must we do to make the best use of what we have? Should we hoard our resources for fear that we too will become a deficit nation in materials? Should we deny the export of these materials in the raw or semi-finished state? And in thinking of these matters one must think of Canada not as a country of 15 million people but of double or treble that size.

Even under the most optimistic estimates of future population there seems little fear of there not being enough of the non-renewable resources for our own use. In addition to the proven reserves that are now being worked, there are other known deposits of great size, and undoubtedly there are still more important reserves that have not as yet been uncovered. But apart altogether from the abundance of our supply, there is the tendency towards greater efficiency in use and the development of substitutes that must be taken into account. In general terms, three tons of high strength steel now do the work of more than four tons of carbon steel; light metals are being substituted for steel; and there is little doubt that in increasing measure plastics will substitute for metal. With technology continually working in the direction of this substitution, it seems clear that our course should be to encourage the greatest possible consumption of the materials now commonly in use. Provided we as a country are at the forefront in the development of new and better ways to use our non-renewable resources, we will be wiser to do this than to curb our development for fear of running short. With all that has to be done to open up this country, and with vigorous competition from other countries, we cannot hope to succeed by any policy that suggests hoarding.

Suggestions have been made that it would have been wiser not to permit the export of iron ore from Labrador in its primary form, the idea being that those reserves should be held to be matched with the coal of the Maritimes as the basis for a greatly expanded steel industry. Such a programme, however, would only be possible if there were some reasonable assurance of markets for the finished steel. The Canadian steel industry already has, under the impetus of recent demands and in consequence of special incentives, materially increased its capacity, and further expansion of a size to justify the opening up of the Labrador reserves would seem to be some years away. By permitting the export of the ore, as such, we take advantage of an existing demand and we get immediately the opening up of a vast new area of our country.

The Labrador development and the building of the new town at Lynn Lake are properly much in the news. The new railways that each need are important extensions of our transportation system which is the first essential to opening up the North. Further opportunities of similar nature are known to exist, such as the great reserve of lead and zinc at Pine Point on Great Slave Lake. Pine Point, however, is some 800 miles north of the American border, and much of the market for the metals, as the Paley Report shows, will come from the United States. Our concern should be to see to it that Canada is in a position to fill that demand when it materializes, for we are not the only source to which the United States can turn. More exploratory work no doubt remains to be done before actual developments such as Pine Point can be undertaken, and those who eventually risk the large amounts of capital that will be involved will have to see the probability of commercial success. But the biggest single problem to be overcome is one of distance—a problem that has been inherent in all of Canada's development thus far and one that we must, as a national problem, continue to face in the future. It is worth remembering that distance was overcome in the past by taking risks which involved amounts that were a much greater proportion of the then national income than what is called for today in the further opening up of the North.

With the huge reserves of minerals that undoubtedly exist, with technology continually fostering substitution, and with our prime requirement to extend the developed areas of the country, we should encourage projects that will open up the more remote areas and we should not be unduly concerned about the degree of processing that is involved in any export demand.

INCENTIVES FOR RISK-TAKING

There can be no doubt at all of the importance of our natural resources to our national development. We are continually being reminded that one out of every seven Canadian wage-earners is dependent on the forests; that Canada supplies 90% of the world's requirements of nickel; that Canada's No. 1 Northern Wheat is the standard of the world; and that Canadians enjoy the cheapest hydro-electric power of any country in the world. The American press, which has recently discovered Canada, talks of our resources in the most glowing terms, and even the sober-minded London *Economist* describes what is going on in Canada as ". . . . as exciting and impressive as any achievement in industrial civilization."

It is easy, however, to count too much on our extensive natural resources as an assurance of our future well-being. Without natural resources we would, of course, be in a very different position, but the fact remains that resources in themselves are worth little or nothing until human effort is expended upon them. It is comforting to know that there are tremendous oil resources in the Athabaska tar sands, and to feel that some day they will be available to us as a source of energy. At present, however, they are not making any contribution to our welfare. Huge timberlands, large areas of potential farm-land, extensive water-power and untold mineral deposits are available to us, but they will lie idle, and indeed some will deteriorate, unless there are people with the initiative and the energy to make these resources contribute to our welfare.

The basic requirement for the future is people—people who have the vision, the opportunity and the incentive to pioneer new ventures. We have, of course, passed through what is generally thought of as the pioneering stage in this country—the aeroplane, the geiger counter, the seismograph, the bulldozer, and the great variety of modern equipment have revolutionized development—but we still have a lot of pioneering to do in the sense of big risk-taking, opening up new territory and establishing new industrial ventures.

Estimates of the population that this country can support vary a great deal, but few of the experts would put the minimum below three or four times our present population. Whatever the figure, we have a country that can support many more people than now occupy it—and no small group such as our present population can hope to control and exploit to their own advantage the tremendous resources that are ours. We must pursue an imaginative immigration policy—we must open up new territory—and we must be searching continually for a system that will encourage the risk-taking that is inherent in such a programme.

No better system has yet been found for encouraging risk-taking than that which provides some substantial benefit for the risk-taker who is successful. A good example was the original arrangements that were made for the building of the first transcontinental railroads. The railways, in consideration of their undertakings, were given extensive land grants which would be of value only if the railroad undertaking itself were successful. Nowadays, however, the question arises as to who should take the risks and who should get the rewards. Some will argue that because natural resources belong to the country and to the people generally, and because modern methods mean that resource development must be on a big scale, the undertakings should be by governments so that the rewards will accrue to all the people. But the function of government is to regulate and stimulate—not to operate. It is not the job of government to undertake with the public's money the particular types of risks that are inherent in resource development. Neither are governments likely to have the skill, the know-how, or, in fact, the power of decision that is necessary to manage a business in a competitive world.

The last fifty years have seen a greater advance in the volume and variety of goods and services made available to the public on this continent than to any other people in any other comparable period of time. In the early part of this half-century, it is undoubtedly true that the private gain accruing to the risk-taker was disproportionate. But the fact remains that it was under that system that the United States experienced its greatest development. It is reported that in the early 1900's Andrew Carnegie had a personal income of something over $22 million per annum, and there were no income taxes in those days, and a dollar then was probably worth about three today. In today's terms, he apparently had an annual income at his own disposal of some 65 millions of dollars.

Few people would advocate a return to those days, but there is danger that we are now swinging too far in the other direction—that in our desire to even things up a bit we are in danger of discouraging the risk-taker. We live in an age where the emphasis is on security—family allowances, old age pensions, unemployment insurance and the like. This is not the place to argue the merits and disadvantages of these various programmes, but one cannot help but be impressed with the fact that they now account for something between a fifth and a quarter of the total budget of the federal government, and the annual outlay amounts to over $1,000,000,000. In contrast to this is the amount spent on what might be called "opportunity" as distinct from "security". Though comprehensive figures, unfortunately, are not available, the amount included in the federal government estimates for the current year that might be classed under this heading is certainly not in excess of $250,000,000 and probably would be much less under a more precise definition. Provincial expenditures of like nature would have to be added to both sides, but the aggregate that could be classed as an investment in opportunity seems small in comparison with the amount spent on security. There is the additional fact that well-planned expansion of the economy would of itself provide security for the future and would minimize the need for, yet underwrite our ability to carry through, what we have already taken on in social welfare.

It is not necessary to discuss the desirability of particular social welfare payments; nearly everyone will agree that they are all, in themselves, desirable, and little is to be gained by reviewing those that have already been taken on. Once they have been embarked upon there can be no turning back. But there are constant requests for increases in and additions to these payments and the question is, if they be adopted, will they be at the expense of other things that are fundamental to our development?

Apart from defence expenditures, which are in a special category, social security payments are the biggest single factor in determining the level of taxation. In Canada this level is now about a quarter of the gross national product, and is raised in very large measure by taxes on income—first by taking about half of the profits that are made by a corporation, and then by a graduated tax ranging up to 40, 50 and 60% on what is distributed to the shareholders. What taxation at this level does do is to encourage outlays, many of them wasteful, that can be taken as an expense in calculating taxes; it may encourage the speculator who is looking for a quick tax-free capital profit—but it is not much of an encouragement to the risking of large amounts of capital in long-term resource development.

It will be argued that our tremendous resource development of recent years belies this argument, but it is important to remember that much of that development has been influenced by factors that are not ones which we want or expect to see continued. The tremendous world demand for non-ferrous metals, for iron ore, and for oil, and indeed for a great many of the things that we produce in Canada has risen in large measure from the defence budgets of the free world and from the disappearance for political causes of various sources of supply that used to serve a large part of the free world. For nearly fifteen years we have had and have become accustomed to a booming world demand for our products that has been in very large measure stimulated by war or by fear of war. Will anyone argue that the demand for aluminum, for iron ore, copper or nickel has been unrelated to defence budgets, or that the demand for our food products has not been affected by the artificial division of Europe, or that the development of our oil resources has not been encouraged by the hazard of supply from the Middle East? These spurs have undoubtedly had a lot to do with our basic resource development of recent years. Yet we can't expect these inducements to continue—indeed, we hope that they won't continue, and much effort is devoted to minimizing them.

Looking to the future, two things seem of great importance —we need more incentive for risk-taking and a better balance in government expenditures between "opportunity" and "security". In an expanding economy the incentive of lower tax levels does not necessarily mean smaller government revenues and would not be inconsistent with some increase in expenditure on opportunity. What is to be feared is that we will tend to accept present taxation levels as normal, that as defence expenditures decrease, it will be assumed that the corresponding amount of money is all available for other purposes, particularly social welfare, and that we may lose sight of the basic incentive of profit and private gain to development, expansion and risk-taking.

TARIFF POLICY

In George Bernard Shaw's play *The Applecart,* there is a delightful scene in which the United States Ambassador to the Court of St. James conveys to King Magnus the United States decision to cancel the Declaration of Independence and to return to the British family of nations. The King's first reaction is, "The devil you will," and a little later, when the American Ambassador explains that this is really a merger into a bigger and brighter concern, the King replies that though earlier he had dreamt of a reunited English-speaking empire, now that he is older he finds the reality less attractive than the dream.

The chance of Shaw's fantasy coming to pass is probably as remote as the possibility of the elimination of all tariffs between Canada and the United States, and a completely free movement of all goods across the border. But in any event King Magnus had the right idea. Tariffs are only one method of shaping economic policy, and if we were to throw our lot in with the United States on tariffs, we would be forced into accepting numerous other fiscal measures over the design of which we would have no control whatsoever. It would, for example, be impossible to think of the free movement of agricultural products north and south across the border unless there was comparable price support legislation in both countries—and there is little doubt as to where the relevant decisions would be made.

In order that there be a political entity known as Canada, we have accepted certain basic costs resulting from climate and geography which find their way into practically all phases of our economic life. One of the ways in which we pay for these is through protective tariffs that have enabled Canadian industry to grow and develop.

The other side of the medal, of course, is that we have been and are bound to continue to be world traders in a very important degree. Unless we can sell our products in world markets, we cannot continue to exploit our resources to our own advantage and to that of future generations of Canadians. As in so many other things, the desirable course lies between these two extremes of free trade on the one hand, and a highly protected economy on the other.

This is one field where it is particularly difficult to generalize —so much depends on the degree of development of the particular industry concerned, the prospects for its further development on an economic basis, whether or not it has access to other markets, its ability to meet changed conditions, and how any change should be brought about—whether suddenly, gradually, or after a stipulated period of time. Our general objective, however, must be towards the opening of new markets for our increasing production, and this will call, in the aggregate, for a *quid pro quo* of tariff reductions on our part. However, it is important that our tariff be kept up to date with the changes that are taking place in technology. Industrial processes change, synthetics replace natural products and new products are developed for which no proper tariff classification exists. A tariff that was reasonable for the process in use some years ago may now be too high, or equally well may be too low. As and when we can gain better access to other markets for our products, we should be prepared to accept a general downward trend in our tariff, but an iron-bound rule of no new or increased tariffs would mean a denial of many new products, skills, and know-how, to the serious disadvantage of our resource development programme, and the rounding out of our industrialization.

OPPORTUNITIES FOR THE INDIVIDUAL

It is in large measure to the existence of our natural resources and the use we have been able to make of them that Canadians owe their present state of material well-being. And it is these resources that provide the opportunity for the future. But opportunity for further development, for profitable capital investment, for growing markets, and for all the material benefits that go with a high and rising standard of living will mean little unless there is opportunity for the individual to lead his own life, to choose his occupation, and if he wants to, to be his own boss.

Yet the very gains that we have made in the utilization of our resources—the improved modern methods of discovery and exploitation and the economics of mass production nearly all lead in the same direction as far as the unit size of the undertakings is concerned. There is a strong tendency, an almost inevitable requirement, that much of our resource development be undertaken as big ventures involving large amounts of capital at risk and calling for extensive administrative organizations. What then is to be the position of the individual who wants to be on his own and does not want to work for someone else? Our future development would indeed be dearly bought if there were no room for him, the small operator.

The use of natural resources for farming, fishing, and trapping provides occupations well suited to small operators who have only modest amounts of capital available. Furthermore, the individual's position in these fields is protected in considerable measure, and quite properly, by such things as research into production methods and conservation techniques carried on for his benefit at public expense. Support price programmes work in the same direction. It is worth a good deal to preserve these opportunities for the individual.

In the fields of harnessing energy, exploiting minerals and harvesting the forest, the situation is different. It is on the products of these resources that we rely so heavily for our exports. We must sell in world markets in order to buy the many essentials that we do not have—most of the natural fibres, vegetable oils, citrus fruits, and much of the capital equipment that we need for our future development, to mention only some of our requirements. Furthermore, the greater development and industrialization which we hope for and of which we are undoubtedly capable is unlikely to diminish this need for imports. The history of our development thus far has shown that as our industrialization proceeds and the value of our exports increases, our standard of living increases and so does our demand for imports. Since we must trade in world markets we must be competitive, and for this purpose we must take advantage of modern technology, modern conservation methods, and the economies of mass production. We cannot afford the luxury of pricing ourselves out of the market.

In some minds the resulting tendency towards bigness will conjure up the bogey of trusts, monopoly, and all the evils that are sometimes attributed to big business. But industrial development on this continent has shown time and again that bigness, resulting in a dominating position as buyer or seller in any market, brings about its own remedies. Thus, for example, the big employer has induced big labour unions, the big food packer has been met by the chain store, the household goods manufacturer by the department store and mail-order house, the fertilizer manufacturer by co-operative buying on the part of the farmer. This tendency by which a dominating position develops a counteracting force, coupled with good anti-trust and other legislation under which it can be determined whether or not the public interest is being served—and that does not regard bigness of itself as an evil—should provide the necessary protection of the public.

The important point is that the success of the development of our natural resources is of itself the best guarantee that we can have that there will continue to be opportunities for the small operator. One has only to visit new developments, such as the iron ore project in Labrador, the building of the new town and aluminum smelter at Kitimat, or a major forest-management undertaking, to see the multitude of opportunities that are opened up: a good market for the products of the farm and fishing-grounds; numerous opportunities as sub-contractors to carry out part of the programmes of these major resource developments; an expanding demand for the professions, the distributive and service trades, and light manufacturing; fields in which a business can be begun in a small way and either kept small or expanded in accordance with the owner's wishes and capabilities.

It is our good fortune to have tremendous natural resources —resources that the world needs and wants. We are not alone in this, but we have in addition stability of government institutions, a system of justice and a general reputation that will attract capital investment which we will need for further development, and we have the ability to support a much larger population. Few countries have this happy combination of circumstances.

We have, therefore, great advantages and opportunities which we should seize. Canada can be built into one of the leading nations of the world. It is not a question of being the biggest or the best—it is a matter of taking full advantage of what we have for our own benefit and because world prosperity is indivisible. What then must we do? We should, I suggest, bind the country together by developing greater flexibility in the use of our most important resource—energy in its various forms; we should adopt policies that will encourage good conservation practice; we should not hoard our material resources; we should encourage risk-taking; we should work in the direction of freer international trade; and we should not be afraid of mere size; remembering always that the purpose of all these endeavours is the welfare and freedom of the individual.

THE CHALLENGE TO SCIENCE

Reginald Killmaster Stratford

B.S.A., M.Sc.,
D.Sc., LL.D., F.C.I.C. Scientific Adviser,
Imperial Oil Ltd., Director of Research,
Imperial Oil Ltd., 1947-51; President
Research Council of Ontario since 1951;
Lecturer, Ontario Agricultural College,
1921-22; University of Lyons, France,
D.Sc., 1924; past president, Chemical
Institute of Canada.

THE CHALLENGE TO SCIENCE

In times of shallow optimism the profounder natures are pessimistic. —LESLIE STEVENS

IN ADDRESSING this distinguished gathering today on "The Challenge to Science" I feel like a little ship setting out on a vast sea. I am fully aware of the uncertainties involved, of the storms, the hidden shoals and the treacherous currents I may encounter. It would be much safer for me to stay at home. Yet I realize that nothing can be accomplished without facing hazards. I hope eventually to reach port where I may present my cargo so that you, the buyers, can evaluate it.

A scientist is the complete antithesis of a propagandist. He and his brother, the artist, are introverts while the propagandist is an extrovert. In other words, a scientist is a poor salesman. He approaches his subject in a critical frame of mind and to many people he appears to be a pessimist. While this is not actually the case, he must take an objective view of any sub-

67

ject he studies. I shall endeavour to approach my subject in this way and, if at times I present a gloomy picture, this is because my training as a scientist has accustomed me to look critically at both sides of every problem. A propagandist cannot afford to be objective because, in order to sell, he must always feel sure that he is right.

Many books and articles have been, are being and will be written about Canada. Most of them are for external consideration, such as CANADA, NATION ON THE MARCH.[1] Very few are written critically for internal consideration. I am afraid that my paper falls in the latter class because I sincerely believe that scientists, together with other leaders in our present society, are faced with the greatest social challenge in history; this in spite of the fact that most of our people have a higher physical standard of living than they ever enjoyed before.

When we, the authors of this Conference, were asked to prepare papers, it was suggested that all endeavour to take a long rather than a short view, indeed, to look ahead for fifty years. Now whether or not the scientists are willing to do their share and take an active part in serving society, there undoubtedly will be as many or more changes in the next fifty years as there have been in the past half-century and the fruits of science will, as in the past, account for most of these changes.

If you expect a glowing prophecy of our life as it will be fifty years from now, I am sorry to inform you that you are in for a disappointment. I propose to point out some of the problems that face us today, what mechanism we have—and will need to have—to meet their challenge and to warn you that years of research will be required, particularly in the field of sociology, before we dare predict the route that should be followed.

[1] *Canada, Nation on the March*, Clarke, Irwin, Toronto, 1953.

Toynbee [2] recently pointed out that there have been three great revolutions in history. The first was caused by the horse-drawn chariot, the second by the steamboat and the last by the jet plane. Each of these developments extended man's sphere of interest. Toynbee also stated that history follows a very definite pattern and that a recurring sequence of events becomes apparent in the rise and fall of succeeding civilizations. From such a study he claimed it was possible to predict what might be expected to happen to our present Western civilization. No doubt this is true except that, thanks to science, today's cycle is speeded up enormously. The impact on our mode of living of the motor-car, the radio, television and the jet plane, to say nothing of the atomic bomb, becomes apparent in a few months or years, whereas, before science developed these modern devices, generations were required to accomplish any radical change. The results produced have not always been an unmixed blessing, and in the case of speed have often proved devastating. In the old days, when a man walked along a road at four or five miles an hour and tripped and fell, the chance of a fatal accident was rather slight. If he was in a horse-drawn vehicle travelling at the round rate of fifteen miles an hour and had an accident, it could be more serious in nature. Today if, travelling along the same road at sixty to eighty miles an hour, he meets with an accident, it is apt to be fatal. While we may say that history repeats itself, new developments, no matter of what type, are put into use many times more rapidly now than they were before our age. Such rapid assimilation has a far greater effect upon the people than a change that takes place more slowly. It is because of this acceleration that history may not repeat itself.

Today one's contacts and friendships are not limited by distance, as was the case a hundred years ago. If one is a

[2] Toynbee, A. J., "Men Must Choose" (*Atlantic Monthly*, pp. 27-30), January, 1953.

lawyer, a businessman, a scientist, or a plumber, he knows much less about the interests and problems of people outside his own profession, than he did fifty years ago. For example, I have more friends in Toronto, Montreal and outside of Canada than in the locality where I have lived for almost thirty years. These friendships were made through my contacts with scientists and people interested in industry. I regret to say that I have relatively few contacts with doctors, lawyers, and local business managers and others in my home city who in another era would have been my friends. In one sense my interests have been narrowed, and I have been able to participate very little in community affairs. This is true of most people in responsible positions, and the fact creates one of the main reasons why there has been a decided drop-off in community interest and leadership.

Undoubtedly the many groups that go to make up our society are strong within themselves but, because there is little, if any, co-ordination one with the other, it has been difficult to maintain a balanced community. Just as "a forest is a triumph of the organization of mutually dependent species"[3] so a great society is a triumph of mutually dependent groups of people. If we want to make our society great, the various groups which compose its structure must be prepared to work more closely together for mutual good. Because science supplied the tools that speed up the changes which otherwise would have taken generations to accomplish, scientists have a definite responsibility to society and, if they continue to supply tools which will permit still further acceleration in the future, their responsibility will be that much greater.

The scientist, as we know him today, is relatively new in our society. His predecessor through hundreds of years studied to unravel Nature's secrets and only accomplished this through

[3] Whitehead, A. N., *Science and the Modern World*, p. 239, Macmillan N.Y., 1926.

long tedious hours of work with primitive equipment, and in many cases in laboratories which were little better than holes in the wall. The exchange of information between one scientist and another was a most haphazard and difficult procedure and was made still more complicated by the lack of common language, symbols and terminology. It was only toward the end of the nineteenth century that, due to improved means of communication and the adoption of universal scientific symbols, men of science were able to meet each other more frequently and talk more intelligently. This, therefore, was the beginning of what we know today as modern science. Until recently most scientists worked in or near universities and for the most part had little interest in the industrial application of their discoveries; in other words they were true scientists with only one objective in mind, which was to probe the mysteries and find explanations for phenomena occurring in nature. During the latter part of the nineteenth century there arose a number of monumental figures in science on this continent such as Bell, Edison and Steinmetz, whose names became household words because their discoveries had direct application to daily life. It was during this period that a number of industrialists commenced to realize the economic value of the scientist's work, and in ever broadening fields the scientist and the industrialist worked more and more closely together. The inevitable result was that scientists were drawn away from quiet contemplation in their small university laboratories to those large, elaborate and highly organized institutions in which modern research is carried on. The significance of all this is that in the past, while relatively few men working alone laid the foundation for our present technical knowledge, they had little direct effect upon the society of their day. Today we are spending millions and millions of dollars annually on research and the result of this work definitely and almost immediately affects world society.

It might reasonably be argued that the scientists of old had little, if any, responsibility to society, for in most cases the product of their labour was of no particular interest to people in general. This is no longer true today as nearly all scientific effort, particularly on this continent, is directed to some practical application, and little work is carried on for the mere joy of discovery.

A natural question now arises. If we say that scientists as a group have an important responsibility to society, what is the extent of their responsibility, and how does this fit in with other groups such as industrialists, propagandists, humanists and sociologists?

If we ask the scientist, as I have done on many occasions, what in his estimation is his responsibility to society, he will probably answer that he has no responsibility except to his science. What society does with his creation is not his affair.

The industrialist (and it must be admitted that many industrialists are not happy in this situation today) will tell you that his responsibility is primarily to his shareholders, to his employees, and, to a lesser extent, to his customers; but he admits little responsibility to society in general. Notwithstanding industry's large contribution to research, the question of conservation of materials and the more intelligent and reasonable use of the products he has to sell is overshadowed completely by the competitive situation. During the last half-century industry in Canada has grown from a relatively small entity to a force that in many cases challenges the authority of government. Certainly, as Einstein [4] pointed out, our governments today do not fully know how to control this situation.

The propagandists, and in this group I include newspapers, radio, television and the moving-picture people, unfortunately devote too much of their effort to sensationalism and do not use

---

[4] Einstein, A., *Out of My Later Years,* Philosophical Society, N.Y., 1950.

these wonderful gifts of Science to the building of a finer society. In fact, the most powerful elements of propaganda are in many ways nullifying the efforts of our institutions of learning. The situation is particularly bad on this continent, where even the restraint of good taste is often non-existent. For example, we have newspapers who send photographers to take pictures of the victims of an accident rather than to their aid. As for the news, it would appear that it has to be of the most sensational type before it can be acceptable to people who deem themselves the most "highly educated public" in the world. I know many thoughtful men today who read the newspapers resentfully and have given up going to the pictures, who never turn on the radio and would not have a television set in the house, not because these contributions of science are not wonderful in themselves, but because these marvellous mechanisms are not put to the high standard of use which would justify the creative genius of their inventors.

Unfortunately our generation often thinks of modern labour-saving devices or mechanical communication systems as goals in themselves, and not as means whereby the individual may be freed to contemplate and enjoy all that is richest and most desirable in the treasures of the ages. Basterfield[5] very aptly expresses the situation when he says people have come to believe that "metaphysics and theology are elaborate nonsense; and that art, music, and letters are evanescent and more or less entertaining phenomena produced by peculiar minds which appear in every phase of human history but need not be taken seriously." The social sciences also are almost completely neglected today in spite of the fact that, thanks largely to applied science, we are in the midst of a social upheaval, the possible consequence of which no man can foresee.

It might be well to dwell in more detail on the role that

[5] Basterfield, S., *The Place of Science in a World View*, p. 5, University of Toronto Press, 1953.

science plays today in the fields of industry, natural resources, and human society. Industry undoubtedly claims the greatest effort from science and pays well for its contribution to research. The result is apparent to everybody. Research in relationship to our natural resources is remarkably well taken care of by our governments. What has been seriously lacking is the rapid and effective application of known scientific facts to forest management, proper land use and general conservation of natural resources. In Canada, apart from medicine, science has made little contribution to urban and rural social problems as affected by our mechanical age. Our lack of knowledge on this subject is a threat to the stability of our society.

Let us examine the role scientists are playing today, the extent of their responsibility to society and, where this is not adequate, suggest what might be done about it in the future. Because the subject is so complex, an effort will be made to go from the general to the specific, in other words to draw upon conditions which exist throughout the Western world as they apply to Canada.

There are three broad classes of scientists. We have a limited number of brilliant, original thinkers of whom Bertrand Russell [6] said there must of necessity be very few until by some new method man's congenital aptitudes have been increased. In Europe such men still have much freedom of action and are respected for the originality of their ideas. On this continent the exceptional individual, whether he is an artist or a scientist, does not have a particularly happy time because the public in general (and personnel departments in particular, both industrial and governmental) have come to believe that anything out of the ordinary is queer and undesirable.

[6] Russell, Lord Bertrand, "Education's Place in a New Age" *(Saturday Night)*, March 7, 1953.

Robert R. Young [7] expressed the case clearly: "If this planet is to endure, we must be taught that the path to truth is not a collective one, that it can be attained only through the independent and critical approach, that it is far more important to criticize than to commend, to dare than to conform. Men are not sheep nor mobs, but fashion frequently decrees them to be so." All scientists are not necessarily odd, all odd people are not necessarily clever, but, if by chance a brilliant person is a little different from the rest of society, we should be only too glad to accept him as he is.

What makes the situation still more difficult on this continent for an original thinker is the great difference in salaries paid by our industries and universities. Many clever men gravitate to large research laboratories where there is little freedom of action, and, because they are obliged to do more development research than fundamental work, outstanding individuality is lost and the promising scientist frequently becomes an indifferent technician.

Next to the brilliant scientists come the clever, systematic people who, under good leadership, make excellent contributions. They constitute the larger number of men working in big research organizations, and they are responsible to a large extent for the excellent development work that has made modern industry so successful. As long as the programme is reasonably well defined, these men go to work with a will, but, unless they have first-class leadership, they are just as apt to go in the wrong direction as the right. For the most part this group of scientists is not made up of original thinkers, and, in many cases, these men are not too well grounded in fundamentals. Those who are less well trained usually feel that science is the beginning and end of all things and that other

[7] Young, Robert R., "A Marriage of Business and Education", (Presented at the Annual Barnard Forum at the Waldorf Astoria, N.Y., February 14, 1953).

forces in life, such as the humanities and social sciences, are of little account.

Lastly there are the technicians. Whether university graduates or not, these do a vast amount of work and are essential to any research and development group, but their contribution to scientific discovery is negligible. In other words, they are essentially craftsmen.

Turning now from a broad classification of scientists to their fields of effort and the type of work they do, the subject can roughly be divided into four divisions.

(1) UNIVERSITY RESEARCH. In Canada, while the university effort is not large, it is reasonably free of what might be called directed research, that is, work being carried on for some outside agency, usually government or industry. In the United States this problem is a formidable one today and many educators are fearful lest the universities lose their independence in research.

Our universities are finding it hard to acquire and hold brilliant scientists due to their inability to pay such men adequate salaries. Another serious shortcoming is the lack of over-all balance in research subjects. It is not suggested that each university be equally strong in every department, but in the over-all Canadian picture an attempt should be made to maintain a balance between the physical and social sciences and the humanities.

(2) GOVERNMENT RESEARCH. On a per capita basis Canada's 1951 federal expense ($6.14) compares reasonably well with that of England ($8.48) and the United States ($8.44). There is an appreciable amount of fundamental work being carried on in many departments of government, both federal and provincial, but on the whole the research is of an applied nature and directed towards solving some particular problem. In my opinion the calibre of personnel employed and the

quality of the work is very high. There is, however, at present a lack of facilities and personnel to carry through the development stage many discoveries made by the scientist in government service.

(3) INDUSTRIAL RESEARCH. In Canada there are only a few companies which have what could be properly called research departments, as most branch industries in this country depend for their scientific direction upon their parent company either in the United States or Britain. In the United States most industrial research is in the development field and this accounts for the tremendous success of American industry during the past half-century. To obtain some conception of the magnitude of this undertaking, of the total annual expenditure on research in the United States of three billion dollars, more than two billion is supplied by industry, approximately eight hundred million by the federal government, and the balance is spent by universities and research institutes.

The danger in the present situation is that, when new ideas fail to appear (and these largely come as a result of fundamental research), the huge industrial development groups will have great difficulty in justifying their existence. Many industrial scientists are aware of this situation and are trying to support more fundamental research both in their own organizations and at universities.[8] The industrialist, however, is frequently reluctant to invest such risk capital without much prospect of a return for a period of five or ten years.

(4) INSTITUTIONAL RESEARCH. There are a number of important research institutes in the United States financed almost entirely from private funds. In Canada there is an excellent example of this in the Ontario Research Foundation. In Britain shortly after the First World War the government

[8] Hill, Julian W., "Financing of Research—Industrial Free Support", (Presented at the Engineering College Research Council, Louisiana State College, February 26, 1953).

set up a Department of Scientific and Industrial Research which has encouraged research on a co-operative basis. At the present time there are forty-two Institutes assisting different groups of industries operating under this scheme.

In Canada five of the ten provinces have established Research Councils, most of which are completely different in character. In my opinion, each province should have a research council and their organization, objectives and outside contacts should be similar in character. In this way greater use could be made of the exchange of information between the councils in the different provinces and the federal government.

The four groups, university, government, industrial and institutional, could link and co-ordinate their work much more closely than they have done in the past. This would present a wider field for the leadership of our brilliant scientists, would reduce unnecessary duplication, would keep research costs to a minimum, and would permit each group to make the best of its own particular type of research, fitting this in with the best of the other groups. If we were to expand group or institutional research, the small industries in the country could make better use of the latest scientific discoveries. In brief, by closer co-operation of all research activities throughout the country both industry and government would profit and the people of Canada would benefit.

Let us now turn to the scientist's professional organizations in order to see what role they play in Canada's affairs. Nearly every group in the technical or scientific field has its own organization, representing chemists, engineers, agriculturists, physicists and others. For the most part these Institutes have three objectives. First, such groups serve as a means for the exchange of technical information among their own members. This function is well carried out today. Papers are presented at the annual conferences, and later published in scientific journals which serve to advance scientific thought and to establish the reputation of the scientist. Secondly, the annual conferences and frequent technical meetings create a spirit of good fellowship and permit an exchange of ideas amongst the members of a particular science. Thirdly, the professional institutes, as the name implies, attempt to clarify and promote the professional standing of their members. In other words, professional institutes help scientists to gain not only prestige from their publications, to make new and interesting friends, but also to obtain some protection in their own field of endeavour. This is all to the good. Unfortunately, these various groups fail to relate their particular sciences one to the other, nor are they in a position to study the effects of scientific developments on society in general. It is true that a short time ago a professional council was organized in Canada and functioned for a few years. This group was composed of presidents of nearly all the professional institutes. Undoubtedly some good was accomplished, but the council was never given sufficiently inspired leadership to carry it over the early formative years and as a result met an early death.

To summarize the foregoing, the scientist has turned his attention largely to the mechanical aspects of our present-day life. He has been absorbed by industry where there is a marked tendency, particularly on this continent, to standardize even the creative minds. This has resulted in a reduction of first-class fundamental work. While Canada is carrying on a reasonable amount of research, the effort is not as well co-ordinated or balanced as it might be. Except in large industries, the development phase of research is not sufficiently stressed so that, while the universities are doing a certain amount of fundamental work and government departments are carrying out a good deal of applied research, much more use could be made of our present fund of knowledge if the development phase of research was more generally applied. Lastly, while

Canada has fostered a number of professional institutes, these have never been well co-ordinated and scientists have been unable to speak with one voice on matters of national or world-wide importance. With all their present shortcomings, scientific organizations in Canada could very easily be brought together to form a spearhead for the programme which will be outlined later in this paper.

Whether we like it or not, due to the concentration of people in urban centres, we are bound to lose more and more individual freedom as time goes on. This is apparent to anyone who travels along the East River in New York or through the outskirts of our large cities. Here is proof that true freedom, as we knew it fifty years ago, no longer exists, a condition which seems inevitable in modern society. It would therefore appear desirable that every individual and every group of individuals should endeavour to adjust the bonds which limit their freedom in the way that hurts the least.

In my opinion the difference between a socialistic state and a true democracy lies not in the direction in which society moves but in the question of who holds the reins. In a socialistic state there are relatively few in control and these adopt a paternalistic attitude toward the rest of the people. In a true democracy it is the people who, through their small and large organizations from one end of the country to the other, guide and moderate in successive steps the policies of the various governments, municipal, provincial and federal. If we are to be a fine democracy, it is most important that we should have an educated and enlightened people. Contrary to general opinion on this side of the water, true democracy is most effective in the highly organized Scandinavian countries. For example, when I visited Denmark two years ago, I found that in the field of agriculture the interest in the application of science is so enthusiastic that it is the Farmers' Federation and not the government that pays for seventy-five per cent of the cost, and also directs the agricultural advisory service. (In Canada, by contrast, the government pays all.) In Denmark there are three times as many specialists in the agricultural field as there are in Ontario. The farmers sit on the research boards and also pay directly for all the analyses which control the quality of their produce. To a varying degree this is true of other activities in Denmark. It is also true of other Scandinavian countries.

In my opinion the apathy in Canada toward social affairs is undermining our present society. This is particularly true of the scientist. Therefore, I would like to turn now from a contemplation of the role science is playing in our modern life to the problems it should tackle in the next fifty years if Canada is to become still greater in every respect. Little need be said about the relationship between science and industry. Industrial scientists should certainly press for more fundamental research; otherwise the well which provides their livelihood will dry up and they will be out of employment. They should also see that the universities are not robbed of all their first-class men or, through the lack of good teachers, the quality of our graduates will deteriorate. Lastly, the industrial scientists, probably through their professional institutes, should restrain the propagandists from distorting the truth in connection with new scientific developments. This abuse is all too common today, and, if continued, will eventually lower the respect of the public for science.

The conservation of our natural resources should be the concern of all scientists and, through their professional institutes, they should play a most influential role. The present waste of our forests, soils and many other natural resources shows an utter disregard on the part of Canadians for the well-being of coming generations. In most of these fields corrective measures have been started but the work is carried out on much too small a scale. It is here that the industrial scientist with his appreciation of development research could be of great help.

Modern society, with all the changes that have been brought about by scientific invention, is crying out for systematic study: not the kind of research that a professor accomplishes with a few dozen students in a matter of one or two months, afterwards publishing his results in a popular Digest, but long systematic studies of the human being under different environmental conditions. This important field has been neglected in Canada for three reasons: first, there is no monetary return; second, the subject is extremely complex, particularly in the field where the humanities play a major role; and, third, because years of careful study are needed before sound conclusions can be reached.

There is no denying that the study of the human being and his place in modern society is most difficult, but this fact presents the best reason why no time should be lost in commencing elaborate studies. The final use that should be made of such findings must rest in the hands of the humanist, but his chances of error are much fewer if science has contributed to his fundamental knowledge, and if prejudice and personal bias play a minor role.

It is Lord Beveridge's view [9] that "the science of human society should now have first call on all our resources and effort; and consequently such sciences should receive in full measure the material means they require for their development as sciences of observation and not as arts."

There is practically no end to the number of sociological problems that need systematic study, a solution of which might very well have a profound influence on the future of our people. Here are a few of those which I consider most important:

[9] Beveridge, W. I. B., *Voluntary Action,* Allen & Unwin, London, 1948.

1. Education versus propaganda. Are the objects of education being fulfilled or defeated by our newspapers, radio, movies and television?

2. The real significance of our present system of instalment buying. How extensive is it and what effect does it have upon the stability of home life?

3. How are we using our leisure time? Should there be more directed recreation? Should adult education be extended and, if so, to what extent? A study of this subject as it is handled in Northern Europe should be most valuable.

4. Are we wise to encourage single dwellings that cause our cities to sprawl out for mile after mile, increasing the cost of living as well as the difficulty of transportation and of providing educational and recreational facilities? What are the advantages and disadvantages of modern apartment blocks?

5. How wrong are we not to put more time and effort into city, town and country planning? It is true that since the war our governments have been trying their best to induce municipalities to plan ahead, but there is such a huge educational problem that so far very little progress has been made. A good example of the difficulty occurred in my home town, Sarnia. In 1941, a master plan was drawn up by Norman Wilson, the famous city architect, envisioning a city of 75,000 population. It was a beautiful plan, and because the recommendations were so thoroughly scientific, a joy to any scientist. In spite of its many good qualities, the plan was not adopted largely because the businessmen, bankers and other leading citizens in the community did not appreciate the need of planning for the future. In the last ten years the city has grown from a small industrial town of 20,000 population without much physical character to double the size, still with no character. Today, in spite of the adoption of a belated plan, the city is a complete hodge-podge. I hate to think of its appearance in ten years' time. All this difficulty could have been

avoided if the people had been educated to appreciate the significance of city planning.

6. What are we going to do about noise? What are we going to do about air and water pollution? Surely, if science puts its shoulder to the wheel, these problems can be solved.

The first step to be taken, if my plan for the future means anything, is to expand many times our departments of sociology in the universities across Canada. Because the human element occurs in all such studies, the fundamental research should be carried on at universities where there will be no threat of political influence. Our governments and industries should support this work most generously because it will provide both these groups with a sound basis upon which to build future policies.

Strange, is it not, that, in spite of the almost unbelievable wealth on the North American continent, our governments hesitate to support the arts or pay university scientists what they are really worth? For example, the present federal government has dawdled and dawdled with the recommendations made three years ago by the Royal, more popularly known as the Massey, Commission [10] as to the advisability of setting up a Canada Council. Happily the intention of establishing such a Council has now been announced.

Relatively few people have great vision and still fewer are able to translate such vision into action. The important thing is to seek out and find our most gifted artists, architects and scientists, let them form the nucleus of the council, give them the observations, information and conclusions of the large group of clever researchers who have studied our society for several years, and say, "With this knowledge in your possession show us how to mould our society into something that is enduring and great."

[10] Royal Commission on National Development in the Arts, Letters and Sciences 1949-51, Edmond Cloutier, Printer to the King's Most Excellent Majesty, 1951.

I should like to cite two examples of recent success directly due to giving head to artists and scientists. One is the wonderful picture of the Coronation, "A Queen is Crowned", its commentary written by Christopher Fry and delivered by Sir Laurence Olivier, and its music composed by Malcolm Sargent. These gifted persons were backed by the technical excellence of the J. Arthur Rank Organization. The other example occurred in Canada. Accepting the invitation of a man whom most people considered an impractical dreamer, a few great artists from England came to our little Stratford-upon-Avon in Ontario and with the help of architects, scientists and the financial support of many people, produced two obscure Shakespearean plays so beautifully that over sixty-five thousand people, little versed in Shakespeare, came dubiously, sat spellbound and went away thrilled. Truly we are ripe for great deeds.

For purposes of simplicity, I will illustrate my ideas only in connection with the physical aspects of the suggested plan. A select group of leading architects and scientists appointed through the Canada Council or some similar organization should be charged with the responsibility of planning our future cities, towns and rural areas, based on the findings of university sociologists. But the vision of the seers must have the stamp of approval of the practical, forceful, successful people. Therefore a group made up of businessmen, government officials, humanists and scientists, should be given the responsibility of estimating costs, time required and sequence to be followed in completing the project.

Up to this point relatively few people are involved and the cost is slight. Possibly five years will be necessary to do the preliminary work. The next step will need many more workers and will be much more difficult to organize. Those required for this phase of the work can be roughly divided into two groups. The first will work out all details of the master plan and afterwards supervise the building operations, and the second, a very large group, will execute the work over a period of some forty or fifty years. I visualize a period rather like that of the Middle Ages in England and other parts of Europe when the beautiful castles and cathedrals were built. The architect, part artist, part scientist, drew the designs, the specially trained personnel worked out the details, and the craftsmen and artisans constructed the buildings.

Now there will be no difficulty in getting the artists and the imaginative scientists to devise a plan; after all, they are brothers under the skin. To bring together enough qualified citizens who would consider it a privilege to support the master plan should not be too hard. The third group, though not too different from the first two, would have members more diverse in character, who would, I am sure, do their part because there lies latent in nearly every man the desire to make a definite contribution to his country. Unfortunately many, because of day-by-day demands upon their time, hesitate to take on outside commitments.

Ultimately there will have to be some inducement to call up the full co-operation of this important third group. The practice in Europe of bestowing honours has resulted in many fine contributions for the public good. As the present Canadian government refuses to allow titles, our universities have stepped in to fill the breach, annually giving a large number of honorary degrees. In most cases, the universities are taking over the prerogative of the government in acknowledging public service. It is suggested that the State devise some means of public reward for those who make important contributions to society. Another suggestion is that, as a man's income increases, he should be expected to give more and more of his time to public service. The fact is that the federal government today at least recognizes the need for voluntary contribution in money by allowing a generous amount to be deducted when computing taxable income, both individual and corporate, for contributions to such institutions as universities, drama festivals, symphony orchestras and charities. From the higher personal salary brackets and corporation excess profits, individuals and companies could donate a very substantial sum. Unfortunately these gifts today are not nearly as large as one might expect. I feel the explanation may be that the donors do not get adequate recognition for gifts to community and national projects. The assurance of further contributions in time and money from our people would certainly release a great deal of voluntary energy that could well be utilized. On first thought, this suggestion may sound completely fantastic but actually it is not so impossible. Today, with shorter and shorter working hours, men in every walk of life have more and more leisure. Would it not be better for the man, as well as for the country, if he were to spend at least part of this time on creative social work and not purely on amusement?

After the artists, architects and scientists have done their work, and the organizers and the administrators in our communities have approved the general plan, there remains still another aspect to be considered. It will then be time for the propagandists to play their role, and sell the idea to the general public. Up to the present, the propagandist has profited from the cult of the psychologists by selling ideas to the public, whether good or bad. On this continent they have certainly served up a mixed grill. It would be most interesting to see what this same system would accomplish in selling the idea of an all-comprehensive master plan of Canadian life.

Assuming the propagandists have sold the idea to the public, the next step would be to put into execution the master plan conceived by the seers, approved by our advisers and worked out in detail by regional groups of scientists, businessmen and other leaders across Canada. We are now ready to call on the

vast army of craftsmen and technicians who will be responsible
for the physical work. How can these men and women, who
are essential to such a social scheme, be encouraged to give
their time, energy and money to execute the master plan?
Fortunately, this may not be too difficult. If they had not
put their shoulder to the wheel in the past, the beautiful
buildings of Europe would never have been erected, Canada
would not have the great industrial empire that she has today
and we would never have armies to fight our innumerable wars.
What is needed is a vision, clear and bright, and with good
leadership we will, as in the past, have craftsmen who become so enthralled with their task that they embellish and
enrich the designs of the architects. Naturally a large amount
of money will be needed to execute such a scheme. Have
we not a superabundance of just this commodity today with
which we are able to build industries without number, to
satisfy the desire of individuals for innumerable gadgets and
mechanical paraphernalia, and, when we are under the threat
of war, to spend unimaginable sums?

So far I have tried to show the strength and limitations
of our present society, for which science is largely responsible. I
have indicated the role that Science is playing today and, if
we are to have a country that is really great in every respect,
I have tried to indicate what will be required of the scientist
and his fellows in the future.

Who am I to suggest the type of society we will have in
fifty years? That should only be envisioned after this vast subject
has been carefully studied by many qualified people. I, a
scientist, have suggested to you today a scheme of operation
that could accomplish great things. After the enormous industrial expansion slows down in the next few years, man-
power and much mechanical equipment will be at hand. Surely
the people of Canada whose forefathers did not hesitate to
go west in pioneering days, who were courageous enough to

build two great railroads spanning the continent (even though they did overdo it a bit), who fought valiantly in two World Wars, will, if given leadership, create a society nearer to our hearts' desire. I cannot believe that we will long accept the present stupid philosophy that to achieve idleness is the goal of life, but rather will hitch our wagon to a star such as that which this summer brought a few great artists from England to our little Stratford-upon-Avon. Naturally, it is impossible to see the end of the journey but we must set out upon it and, as the picture unfolds, pursue the most promising avenues. What I have envisaged requires a higher general standard of education than we enjoy at the present time, a more inspired leadership, and a willingness on the part of a vast number of people to give their time and energy to social problems.

In spite of what I said at the beginning, perhaps, after all, I will raise the curtain and for a moment look fifty years ahead, even though this is a risky thing to do. I see a country where poverty does not exist, where there is a balance between our cities, towns and country, between the work we do to make a living and that other work which enriches our minds and further improves our way of living; I see recreational facilities of such magnitude that every Canadian has an opportunity to participate; I see a land where the approaches to our cities, instead of the eyesores that they are today, plastered with signboards, are planned and made beautiful by landscape architects; and I see the cities themselves where there is some general design in building, and where beautiful parks and gardens abound. Some may feel that this outline is too idealistic. My answer is that the suggested plans for Canada are already in existence in other parts of the world, chiefly in the northern European countries. Surely a young and growing democracy like ours can adopt such schemes more easily than older and more settled states.

In our maturity we should come to realize that our scientific and industrial effort, great as it is, is not the goal but only a means of freeing men and women that they may enjoy the rich, good life that has been dreamed of through all the ages. By good example and good teaching, we can use our leisure time to bring this state into being so that in place of unrest, hysteria and the sense of insecurity that is so prevalent today, we can create a country of which all can be proud, each one serving where he is most gifted to serve; a country where there is no unnecessary waste, where every acre of land is producing its maximum and where ruthless exploitation has disappeared. Then and then only can the scientists of today and tomorrow be truly proud of the part they play.

Never before in the history of the world have such great achievements been possible. The tools are at hand. We need the faith and the vision.

> "When the high heart we magnify,
> And the sure vision celebrate
> And worship greatness passing by,
> Ourselves are great." [11]

[11] Drinkwater, John, *Abraham Lincoln,* Houghton Mifflin, Boston, 1919.

BIBLIOGRAPHY

ABRAMS, FRANK W.: "Corporations and Education" *(The Lamp)*, Standard Oil Company (New Jersey), March, 1953.

BEVERIDGE, W. I. B.: *The Art of Scientific Investigation,* Heinemann, London, 1950.

FITZPATRICK, EDWARD A.: *How to Educate Human Beings,* Bruce, Milwaukee, 1950.

HENN, T. R.: *The Apple and the Spectroscope,* Methuen, London, 1951.

JAFFE, BURNARD: *Crucibles* (The Lives and Achievements of the Great Chemists), Simon and Schuster, New York, 1930.

SPEAKMAN, H. B.: *Faith of a Scientist,* Clarke, Irwin, Toronto, 1949.

"An Artificial Growth", *(Saturday Night)*, May 16, 1953.

"Physical Science and Human Values" (Symposium), *Nature,* p. 751, Nov. 13, 1948.

"Research in Canada" (Papers given at Symposium, Chemical Institute of Canada, June, 1945), Published by Imperial Oil Limited, 1946.

"Science and the Humanities at the Universities", *Nature,* p. 789, June 14, 1947.

"Science and Society", *Nature,* p. 211, February 9, 1952.

Springs of Canadian Power, A Chatham House Information Paper, Royal Institute of International Affairs, London, New York, 1953.

THE CONTRIBUTION OF INDUSTRY

Douglas White Ambridge

C.B.E., B.Sc. President and General Manager, Abitibi Power and Paper Co. Ltd.; President, Polymer Corporation, Ltd., 1945-47; Director, General Shipbuilding Branch, Department Munitions and Supply, 1941-44; member, Canadian Trade Mission to South America, 1952-53; Director, Polymer Corporation during plant construction, 1942.

THE CONTRIBUTION OF INDUSTRY

THERE must be in this great nation of ours dozens of men who are better able to speak for industry at this gathering than I. When I was invited to come here and lay my thoughts before you I tried to think of some reason for the invitation. I have concluded that the old story of the willing horse probably accounts for my presence here today. I am highly honoured to have the opportunity of addressing so distinguished a group of my fellow countrymen, and I thank our hosts for having conceived the idea of this serious effort to appraise the future of our growing nation.

Man has always been fascinated by prophecy. He is always trying to peer behind the black velvet curtain which a merciful God has interposed between the NOW and the TO COME. Charles Kettering once remarked, however, that all of us should take an interest in the future because all of us are going to spend the rest of our lives in it. But the history of prophecy among civilized men is a melancholy one. Hundreds of thousands of writers, poets, scientists, even stock-brokers, have written millions of words describing the future. Few indeed of this great throng of seers have enjoyed re-reading their writings a few short years after the ink was dry upon their manuscripts.

Our hosts were wise to admonish the several prophets who are appearing before you to confine their predictions to the next fifty years, a short time indeed in the life of any nation, of any race, of any creed or of any way of life. The chances of hitting the target are greatly enhanced if the range is short, as any student of ballistics will tell you. Most men find it difficult to cast their minds very far ahead, and I am no exception. Business leaders spend most of their time think-ing of the next annual report, politicians of the next election, labour leaders of the next contract. The effort involved in trying to push aside the black velvet curtain is, however, an exercise which I can recommend to my listeners. You will find it arduous but interesting. When you lay down your pen and put away the history books you will enjoy a sense of relief and well-being, like the man who made a practice of knocking his head against a wall because he enjoyed the feeling when he stopped doing so.

If we were to divide the unending years to come into a series of half centuries, certainly the next fifty years, the first term in the series, to use a mathematical phrase, would be to us in this room the most important. Few of us will be alive in 2003 but a great many of our children and grand-children will be active men and women, bearing, we hope, their responsibilities and making their contribution to the life of the nation. Surely, when one reflects on the matter, it is a part of our duty to these descendants of ours to write down something of what we have learned during our life-time. We can at least say to them: "We have worked and hoped and struggled. As a result we have found there are forces in the world which you will have to learn to deal with if you in your turn are to live happy and useful lives. Many of these forces are beyond the control of individuals, but most of them can be used to help you on your way if you understand their nature and use their power for the general good of mankind and the particular good of your own country."

I feel, of course, a great responsibility in setting down my ideas, knowing that they may in some small way be read and acted upon by some of my own descendants. I would not like to think that my grandsons would some day be ashamed of their old grandfather for having misled them on the road of life.

I propose to speak my mind. It is to me inconceivable that so eminent an organization as the Westinghouse Company would invite anyone to speak before a distinguished audience and expect him to deliver himself of the usual platitudes which one hears on the hustings. A speaker on this platform has an unique opportunity. He has no need to be elected to any office; he has no power to promise any of his hearers anything either good or bad, and he is not likely to be called upon to account for the invalidity of his predictions because he will have been gathered in to his fathers long before the end of the next half-century.

"Define your terms", cried Pascal three centuries ago, and this is still good advice. It makes one mark out the boundaries of the field which is to be the scene of the game we are to play in. Our hosts have left these boundaries largely to me, and I have marked them out without a tape measure so that I admit I do not know whether the area enclosed is of regulation size or not.

That incomparable industrialist, Henry Ford, at the end of one of his books wrote the specifications for this field in these words: "Mankind passes from the old to the new on a human bridge formed by those who labour in the three principal arts: agriculture, manufacture, transportation." I intend, then, to speak of industry as including these "three principal arts".

It is only very recently in the history of civilization that it has been possible to couple agriculture with manufacture or with transportation, but today the dividing lines between any of the three are so hazy and indistinct that it seems to me desirable to group them together, at any rate for the purposes of this discourse. We must now give some thought to the placing of the goal posts in this area which Henry Ford has enclosed for us. We must try to define the ultimate purpose of agriculture, manufacture and transportation. We must think about the goals towards which mankind is making its slow advance.

Macneil Dixon in his famous Gifford lecture, "The Human Situation", has this to say:

"To accomplish anything you need an interest, a motive, a center for your thought. You need a star to steer by, a cause, a creed, an idea, a passionate attachment. Men have followed many guiding lights. They have been inspired by love of fame and love of country. They have pursued power, wealth, holiness. They have followed Christ, Mahomet, Napoleon. Something must beckon you or nothing is done, something about which you ask no questions. Thought needs a fulcrum for its lever, effort demands an incentive or an aim."

What is true of men themselves is true of their organized activities. The three principal arts it seems to me also "need a star to steer by", and in this paper I intend to develop the idea that Canadian industry should have a plan and a goal towards which it must struggle during the next half-century.

No one who in any way appreciates the extraordinary changes which have occurred in the human situation in the last century can doubt that the purposes which mankind has today are vastly different from what they were before the Industrial

Revolution. Mankind has seen a vision, and mankind is convinced today that the achievement of happiness, not only its pursuit, is possible and in time probable.

Whatever any one of us may think of it we must all of us recognize that this vision has unloosed forces which are beyond the power of any man to imprison. We must try to understand the nature of these forces and so bear ourselves that we make their energy useful in the never-ending battle against poverty, disease, ignorance and all uncharitableness. Let us then concede that the ultimate purpose of the three principal arts—agriculture, manufacture, transportation—is the increasing happiness of mankind. This to me is indeed a challenging thought but on reflection not a new one. Most of us have it in our minds all the time.

Surely the farmer ploughing in his fields is not doing his work solely for himself and his own family. He does not plant a hundred acres of wheat to feed himself. He does not plant it because he likes to see his fields get green, then gold. He does his work and plants his fields and tends them because he knows deep down in his heart that the work he does contributes to the well-being of the race. Surely the men who work our great railways do not pour their energies into their tasks because they like to watch the trains go by. Few workers in industry ply their trades and draw up their plans simply because they must make a living.

The wine of life is to most men the inner satisfaction which comes from being part of some unfolding, some development, some growth. I have seen too much of men in every station of life not to know that very few of them live their lives strictly unto themselves. More and more does mankind realize that any man's happiness depends to an increasing extent upon the well-being of our race as a whole. These are strange words for me to speak at this stage of the tide in the affairs of men when the news of the day is mostly of wars and rumours of wars.

If most men are not greedy, selfish or depraved, if most men have seen the vision I spoke of, how then account for the bestialities of the concentration camps, the persecution of the Jews, the deliberate and planned starvation of millions by the autocrats who rule some of the nations which inhabit our globe?

Let us remember that most men are easily led. Let us remember that a downright wicked man often possesses the power of leadership. When such a man comes to the head of a nation terrible things happen, as the whole history of mankind shows. One of the greatest advantages of our democratic form of government is the fact that free elections often effectively prevent a downright wicked man from seizing and holding power for very long periods. It is true that the democratic procedures have not been able, as yet, to eliminate stupidity from the seats of the mighty, but then stupidity and wickedness are two different things. Stupidity can delay progress—wickedness can completely alter its direction. It is true, of course, that downright wicked men have seized and held power in the smaller political entities, such as the government of cities, but few of them have wielded national power in democratic nations. Certainly the converse proposition that wicked men can and do seize and hold power in autocracies is self-evident.

As long as this state of affairs continues among men, as long as the thoroughly depraved and wicked can achieve the topmost positions of power, we, the enemies of despotism, will find the road towards the final defeat of poverty rough going. We will often be frustrated; we will be angered; we will, when the occasion requires it, fight and lay down our lives. We have not chosen the primrose path. But I do not fear that the day will ever come when man will give up

trying to move forward along this rough and thorny road
at the end of which shines this vision of a race of men freed
from their ancient enemies: poverty, disease, ignorance and
all uncharitableness.

We who have had the entirely undeserved good fortune
to have been born into those communities from which the
ancient despotisms have been banished *must not* stand still and
wait until the rest of our race has rid itself of the rogues and
robbers who rule it now. What then must we, the fortunate,
be doing to move ahead this great array of free men which
stands at the head of the human procession on our rough
and thorny road? What, to be specific, must we, the leaders
in the "three principal arts" in Canada, be doing?

You may say to me: "What can we do? We are an
insignificant group on this earth. Who will listen to any plan
we may devise? Who will look at any star that we may
choose?"

Let me remind you of some pages in British history. At
the end of the Middle Ages, say at the beginning of the
sixteenth century, the population of England and Wales was
somewhere between four and five millions. The English historian, G. M. Trevelyan, tells us that more than four-fifths
of the population lived in the rural parts and that the bulk
of the population cultivated the land or tended sheep. Yet in
this island, sparsely populated with farmers and shepherds,
lived a nucleus of greatness such as this world had never
seen. For centuries there has flowed from Britain a great
stream of spirit and genius which has revolutionized the world
in all its aspects, including the three principal arts with which
I am dealing: agriculture, manufacture, and transportation.
Let us remember that we are the descendants of the men
who lived in Britain when she had a population less than
a third of ours today. Let us not be shy or diffident when
we approach the tasks that lie before us. Our ancestors

did not waver or we would not today count ourselves among the fortunate peoples of the earth.

We Canadians can do great things in the next half-century, but if we are to do them we must throw away some of our habits of thought. We must become accustomed to our newly-won status as a nation. We must regard our neighbours and our parents as a wise young married man just starting out in life regards his. He indulges his parents; he watches his neighbours with a wary eye, and he keeps on good terms with both.

No one that I have ever heard of has proposed a plan which provides for the increasing happiness of mankind if the population of this planet is to keep on increasing as it has been doing since the Industrial Revolution. That much reviled clergyman, Malthus, told us in 1798 that "the power of population is indefinitely greater than the power in the earth to produce subsistence for man." All of us have heard that this is old-fashioned, that we ought not to doubt that Providence will provide and that somehow or other the population of the earth, however great, will be fed, housed and clothed. I, indeed, have never heard of anyone who ever set a limit to the number of human beings which can be accommodated on this over-burdened planet.

As an engineer I cannot believe that the number of "God's chillun" who can live with some measure of human dignity on this earth is unlimited. Furthermore, I am convinced that it would be wise for us to call a halt to the "devastating torrent of children" which at the moment threatens to overwhelm us. There are few who do not agree with this idea. There are many who believe that somehow or other (methods not specified) the "torrent" will subside in God's good time and that then everyone will live happily ever after.

I do not subscribe to this *laissez faire* philosophy because I think I see a better way to get more positive results in less time. It seems to me to be unnecessarily naïve for anyone to pin his faith upon any of the chemical or physical methods of putting a stop to the "devastating torrent". The problem of checking population increases is not likely to be solved in those areas where the problem is most urgent by a course of lectures, because the reduction of the birth rate is not a physical or a chemical problem at all. It is an economic problem and it will not be solved until we attack the economic causes which underlie it.

I have no time now to enter into a discussion of the population problems of the various nations, but all of us know very well that high birth rates are a characteristic of the less fortunate peoples and that where high birth rates are the rule people are subject to famine, poverty and disease. Few of these people in high birth-rate areas enjoy their brief sojourns on this earth because their lives are largely spent in a struggle for existence.

I have said that the problem of population is an economic problem and will eventually be solved by economic remedial measures. Permit me for a moment to develop this idea. We must be careful in our thinking to distinguish between two concepts: "the standard of living" and "the scale of living".

A distinguished American economist, Dr. Willford King, has this to say on the subject:

"The term 'scale of living' is merely a name describing the broad characteristics of the individual's way of life. It includes the quality of his meals, the conveniences of his dwelling, the up-to-dateness of his clothing and the expensiveness of his amusements. Usually its altitude is determined by what the income of the family will buy . . . Careless writers, however, continually confuse this with the 'standard of living'—a concept of outstanding significance.

"While the *scale* of living is something objective which can be observed by others, a person's *standard* of living is purely mental or subjective. *The standard of living* of an individual is defined by economists as being 'The aggregate of wants taking precedence over marriage and a family.' That is, it includes all those services and material goods which to the given individual seem so fundamental to a decent existence that, before they will be given up, he or she will abstain from marriage and will refrain from increasing the size of his or her family. *The standard of living,* therefore, dominates the actions of the individual in the most vital of all matters. As a result it seems safe to say that the prosperity of any given nation is generally influenced more by the prevailing level of the standards of living of its inhabitants than by all other forces combined."

This, it seems to me, removes some of the difficulties which beset the minds of those of us who seriously study and struggle with the population problem. If we can, by some means or other, raise the *standards of living,* as defined above, in the less favoured nations, then we have put into action the most powerful check on procreation known to man, and we will be well along the rough and thorny road on which we must journey.

This is not, of course, a new idea. I feel sure that it has been the basis for the magnificent contributions by the people of the United States toward the easing of the burdens of those of their fellow-men who are in sorrow and in need, that series of acts by the American people which Churchill has called "the most unsordid acts in history".

But although it is not a new idea it is by no means a very old one. When the people of the United States set out during and after the second World War to rescue the nations from the bonds of poverty, disease and ignorance, they set themselves a task which was new to them and new in history. Mankind has had no experience in gigantic national efforts of this sort and there is still hardly more than a mere decade of experience on which to base the future course of great international efforts to bring about higher standards of living for the masses of men.

If, however, we have only a dozen years of experience we must at least use what we have. We in Canada have had a modest share in some of the great American efforts and we have helped in such Commonwealth schemes as the Colombo plan. It is my conviction that as the years roll by we in Canada will be wise if we spend at least as much thought on what we can do for others as on what we can do for ourselves. This is no priggish declaration. It is based on what I think we *must* do if we are to avoid the frightful dangers of an over-populated world.

It is fair to say, I think, that the short experience we have now points clearly to the danger that international rescue operations have so far tended to increase the "scale of living" rather than to improve the "standard of living" amongst the less favoured nations.

The British regime in India certainly raised the "scale of living" in the famous sub-continent. The "standard of living" was not improved and the result was that the population increased year by year, pressing inexorably upon the means of subsistence. Today there are many more millions in India living in misery than there were when first the East India Company began its work.

The problem of raising the standards of living is "some problem", if I may be allowed to borrow a Canadianism from Churchill. It will require the best tools which we, the fortunate, possess if ever we are to solve it. It will not be done over night. It will not be done haphazardly and it will not be done providentially. If it is to be done at all, we, the fortunate inhabitants of North America, must play the leading part, using the best intelligence and the best methods we have at our disposal.

All of us know that industry in North America will grow, that the population of the continent will increase and that there will be many more refrigerators, air-conditioning machines and motor cars at the end of this century than there are now. We know, too, that the industrial potential of both Canada and the United States will be greater, much greater. How can we use this increased potential, this greater power for good, to the best advantage?

It is easy to say, "Let us use it for ourselves. Let us see that every garage in North America has two cars, every deep freeze a dozen fowl. Let us see that there is security on this continent and that every man, woman and child has everything they think they want from the cradle to the grave." Anyone who believes that this should be the objective of industry on this continent for the next half-century fails to understand the human situation that exists today.

I am convinced that if we, the fortunate inhabitants of North America, try to build for ourselves "an island of prosperity" amidst the boiling seas of the world today we will not only fail miserably but we will be engulfed by disasters that we can only dimly imagine. We can see already how things are going. We see the most powerful nation in history devoting vast sums to defence. We see our own country doing the same. Both North American nations are spending their substance on building fences round their gardens to keep the rest of humanity out. Before we are much older we will realize that we are coming to a time when we will be spending nearly all we have on the fences with very little left over for the gardens. We may very well end by having a bristling wall round a bare barracks square.

Must we do this? Is there no way out? It is the purpose of this paper to suggest that there is a way out and that industry and especially Canadian industry can, if it will, lead the way.

It seems clear to me that if the *standards of living* of the less favoured nations could be raised the pressure on our North American "island of prosperity" would be greatly reduced. How do we go about raising these standards of living in far-away lands?

How did we raise our own? Surely the method we used on ourselves will not be entirely useless elsewhere.

It appears that most of us are agreed that our North American standards of living today are the result of the success which has attended the labours of those engaged in agriculture, manufacturing and transportation: in short, the success of industry.

It is my humble opinion that successful industry is the most powerful tool we can use in raising the standards of living of mankind and it seems to me to be clear that this powerful tool we have fashioned should be used abroad and, more important, that it should be used by those who have demonstrated at home that they know how to use it. If these ideas are sound then we come naturally to the conclusion that industry should be the major factor in the vast task of increasing the happiness of mankind which I take it we are all agreed is the ultimate purpose of all human effort.

I have said that Canadian industry can play a leading part in the great task which lies before us, and I suppose I should provide my listeners with facts and figures to show how big Canadian industry is, how fast it is growing and how big it is likely to be in ten years, in twenty and at the end of the present century. I have not done so because there is such a profusion of figures available to the diligent that I feel that this distinguished audience has been fully fed on figures and that consequently my listeners will be more interested in ideas than in the mathematical extrapolations which discussions of statistics always lead to when the future is being probed.

Canadian industry occupies an extraordinary position in

the world today. It is a place of vantage and a place of opportunity. This is so for many reasons. In the first place, Canadian industry produces much more of a great many goods than the population of Canada can consume, and this state of affairs is likely to continue for the next fifty years. Canadian industry must, therefore, export a substantial part of its production if the scale of living of Canadians is to be maintained at a level which can only be secure if there is full employment.

In the second place, it is highly important, in my view, that Canadian surpluses should be sold as far as possible in countries other than the United States. If we should ever content ourselves with selling our produce mainly in the United States we will find that we have become a satellite nation and we will have thrown away the glittering opportunity of becoming a full partner of the Great Republic in the stirring adventure which I am here describing.

Canadian industry is based upon magnificent resources, and has been and will continue to be well nourished by American capital and American technology. In fact, Canadian industry is a very promising force for good whose strength and talents are badly needed in the world-wide battle against poverty and ignorance and the noisome creeds and absurd doctrines which are bred and thrive wherever men live in the gloom of want amidst the swamps of famine, disease and tyranny.

If, however, Canadian industry is to play a leading part in the next half-century in world affairs then we, the leaders, must mobilize our forces, define our goals, prescribe the methods and acquire the means to do so.

We have recently had a good deal of experience in mobilizing industry in Canada. Urged on by the stern necessities of war the Canadian government and Canadian industry worked closely and harmoniously together for years and succeeded in doing a production job which, I think we can all say with due modesty, was a great and welcome surprise to our parents and neighbours. All of us who played any part in ranging the industrial resources of our nation against the enemy know that in Canada the government understands how to work with industry in the national interest, and that is, of course, highly important.

Team work between industry and government in Canada is easier to achieve because we are a relatively small nation where everyone knows everyone else. Under the leadership of the then Minister of Munitions and Supply, Mr. C. D. Howe, a very effective administrative structure was set up which resulted in extraordinary increases in the production of every sort of war supply. All of this experience is at our disposal and given public support could be used to great advantage again for the purpose of building up the standards of living of our fellow-men. Surely it would be worth our while to use this hard-won experience in a great national effort to forestall and prevent future wars.

You will say to me, "Ah, yes, but the excellent team work which was undoubtedly achieved in war time cannot be duplicated in peace time. Men are human and only under very special circumstances will they work together. Only when the very existence of their country is threatened will they rally and strive for a common goal." This is probably true and one might despair if it were not for the fact that today, all over the world, very special circumstances do, in fact, exist, circumstances which are every bit as dangerous as any which existed when that "blood-thirsty guttersnipe", Hitler, was running loose in Europe.

What are these circumstances? We have in the world today a nation infinitely more powerful than Nazi Germany ever was, possessing a war machine equipped with weapons so dreadful that they are, in fact, beyond the range of the imaginations of most Canadians. This formidable nation is ruled by men whose ruthlessness, even among themselves, is to us unbelievable. These men are dedicated to doctrines which few Canadians have ever read and which still fewer Canadians understand.

Let us make no mistake. It is the unalterable purpose of the Communist rulers to destroy any nation which will not bow the knee to the Communist gods. Let us, furthermore, put little faith in the hopes we sometimes have that sooner or later, somehow or other, these sinister despots who control the Communist world will be overthrown by someone or other, we are not sure just who.

Did the Germans themselves overthrow Hitler? Did the Italians rid themselves of Mussolini? Did the Japanese unseat their war lords?

We are living in dangerous times and I feel convinced that the Canadian public and Canadian industrial leaders would support a national effort to do something distinctly Canadian in the less favoured nations, which would fit them to withstand the blandishments which the ruthless rulers of the Communist world use to lure the unwary into their bottomless traps. What can be done?

In the very sketchy proposals which I am about to make I do not presume to be able to do more than outline a plan of campaign. Nor do I expect that this plan would remain unmodified if it were given serious detailed study. All I hope I may succeed in doing is to stimulate others to think on similar lines to the end that in government and industrial circles, and amongst the public, a favourable atmosphere may be created which will permit the growth of a long-range Canadian plan designed to bring to the less favoured nations some of the blessings which we, in our fortunate homelands, enjoy.

I should like at this point to summarize as concisely as I can what has been the burden of my remarks so far.

I believe that we are living in dangerous times. I am convinced that the two North American nations will not succeed in building and then defending an "island of prosperity". By the time the defences are deemed to be adequate the prosperity will have disappeared from the island. I believe that the dangers which threaten us are very intimately related to the poverty which permeates the less favoured nations and that in turn this poverty is due largely to the "devastating torrent of children", which presses unremittingly on the means of subsistence in great areas of the inhabited earth. It appears to me that we can only effectively check improvident increases in population by increasing the standards of living (in the accurate sense of that phrase) of the peoples concerned. It is clear that successful industry is the most powerful tool we can use in bringing this about and it follows that the people in our fortunate countries, who know how to use this tool at home, should be mobilized to use it abroad. Canadian industry can be mobilized because it is relatively small, relatively compact and has recently had a great experience in close and harmonious working arrangements with government. Canadian industry in the next half-century could be the spearhead in a vast adventure to which the final defeat of poverty would be the glistening goal.

H. de N. Kennedy, the official historian of the Department of Munitions and Supply, describes the various steps which led to the establishment of the Department and the wide powers which were given to the Minister in charge.

He tells us that:

"The Department of Munitions and Supply became the center from which all war production radiated, Canada being the only country of the United Nations that procured all war supplies through a single agency . . .", and goes on to say,

"Most of the work of the Department was done in four large temporary buildings in Ottawa where conferences could be held quickly, and advice or information relating to almost every industry in the country obtained without delay." And he pays this tribute: "A great debt of gratitude is owed to those industries which loaned to the department the services of leading executives, engineers and technicians and to the many permanent civil servants who contributed their experience and advice."

It seems to me to be entirely possible and practicable for the Canadian Parliament to pass what might be called an Anti-War Measures Act. Parliament could well bring into being such bodies as an Anti-War Production Board or an Anti-War Depreciation Board.

But before anything like this could be done the people of Canada would have to be convinced that such measures were worth while, and that the establishment of a long-range (very long-range) programme for the lifting up of the standards of living in the world would be of more value in the long run than the spending of billions upon what we call defence.

It has not been difficult to persuade the people of Canada that enormous expenditures on defence are necessary. Mr. J. H. Perry, Director of Research of the Canadian Tax Foundation, in a recent speech, made the statement that: "The Canadian defence bill in 1953 will account for more than 40% of the total federal expenditures, and it looks increasingly as though Canada is in defence spending to stay."

I agree heartily that Canada is in defence spending to stay and I wonder whether the kind of defence spending we do is in the long run very effective in bringing about real peace on earth. So far the methods we are using have brought about an uneasy state of world tension and an armament race which makes the races for armed power of a few decades ago look like Saturday afternoon regattas. We must all admit in our hearts that the way we are going about defending ourselves is not the long-term answer to the problem of reducing the pressures upon the North American "island of prosperity".

Let us, then, use our imaginations. Let us be as fantastically optimistic as were the builders of the C.P.R. or as full of faith as were the Fathers of Confederation. Let us make up our minds that something new must be added if we are ever to achieve real world peace.

I believe firmly that the Canadian people would support some alternative to the present dreary plans which call for tremendous outlays on vague and controversial programmes extending into unlimited time. The leaders of the people, their representatives in Parliament, must some day recognize that we are all wending our way down a blind alley, and must cast about in their minds for some way out.

This is where the leaders in Canada of the "three principal arts"—agriculture, manufacture and transportation—the leaders of industry, must see their duty and do their utmost to persuade and convince the leaders of the people that there is a way out of this blind alley and that we should be up and doing something to find it.

If I, myself, were capable of sounding this call to arms against armaments, I would undertake it, but as Mark Antony once declared:

"I am no orator as Brutus is;
But as you know me all a plain blunt man.
. . . For I have neither wit, nor words, nor worth,
Action, nor utterance, nor the power of speech
To stir men's blood: I only speak right on:
I tell you that which you yourselves do know;"

There are in Canada many men who could sound this call and if I were to succeed in getting them to take up the cause I would not have lived in vain. What would I ask them to advocate?

I propose that the leaders and moulders of public opinion should press for the establishment of a government department whose duty it would be to assist Canadian industry in a great national effort to lead the world out of the hopeless morass in which we presently wallow.

I propose that this department should, together with industry, map out those areas where Canadian help would be most valuable and most valued.

I suggest that any company willing to go abroad and establish industry should be encouraged to do so by adequate financial arrangements with the taxing authorities based on the experience of the Department of Munitions and Supply during the most recent World War.

I suggest that this national effort be regarded as a part of Canada's contribution to world security because I am convinced that the dedication of a part of our national energies to the cause of mankind will be as effective as some of the defence programmes on which we lavish money today.

What would result from the implementation of these proposals, not next year, not in the next decade, but at the end of this century and from then on into the future?

Dozens, at first, then scores of Canadian companies would, in due course, go out into the world to help the less favoured nations to improve their agriculture, their manufacture and their transportation. These companies would not be what might be called extractive companies whose sole purpose today is the extraction of raw materials for carriage to the home base. They would be companies seriously interested in the success of their foreign subsidiaries in their own scenes of operation. These "cells" of successful industry would be operated not by government civil servants but by industrial managers whose personal careers at home would depend on how successful their efforts were abroad.

As the standards of living and the purchasing power of the people in the less favoured nations slowly but persistently rose would not these nations become (slowly, it is true) better prospects as buyers of Canadian surpluses? It might even be that if success attended this government-backed effort of Canadian industry the effort might come to the notice of the powers that be in the Great Republic. Perhaps we could persuade the American people to join us in our great adventure.

I need not remind my distinguished listeners how small a dose of the proper vitamin will restore an improperly nourished body to health. I need not remind you how a few cubic centimetres of the proper antibiotic will completely defeat an entrenched disease. Would it not be wise to use some of the healing virtues of successful industry in our attempts to bring health to great masses of men who are beset with all manner of aches and pains?

As I come to the end of this discourse and re-read what I have written, the thought strikes me that I have advocated a course of action which the Canadian people could take during the next half-century. I have not as yet made any prophetic declaration that, at least in my view, they will take such a course. And here at the end I must now declare my faith that the Canadian people will not forever content themselves with building a bristling wall round their national garden. Sooner or later the people of this country are going to try to find another way of dealing with world problems.

I hope fervently that the Canadian people will find this other way sooner rather than later. The example of the Maginot Line should not be completely forgotten so soon. When we set ourselves seriously to this task we will soon realize that our great industrial organizations are the most powerful means we have for bringing help to the helpless, and health to the weary, sick, ill-nourished masses of mankind.

When that day comes I declare my faith that the industrial leaders of this nation will be ready to administer powerful doses of industrial penicillin wherever they will do the most good.

My countrymen, is it not meet, right and our bounden duty that we who have been helped so much in the past by our parents and neighbours should now, in the young manhood of our national life, go forth into the world and let our light so shine before men that they may see our good works and glorify our Father which is in heaven?

THE ROLE OF GOVERNMENT

Maurice Lamontagne

L.Sc.Soc., M.A. Chairman, Department of Economics, Faculty of Social Sciences, Laval University; adviser, Royal Commission on Prices, 1949; member, Committee on Combine Legislation, 1950; special adviser, Economic Research Branch, Department of Trade and Commerce, 1946, 1948.

THE ROLE OF GOVERNMENT

WITHIN the framework of the present symposium, several aspects of the role of government have already been covered in previous chapters and others, related to the educational, cultural and international fields, will be reviewed subsequently. Given this perspective, the present essay will be focused on the role of government in economic and social affairs. This is one of the most vital and controversial problems of our time, and is a field where conflicting interests as well as opposing ideologies meet.

In order to keep in line with the general theme of the symposium this essay is oriented toward the future. More precisely, it will attempt to forecast what the economic and social role of government in Canada will be during the next fifty years. It is useless to emphasize the tentative nature of such an undertaking, because it is evident that no serious person would contend that he could give an accurate and scientific long-term forecast, especially in this field where the

119

changes in the variables do not seem to conform to any precise law and where the unknowns can be determinant and numerous.

The forecasting method which will be used is quite simple. We will try first to detect the trends which seem to account for the past. Secondly, past trends will be submitted to scientific analysis in order to see if they ought to be modified before being projected into the future. Thirdly, the forecast itself will be formulated. Regarding this latter adventure, however, we must never forget that the only one thing certain with regard to the future is its uncertainty. This is particularly true with regard to our topic.

(A) EVOLUTION SINCE 1850[1]

The first phase in the application of our forecasting method consists in reviewing the past role of government in Canada, to detect what have been the prevailing trends. It seems that, from 1850 to the present day, a distinction can be made between two periods which largely coincide with two important industrial revolutions. In Canada, the First World War marked the transition between those two phases.

(a) THE FIRST PERIOD OF EVOLUTION

While it is always unsatisfactory to ascribe specific dates to different phases of general economic evolution, it can be suggested that the first period started with the end of mercantilism, when the first industrial revolution received its real impetus in Canada, and, in the political field, with the first years of Confederation.

[1] For a more detailed account and a more quantitative appraisal of the Canadian evolution during the period covered by this section, see: *Report of the Royal Commission on Dominion-Provincial Relations,* Ottawa, 1940; and *Canada's Economic Development,* 1867-1952, Department of Trade and Commerce, Ottawa, 1953.

The first industrial revolution was felt by different countries at various periods and in different ways. Among the countries particularly favoured by the new set of factors, Great Britain was the first to adopt the new techniques; and she was followed by France and, later on, by Germany and the United States. Because these countries wanted to profit most from the new conditions, Great Britain and France adopted the system of free trade, while Germany and the United States, whose new industries could hardly meet foreign competition even on the domestic market, established protectionist regimes.

The industrial revolution meant the rise of manufacturing, new methods of production and substantial changes in the system of sea and land transport. As has been frequently said, it was based on coal, steam and steel. For countries in a favourable position with regard to those factors, conditions created by that revolution offered tremendous investment opportunity and promised ample rewards to enterprising individuals. In such circumstances, industrial development could be entrusted to private initiative, which would produce rapid economic progress provided private enterprise was not discouraged by any system of intervention and regulation. Thus was justified the doctrine of economic liberalism, characterized by the *laissez-faire* principle in the political field, an ideology generally accepted in Great Britain, France and the United States throughout that period.

In the British North American colonies, however, economic conditions were quite different because the industrial revolution had an unfavourable impact, aggravated by the long depression which characterized the last part of the nineteenth century. Their economy was based on international trade, but free trade in England and protective tariffs in the United States, which were brought on by the industrial revolution, gave a hard blow to that essential pillar. Important industries, such as ship-building, were almost wiped out. Nor did the new technology favour these colonies, because coal and iron deposits then known were limited and badly located. Their respective domestic markets offered few opportunities for industrial expansion, because they were restricted to relatively small areas where the density of population was low. Potential investment opportunities existed, mainly in the field of railroad building and equipment, but prospective profits did not seem sufficient to attract private capital. Such conditions were in many ways exactly the reverse of the situation faced by other countries.

It was necessary, then, to find a solution to serious economic stagnation and, at the same time, to achieve the technological progress enjoyed in other countries by providing railroad transport facilities and by encouraging the application of the new methods of production as well as the manufacture of the new products. It was clearly a case where government could not adopt a *laissez-faire* attitude, and where private initiative could not be relied upon either to offset the unfavourable impact of the industrial revolution or to promote long-term economic development. On the other hand, it became more and more evident that the sources of revenue and the borrowing capacity of the governments of the various colonies were too limited to enable them to carry on such heavy responsibilities as separate units. Political integration of some sort was necessary. Thus, Confederation, which was brought about in 1867, can be interpreted as a political adaptation to the unfavourable impact of the first industrial revolution on Canada.

Although the Canadian people had a strong preference for private enterprise, the doctrine of economic liberalism requiring government non-intervention did not fit in with the particular conditions of that period. Consequently, even businessmen strongly favoured the Confederation project which ascribed an important role to the new central government in economic affairs. In general terms, these responsibilities consisted in enlarging, unifying and developing the territory.

The first task of the federal government was to enlarge the territory. It bought the North-West Territory and kept control over all its resources until 1930, thus creating a vast economic frontier similar to the American West. In addition, it induced British Columbia and Prince Edward Island to enter Confederation. Thus as early as 1873 Canada extended over the entire area she occupied until the addition of Newfoundland in 1949.

The unification of the territory meant the elimination of the tariff walls erected between the former colonies and the adoption of a common monetary system. Above all, it required the improvement of the transport system which involved the completion of the canal system on the St. Lawrence and a heavy programme of railroad construction. The role of government in this field took different forms: direct public investment, monetary subsidies, free distribution of land, guarantees for private borrowing. It finally ended up with the creation of a large public enterprise to integrate the network which the government had been obliged to take over.

To develop the territory it was necessary to build up important markets which at the same time would be complementary to each other. Given the unfavourable conditions of the export trade and of technology, such an objective was very difficult to achieve. The first step toward this goal was to ensure that the domestic market would be preserved for Canadian industry. This was the objective of the National Policy inaugurated in 1878. It was thought that protective tariffs would compensate for adverse location factors. As a matter of fact, many industries manufacturing such products as textiles, steel, tobacco, boots and shoes, were greatly helped by that policy, although farmers and consumers in general deeply resented it. These industries, concentrated in the field of consumer goods, played a rather passive role in economic development; they only responded to the dynamic impulse of public or publicly supported investment projects. However, for several decades, these factors were not sufficient to compensate for the stagnation of the export trade.

The end of the century coincided with world economic recovery. For the first time, Western countries felt the full impact of the industrial revolution. One of its most important consequences had been the relative decline of agriculture which meant that those countries were less than ever self-supporting in this respect. In particular, there was a huge world demand for wheat. On the other hand, Western Canada was particularly suited for wheat production and was, thus, in a strong position to compete on world markets. For the first time, one of the results of the industrial revolution in certain countries, that of free trade, favoured Canada. At last, the dream of the Fathers of Confederation, the setting up of an economic frontier in the West, was to become a reality. However, the colonization of the West, in Canada, was to a large extent a government enterprise and not a purely private venture as in the United States. The Mounted Police, not the ranger, dominated the scene. The central government owned the land, brought the people, mainly immigrants, provided directly or indirectly the transport system and made sure that wheat would move within Canadian boundaries at low rates. The rapid colonization of the West, coupled with the huge public investment programme necessary to organize the territory, favoured an intense prosperity and a swift industrial development in the whole of Canada.

Thus, before the First World War, the Canadian economy had finally succeeded in adapting itself to the conditions imposed by the industrial revolution. It had found a satisfactory equilibrium based on the complementarity of its two main sectors. Canada had a new staple product, wheat, which was sold on the international market and which was the dynamic as well as the autonomous factor of economic prosperity and development. On the other hand, her manufacturing industries, primarily oriented toward consumer goods, had adapted themselves to satisfy the main requirements of the domestic market, although they still needed various forms of protection.

The role of government in the achievement of that balance had been decisive. Long-term projects of economic development were inspired, supported and often initiated by the public authority. The birth or the survival of many private industries would have been impossible without the protection of the State. On the whole, private initiative merely responded to the impulse coming from the government. The latter really dominated the investment field and the scene of economic development. Given this situation, it is interesting to note that at a time when the *laissez-faire* philosophy was prevailing in the rest of the Western World, there was no protest in Canada against government intervention and interference, not even from business circles.

In contrast, the role of government in social affairs was restricted to a minimum during that first period. In this field, *laissez-faire* was not only required by the social philosophy generally accepted at the time but it was also made possible by the prevailing social conditions. The economy, based mainly on agriculture and on small enterprise, did not experience wide short-term variations in production. Massive and prolonged unemployment was relatively unknown. Technological immobility was low. Housing was not expensive, because modern conveniences did not exist and almost every workman knew how to build a house, so that the great majority of families could afford to own their own homes. The period of formal education was short. Sickness was treated at home, often without the intervention of the doctor. Children and old people, far from being a liability, could be employed at useful tasks, especially on the farm. Of course, social risks and extreme poverty existed, but, according to the then prevailing standards, they were expected to be solved on the private level. The family was the central institution of social life and it was primarily responsible for the well-being of its members. In cases when it was unable to carry on its responsibilities, private charitable organizations were called for. In the last resort only, local governments could intervene, but their role was to remain supplementary, secondary, and restricted to narrow limits. Thus, in contrast with the economic field, in social affairs political doctrine and concrete conditions coincided, and required a limited role of government.

(b) THE SECOND PERIOD OF EVOLUTION

At the beginning of the present century, when Canada was not yet completely adapted to the conditions of the first industrial revolution, several signs of a second one began to appear. In a sense, however, it was retarded by the First World War and received its real impetus in the twenties. What was the basis of this new industrial revolution, and what would be its impact on the countries of the Western World, and, in particular, on Canada?

The first technological revolution had been based on coal, steam and steel; the second was founded upon oil and water and on metals which became substitutes for steel, such as copper and aluminum. In some fields, it contributed to generalize innovations resulting from scientific and technological discoveries dating as far back as the previous century; in others, it opened new avenues leading to new methods of production and new products. It brought substantial changes in almost every sector of economic activity. In the field of transport, it was characterized by the automobile, the airplane, the Diesel engine, and the electric locomotive; in the field of communications, by radio and, later, television. Wood was used in the production of paper and plastics. New industries experienced rapid growth in manufacturing such products as automobiles, aluminum, paper, electrical appliances, aircraft, chemical products and others. The new industrial revolution witnessed the generalization of mass and standardized production, which favoured large-scale operations, huge plants, a further division of labour and increased efficiency.

The impact of the second industrial revolution on the various countries of the Western World has been too much neglected. In contrast with that of the first revolution, it was, on the whole, unfavourable to Western Europe. These countries had no oil, very limited sources of water-power, restricted forest reserves and few deposits of base metals other than iron. Furthermore, their cultural background and long-established habits did not facilitate the application of the new methods of mass and standardized production. Finally, their limited territory did not provide large domestic markets. This does not mean, of course, that economic development did not take place or that stagnation appeared immediately and to the same extent in these various countries. First, the favourable impact of the first industrial revolution was still felt, although its intensity was diminishing because the industries which it had created were gradually approaching their stage of maturity, and because the resources on which it was based became less accessible and abundant after a long period of exploitation. Secondly, these countries attempted to adapt themselves to new technological innovations. This meant new industries and new investment opportunities. However, economic development in new fields was restricted; because industries were unfavourably located for various reasons, they were limited to their respective national market, and, in many cases, needed tariff protection to keep it. On the whole, it is probably true to say that the economy of these countries is still based upon the old technology and on the old types of industries, and that the main long-term effect of the second industrial revolution has been to increase their dependence on imports and to reduce their comparative advantage on the export markets. Thus it appears that the private sector of these economies, while relatively stable in the short run, is incapable of producing an adequate rate of industrial growth in the long run, because profitable opportunities for autonomous private investment are lacking, at least under present technological conditions. Their economic situation is quite similar to that of Canada when the first industrial revolution gained its impetus. The methods of adaptation envisaged in both cases are analogous: political and economic integration of independent units, increased government intervention as a substitute for vanishing private initiative, and restrictions in the field of international trade. Before criticizing the orientation of policy and the state of social thought in Western Europe, we should take full account of these basic factors and keep in mind the period when even Canadian businessmen were not impressed by the merits of *laissez-faire* and by the advantage of free trade.

The situation in the United States was quite different. First, the full impact of the first industrial revolution was felt later than in Europe, and it more or less coincided with the beginning of the second revolution. Secondly, the new technology favoured the country in many fields. Base metals and especially oil deposits were abundant. The market was large and population rapidly increasing. Mass-production techniques were accepted enthusiastically; productivity rose; so did wages, and living standards, which in turn induced new industrial development. Nonetheless, there were some weaknesses in the basic structure of the American economy. In terms of the new technology, it lacked abundant forest reserves and cheap water-power, and its base metals deposits rapidly became insufficient to meet growing requirements. In terms of the old technology, coal was becoming an ever more expensive commodity and rich iron ore deposits showed signs of rapid depletion. In spite of these adverse factors, some of which are very recent, private initiative had plenty of opportunities, economic growth was rapid, the *laissez-faire* doctrine took the form of a dogma which was not shaken by short-run instability. On the whole, it is probably true to say that the American economy was mainly based on the old technological factors, although to a much lesser extent than in Europe.

In contrast with the first industrial revolution, Canada was probably the country most favoured by the new technology in the Western World. The development of the Canadian Western economic frontier had been viewed during the past century as an essential element in the balance which was to be achieved before the First World War. The Northern economic frontier, which was entirely located in the famous Canadian Shield, had been completely neglected. The new industrial revolution would reveal its natural predominance. It contained abundant and untapped natural resources precisely of the kind required by the new technology, such as wood, nickel, copper, zinc and, above all, cheap water-power. Later on, oil-fields and iron ore deposits were to be discovered, and apparently the outlook for future discoveries is very bright. These factors, coupled with the opening of important markets, especially in the United States, and the inducement to supply the Canadian market with the new products, contributed to produce a rate of economic growth probably unequalled before. For the first time, the rate of Canadian economic development exceeded that of the United States during the second quarter of the present century. Over the long run, prospective profits were high, investment opportunities were great and private initiative was very active.

Thus, for the first time since the industrial era, the Cana-

dian government was in a position to adopt a *laissez-faire* attitude toward economic affairs. It may be said that the doctrine
of economic liberalism was fully applied in Canada during
the inter-war period, at the time when economic unrest gave
rise to new ideologies in Western Europe. The only new
important responsibility undertaken by government in the
economic field was road-building which, of course, could not
be left to private initiative.

It was soon discovered, however, that the movement of
private investment was irregular and that, if left alone, it
tended to create short-run economic instability characterized
by inflation and unemployment. The great depression of
the thirties was the most dramatic manifestation of the new
industrial era. In 1933, private investment[2] had dropped to
18.4 per cent of its 1929 level, and for the first time in
Canadian history it was possible to see all the consequences
of an economic crisis in an industrialized country.

Broadly speaking, governments adopted the same *laissez-faire*
attitude toward short-run problems which they had applied
to the long-term situation. They tried their best to stick
to the policy principles of economic liberalism and to behave
as if they were private institutions. In the field of fiscal
policy, their aim was to reduce their expenditures to a
minimum and to balance their budgets. This produced quite
undesirable results during the depression: public expenditures
were reduced, public investments were replaced by direct relief,
tariffs were increased, the rates of existing taxes were raised
and new forms of taxation were introduced. Thus, the over-
all effect of government policy was to intensify the depression
and to increase social unrest. It must also be noted that,
during this period of hard times, important segments of the
Canadian population lost faith in the structural organization

[2] *Private and Public Investment, 1926-1951, in Canada,* Department of
Trade and Commerce, 1951, p. 17.

of our society and adhered to other ideologies such as social credit, socialism, fascism and communism, which were all pointed toward an increasing role of government.

In the social field, the situation during this second period was different from that of the first. The main source of change has been rapid industrialization. This phenomenon first meant growing concentration of economic power and increasing monopoly elements in industry. The factors of production and the suppliers of raw materials responded to the movement of industrial concentration by attempting to create other monopolies. This period witnessed the rapid development of the co-operative movement, the farmers' associations and the labour unions. Secondly, industrialization, through its various impacts, has given rise to specified risks and needs which cannot be met by the average family. Urbanization has meant that children and old people, who were an asset in a rural environment, have become liabilities. It has also created the need for several community services. The greater division of labour has increased occupational immobility and required more advanced and more expensive education. The widespread use of modern conveniences has contributed to increase the cost of building and furnishing private houses. Scientific discoveries and better education of the public in the field of health have raised the cost of sickness through more frequent hospitalization, more expensive treatments and more frequent consultations of the doctor. In other words, such risks and needs as old age, sickness, housing, education, unemployment and other charges, which could normally be met by the family unit during the first period of industrialization, have become social problems with the second industrial revolution.

Thus, the very conditions which permitted the government to adopt a *laissez-faire* attitude in the economic field obliged the public authorities to assume an increasing role regarding social welfare. If the cost of defence is neglected, the striking change in public finance since Confederation did not take place in the general level of expenditures but in their distribu-tion. With the second industrial revolution, the relative im-portance of transfer payments has increased rapidly while government expenditures on goods and services, including direct investment, have experienced a relative decline. This process of "socialization" of collective risks started in the late twenties but it received its real impetus during and after the Second World War. Some people have denounced this movement as creeping socialism and have given a derogatory connotation to the concept of the "Welfare State", while others have attacked it as an attempt to consolidate and perpetuate the vicious system of private enterprise. In fact, it is probably more realistic to say that the new role of government was not inspired by any given ideology but that it was an indirect impact of rapid industrialization; that it originated from the growing recognition that the second industrial revolution had upset the former state of affairs, and that the family unit was unable to assume certain risks that were no longer exceptional and light but collective and expensive. In other words, private initiative had failed to solve the complex social problem result-ing from rapid industrialization and urbanization in an un-stable world, and public intervention had become necessary.

(c) CONCLUSION

We are now in a position to set out the main conclusions concerning the evolution of the role of government in Canada since Confederation. Past experience shows that the striking fact in that respect has not been so much the extension of government responsibilities as their changing character.

Up to the twenties, government played an active role in the field of a long-term economic development through its pro-gramme of direct public investments and of encouragement to private initiative. It was the real dynamic factor in industrial progress during that period. On the other hand, because of its long-term influence over the Canadian economy and because of other features of the industrial structure, short-term economic instability was not so much a problem; to a certain extent, this explains why the responsibilities of the public authority in that respect as well as in the field of social security were almost negligible.

Since the twenties, however, the role of government has followed a different pattern. Long-term economic development has been taken over by private initiative, while public authorities have assumed new and increasing responsibilities first in the field of welfare and social security and later, especially since the forties, in respect to short-term economic instability.

It is highly important to note the Canadian past experience, because it shows that there is no basic general trend pointing toward an increasing role of government in the same direction. It also reveals that political ideologies have not played a decisive influence in determining State responsibilities. On the contrary, the role of government has been primarily functional in character; it has been adapted, with certain lags, to changing economic and social circumstances, which, in the last resort, were determined by the recurrence and the impact of industrial revolutions.

(B) A THEORETICAL APPRAISAL OF PAST TRENDS

The method of forecasting which is applied in this paper consists of two stages. It requires first a review of past trends and secondly a scientific analysis of those trends in order to see if they are likely to be modified in the future. We will now turn to this second stage.

It is probably time to say that a large number of people nowadays would refuse to project into the future the trends which we have found to account for the past. They would rather agree that we are rapidly moving toward some form

of socialism or perhaps even toward communism. Most of
the political theories which have been developed to forecast
the future role of government reach the same conclusion.
Among those, the Marxian theory is perhaps the most famous.
Schumpeter's thesis[3] is probably even more symptomatic because
it was presented by a scientist who classified himself as a
fervent supporter of the capitalist doctrine. Such unanimity
of opinion is impressive indeed, and before dissenting from it
we must provide a better scientific account of the facts than
the one on which it rests. It is, of course, impossible to meet
such a challenge in this short essay. However, some suggestions, susceptible of leading to an alternative theory, will now
be outlined.

From the above interpretation of Canadian past political
evolution, it is possible to build a general model describing
the behaviour of government in three important economic and
social sectors, that is, long-term industrial development, short-
term economic stability and social welfare. The main deter-
minants of that model are the consequences of industrial
revolutions and the different objectives sought by government
and private initiative.

There are two main possible versions of the model. If a
given industrial revolution has an unfavourable impact on a
particular country, this means that the long-term prospective
yield of new investments is small, that private initiative is
unable to provide an adequate rate of economic growth and
that, if the private sector of the economy is left alone, long-
term stagnation will result. However, this does not correspond
to a stable situation. In the normal case, government intervenes
by assuming a dynamic role in the field of economic development, which involves a more or less intensive degree of
socialization according to circumstances. Under such condi-

[3] Schumpeter, J. A., *Capitalism, Socialism and Democracy*, New York,
1942.

tions, the rate of industrial progress is likely to be low, not because it is sponsored by government but because it takes place in spite of unfavourable factors. On the other hand, government motivation is such that it need not generate a cyclical type of economic fluctuation; this means that the role of government in respect to short-term stability is relatively minor. Finally, government responsibilities in the field of welfare seem to be determined largely by the degree of industrialization: they are limited, if the country is still in its first stage of development and predominantly rural, but they are extensive and probably at their maximum if the country has reached an advanced stage of industrialization. Canada before the twenties and Great Britain since that period represent those two extreme possibilities.

This first version of our model has its counterpart. If a given industrial revolution has a favourable impact on a particular country, the long-term prospective yield of new investment is high, and private initiative is in a position to provide a rapid rate of long-term economic growth. Then, in the normal case, government takes a *laissez-faire* attitude in this field. However, it is a fact now generally recognized that when private initiative plays the dynamic role in long-term economic development it gives rise to cycles of prosperity and depression; this obliges the government to assume important responsibilities in order to maintain short-term stability. A wide range of policies is designed to attain this objective. Finally, in the field of social welfare, the role of government is likely to increase only slowly after a certain minimum has been provided. With rising and stable levels of income, the urge for extending government responsibilities in this respect is reduced.

The model just briefly described with its two alternatives may be interpreted as leading to an equilibrium theory of macro-politics. It also corresponds to what is sometimes called political functionalism. Some of its features must now be examined.

First, it is an equilibrium theory in the sense that it rests on a balanced relationship between two forces which are at the same time divergent and complementary, namely, private initiative and government action. It emphasizes the complementarity existing between those forces which are viewed as only two different methods of attaining the same objective, that is, general welfare. It is, of course, perfectly compatible with a preference for private initiative, but, if the latter fails to produce either long-term progress, short-term stability or social welfare, it states that government will come into action and fill the gap. Certain political theories have been too much influenced by ideologies assuming a fundamental opposition between private initiative and government action; this initial assumption has been very often the cause of their failure to give a realistic interpretation of political phenomena.

Secondly, it is an equilibrium theory also in the sense that the situation which it describes tends to maintain itself once achieved. Such a situation is stable because it is likely to give the best concrete results in terms of general welfare, which is precisely what most people expect from a given economic and political system. Indeed, the vast majority of citizens do not appraise a given institutional framework in abstract terms or in the light of what is promised by a new ideology but according to its performance and its achievements. What they really want is a satisfactory measure of general welfare and it is only when they are convinced that a given institutional structure does not lead to that fundamental objective that they are attracted by new ideologies. On the other hand, the situation described above is likely to lead to maximum general welfare because it is the only one resulting from the joint action of government and private initiative, each of those forces being in a position to give its most efficient contribution. Any other set of conditions resulting from the exclusive reliance on either private initiative or government action will be less satisfactory in terms of general welfare. Thus, it appears that the theory which recognizes the complementary relationship existing between government action and private initiative is the only one which meets the requirements of stable equilibrium.

Within that context, how can we interpret pure capitalism which is opposed to government action and pure socialism which does not tolerate private initiative? It may be observed that in most countries the first stage of industrialization is characterized by ideologies proclaiming the irreducible opposition between private initiative and government action and requiring the systematic application of one or the other of those methods to every field of economic and social life. On the other hand, experience shows that pure capitalism gradually leads to a situation based on the recognition of the complementary relationship existing between the two fundamental forces of political evolution where the role of each is mainly determined in a given period and in a particular country by the impact of the then prevailing technological factors. It is very likely that pure socialism will follow the same evolution.

Thus it seems that pure capitalism and pure socialism can be interpreted as unstable systems and as preliminary phases to the achievement of the equilibrium situation described by our theory. Both are temporary; they lead to the same stable situation but they follow alternative and convergent paths toward equilibrium. Consequently, countries which go through the capitalist phase are not likely to witness pure socialism. Our theory of political equilibrium is perfectly compatible with those evolution patterns which cannot be accounted for by the Marxian theory.

According to Marx, pure capitalism is supposed to lead to pure socialism and finally to communism conceived as the end of an evolution process or as a system of stable equilibrium.

However, political evolution has shown that, if pure capitalism does not correspond to a stable situation, it is not normally followed by Marxian socialism. On the contrary, up to now, that last system has been applied only in countries which did not go through the capitalist phase of evolution. Furthermore, socialism, in those countries, has been accompanied by nationalism and has brought land reform and industrialization. Those conditions do not correspond to the main features which were supposed to characterize socialism. Indeed, according to the Marxian theory, that system was closely linked with the rise of internationalism; it required the public ownership of all the means of production, which is incompatible with a programme designed to increase the number of landowners; finally, it was supposed to follow industrialization, not to bring it. Consequently, the functional theory presented above, which interprets pure capitalism and pure socialism as preliminary phases to the establishment of equilibrium or as temporary departures from that position, seems to provide a better account of the facts than the one offered by Marxism.

Thirdly, our theory is dynamic because it describes a situation of moving equilibrium. It states that the equilibrium position is moving with changes in the determinant of the model. In other words, equilibrium is characterized by a certain complementary relationship between private initiative and government action. On the other hand, the form of this relationship is determined by the response of the national resources of a given country to the requirements of technological revolutions. That is why it is not static but changing, and the equilibrium position is moving. The equilibrium relationship requires a constant revision and adaptation of the respective functions of government and private initiative. In a given country, as conditions change, equilibrium may require that government and private initiative play the dynamic role successively. In a given period, it may involve extensive government intervention in certain countries and predominant private initiative in others. Thus, even in an equilibrium situation, it is impossible to expect, as some people do, that the functions of government will be alike in all countries at the same time. Such expectations, which are based on a misunderstanding of the process of political evolution, are apt to induce some people to condemn the political situation prevailing in other countries as vitiated by invading socialism or by unfettered capitalism.

It must not be inferred from our equilibrium theory that the stable situation which it describes will always correspond to reality. There are two main sources of disequilibrium. The first is found at the point of transition between commercialism and industrialism or at the early phase of industrialization. Countries very seldom strike the equilibrium position in their first attempt.

They rather move gradually towards it and start from an extreme position which may be described either by pure capitalism or by pure socialism. It is not sufficient, however, to indicate those two paths toward equilibrium; it is probably even more important to explain why a given country chooses to follow one rather than the other. In other words, why do certain countries go through the capitalist phase while others adopt socialism?

A full account of that divergence would exceed the limits of this essay. The following observations, however, seem to contain some elements of explanation. Countries where, for various reasons, private capital is not available domestically or cannot be imported, and where the cultural and social climate is unfavourable to industrialization, are likely to go through the socialist stage in the first period of their industrialization. That type of socialism is dictatorial, strongly nationalistic and favours land reform. On the other hand, countries where the natural resources required by the prevailing technology exist in abundance, where private capital is available or can be

imported and where the cultural environment is not unfavourable to industrialization are naturally prepared to accept pure
capitalism.

There is a second source of disequilibrium which is very
important in relation with our appraisal of past trends and
with our forecast. We have seen that an equilibrium situation
tended to establish itself after a more or less prolonged period
of adjustment, when the natural complementarity between
private initiative and government action was in fact recognized,
and to maintain itself through the constant revision of that
relationship in the light of changing economic and social conditions. Of course, the underlying assumption of that equilibrium
theory is that both government and private initiative are willing
and able to readjust their functions in conformity with the
changing circumstances without too long delays. In other words
and in a more technical language, we assume no lags. However, such delays, caused by structural rigidities or by the
failure to recognize that the equilibrium position is always moving, are possible and they may lead to a temporary disequilibrium.
Viewed in the context of the Western World and from the point
of view of the role of government, they seem to arise when
public authorities do too little or too much, according to
circumstances, either in the field of long-term industrial development or of short-term economic stability or of social welfare.
Although those lags may result from a false appraisal of a
given situation, they usually mean that a pressure group
has succeeded in imposing its own ideology on the government,
with the consequence that the latter does not fulfil in due
time the role required by circumstances.

The triumph of an extreme ideology in the political field,
whether it is based on the exclusive reliance on private initiative or on government action, always brings economic and
social unrest and sooner or later breeds the opposite ideology,
especially in mature societies. When such a process starts, it

splits the population of a country into ideological groups bitterly fighting each other and trying hard to secure political power to promote their own ideology. This situation either brings constant political instability or the temporary consolidation of an extreme ideology by an undemocratic government, which of course leads to a catastrophe. Several illustrations of such situations could be given by reviewing the political evolution of the Western World during the last decades.

The dangers and evils arising from this source of disequilibrium can be avoided if business groups and labour groups can refrain from developing their preference for private initiative or government action into an ideological dogma and, above all, if the government can constantly readjust its role in the light of changing circumstances and act in such a way as to be above the suspicion that it is exclusively influenced by any given pressure group.

We are now in a position to summarize our brief incursion into the field of political science. The above tentative theory can be reduced to the following basic propositions.

1. The process of political evolution leads sooner or later to a situation of stable equilibrium, which is moving according to changing economic and social conditions, and which rests on a combination of forces that can best realize general welfare.

2. That situation of moving equilibrium, which is usually attained after a certain period of adjustment, does not correspond to pure capitalism, which means the systematic reliance on private initiative, or to pure socialism which relies exclusively on government action. It is rather characterized by the recognition of a complementary relationship between the private and the public sectors of our society.

3. This complementary relationship is mainly determined in the long run by the impact of industrial revolutions or by the response of the natural resources of a country to the

technology prevailing during a certain period. Thus, the role of government can be deduced from that main determinant and from the basic features of the behaviour of the private sector.

4. In an equilibrium situation, if the impact of technological factors is favourable to a given country, the main responsibilities in the field of long-term industrial development are left to private initiative, but the role of government in respect to short-term economic stability and social welfare is decisive. On the other hand, if the impact of technology is unfavourable, then the role of government in the field of long-term industrial progress will be determinant but its functions in respect to short-term stability will be greatly reduced while its responsibilities in the field of social welfare will depend to a large extent on the degree of industrialization.

5. Finally, two main sources of disequilibrium have been detected. The first coincides with the passage from mercantilism to industrialism. During that transition period, most countries go through a temporary phase of pure capitalism or of pure socialism, but those two avenues can be viewed as convergent paths toward the same equilibrium position. Once that position has been attained, another source of disequilibrium is still possible. Generally it is due to a static interpretation of the equilibrium position, which is essentially moving; this, in turn, is usually explained by the fact that an extremist ideology is dominating the political scene. For instance, a government may refuse, because of its unlimited faith in private initiative, to take on more responsibilities in a certain field although such a step is required by changing conditions. Thus the static interpretation of the dynamic relationship existing between private initiative and government action causes a temporary departure from the equilibrium position and may leave crucial problems without solutions. If the ideology and the sectional interests which are at the origin of the evil are not too

solidly rooted, the result may be limited to short-run political instability. On the other hand, if they are strongly entrenched, so that delays in solving the important problems of a period are prolonged, then this situation may produce a profound disequilibrium and lead to the temporary victory of an opposite ideology. We may also mention a third source of disequilibrium: the direct intervention of a foreign power to impose by force its own ideology on another country. However, our theory does not take that possibility into account so that the forecast which is based on the above interpretation does not envisage conquest by force or political disequilibrium by conquest.

Our brief scientific inquiry contributes at least to raise serious doubts about the foundation of those political theories which assert that the evolution process leads more or less inevitably toward pure socialism, conceived as a stable system. It also shows that our interpretation of Canadian past experience not only accounts for a single set of conditions which may not repeat themselves but has a much more general theoretical validity. Finally, we are led to the conclusion that past trends are not likely to be modified in the future in Canada and that the model which we have just outlined can serve as the basis of our forecast.

(C) THE ROLE OF GOVERNMENT IN CANADA: A FORECAST

The recognition of the complementary relationship between private initiative and government action has been the dominant feature of our political history at least since 1867, and there is no evidence at present to show that this long-established tradition will be broken. On the contrary, all the facts indicate that it will be strengthened.

First, the present attitude of the Canadian government in

that regard is clear and has been re-stated on several occasions since the publication of the White Paper on employment and income. Only recently, the Prime Minister, the Right Honourable Louis St. Laurent, declared:

"I think all of us recognize the fact that there are some things which it is more appropriate to have done by public authorities than by free enterprise. But I think we are all most happy when free enterprise does what is required to be done and public authorities do not have to intervene."[4]

On another occasion, he said:

"I don't think that free enterprise requires that governments do nothing about economic conditions. Governments can—and I believe governments should—pursue fiscal and commercial policies which will encourage and stimulate enterprise and wise government policies can do a lot to maintain the right kind of economic climate."[5]

Secondly, the major political parties recognize this fundamental complementarity existing between private initiative and government action, although they differ slightly, especially during electoral campaigns, on the emphasis to be put on either of these forces. Basically, those parties, once in power, behave according to the same functional principles.

Finally, it is evident that there are differences of opinion among the various sectors of the Canadian population as to what government should or should not do. However, these divergent preferences have not developed into opposite ideologies. Slogans denouncing the Welfare State or creeping socialism or government controlled by wicked capitalists had to be imported from other countries and were soon found to be unfit for Canadian consumption.

Thus, it may be inferred that the Canadian situation in the

[4] House of Commons Debates, Monday, May 4, 1953, p. 4764.

[5] Statement by the Prime Minister at the Annual Convention of the Canadian Lumbermen's Association, Montreal, February 9, 1953, pp. 9 and 10.

future will continue to reflect the equilibrium position and that the basic complementarity between private initiative and government action will be recognized in fact as it is described by our functional theory. If, in addition, it is accepted that the actual form of that relationship is mainly determined by the impact of the prevailing technology on the natural resources of a country, it becomes possible to formulate a forecast of the future role of government in Canada in the three important fields of long-term industrial development, short-term economic stability and social welfare.

It has been shown previously that the second industrial revolution, which gained its momentum in the twenties and which was based on oil, water and power, electricity, and substitutes for steel, had greatly favoured Canada because her natural resources corresponded to the requirements of the new technology. Now, it is generally recognized that the resources of our Northern frontier are abundant, various and almost untapped. Oil and natural gas production is just beginning, undeveloped sources of water power are still enormous and new mineral discoveries hardly make the news any more. It is fair to say, then, that for the next four or five decades, investment opportunities will be greater than they have been in the past if the present technological factors continue to prevail.

However, the recurrence of industrial revolutions is the inevitable outcome of scientific progress. Such major technological changes are likely to occur when a new and important source of power that can be economically utilized is discovered. The next one will likely be based on atomic energy. What will be its impact? It will no doubt make power a much more ubiquitous factor than it has been in the past, since its source will become easily transportable. Thus the different regions of the world will be almost equally favoured in this respect. However, countries having abundant and various natural resources will still possess a tremendous advantage. Furthermore, its more likely effect will be to create new investment opportunities leading to the development of new industries and new products rather than to slow down industrial progress based on the old technology. The net result of industrial revolutions seems to consist in developing new techniques and new products without destroying the old ones. If those considerations are justified it follows that the forthcoming technological revolutions will increase rather than reduce investment outlets in Canada.

The normal implication to be drawn from this outlook is that private initiative will continue to play the dynamic and dominant role in the field of long-term industrial development in Canada during the next decades. The role of government will be auxiliary and conditioning. It will consist mainly in maintaining a favourable climate for private initiative and in adopting policies designed to ensure that the natural resources will be rationally utilized to the advantage of the Canadian population.

This outlook has direct implications on the future short-run situation. Indeed, there is no inherent mechanism in the private economic sector which guarantees stability at full employment levels. On the contrary, the instability described by the trade cycle is now familiar. The successive phases of inflation and unemployment have their origin in the irregularity of investment expenditures and are amplified by the multiplier and acceleration mechanisms. Basically, the equilibrium situation of the system requires the equality of intended savings and investments. This condition is very seldom realized because these two variables are not determined by the same factors; furthermore, even if it is satisfied, it does not necessarily correspond to full employment. The explanation of such a situation lies outside the scope of this essay. For our present purpose, it is sufficient to observe, as it is now generally recognized, that when private initiative plays the dominant role in respect to long-term development it leads almost inevitably to short-term economic instability.

Two other rather elementary observations must be made. First, the majority of the people will not appraise our institutional structure only according to the long-run performance and the ideological value of private initiative; this means that short-term instability will not be accepted. It is even doubtful if another acute depression will be tolerated. Business groups are becoming more conscious of this danger: they are learning to be more practical in their effort to avoid it and less emotional about their ideological preferences. Secondly, it is gradually being recognized that the private sector of the economy cannot undertake the responsibilities of ensuring short-term stability because they would be incompatible to a large extent with its basic motivation. Prosperity ends when pessimistic expectations on prospective profits prevail. Under those conditions, if a high level of activity is to be maintained, the main initiative must come from outside the private sector of the economy, from an institution which is influential enough to produce a sufficient compensatory effect and which does not respond to the profit motive. Only the government is in a position to fulfil that role.

Thus, if the theory developed in this essay holds, the main responsibility of our government in the future will consist in maintaining short-term economic stability. On the success of this vital role will depend the stable level of general welfare and the survival of private initiative in the field of long-term development.

This objective of government action will require the contribution of each sector of general economic policy. Thus, monetary policy, international trade policy, fiscal policy and public debt management will become the major weapons to fight instability. However, these instruments, to be really effective, must be integrated into a unified plan prepared in advance. In other words, a depression is a danger which is similar in several ways to an aggression. The best defence against it consists in trying to make it impossible and in being prepared to fight it if the attempt to avoid it is unsuccessful. From this point of view, economic preparedness to fight a depression is just as important as military preparedness to resist an aggression. We must also realize that an acute depression might bring a situation which would be very similar to the one which would be created by a successful aggression.

The future role of government in the field of economic stability will be crucial and highly complex. It will require centralized responsibility, growing reliance on expert knowledge and judgment, constant collaboration between the different levels of government and co-operation from private groups as well as from the people generally. We must be conscious of these essential requirements and act accordingly if we want to avoid a situation of large-scale and dangerous disequilibrium. We must not repeat the error of the late twenties and indulge in unjustified optimism. Finally, it must be remembered that the state of our economic preparedness in case of a depression has progressed much less in recent years than has our military defence network; we devote large sums of money for scientific research to develop new military weapons, but many people, even in government, still believe that economic research should be confined to ivory towers.

One of the basic features of our political evolution since the twenties has been the growing role of government in the field of social welfare, which includes aid to education and housing, and various schemes of assistance and of social security. This trend has been so marked that governments in the Western World have been frequently described as "Welfare States". In Canada, this movement will still continue to grow rapidly for a certain period because government will assume increased responsibilities in the fields of education, housing and health. However, with the adoption of stable and adequate schemes covering these sectors, the major phase in the development of our system of social welfare will be completed, since the minimum requirements of the main social needs and risks will have been met. There will be a growing resistance to extending social welfare beyond that point, because people will develop a preference for spending their incomes as they wish rather than pay more taxes. Moreover, the demand for greater social security will be reduced if economic stability is achieved. Thus, after the additions above mentioned have been made, the task of the future will simply consist in the periodical adjustments of the minimum standards provided by the welfare system to the upward trend of our living conditions.

If we relate this general outlook for the future to past experience, it seems that the past and future evolution of the role of government can be divided into three major periods each of which is characterized by a specific dominant feature. Before the twenties, the main objective of government policy was long-term industrial development. Since the twenties, the peaceful activity of government has been concentrated on the field of social welfare. However, the responsibilities assumed in this sector will probably lose some of their relative importance. Finally, the major task which lies ahead for government is the field of short-term economic stability. This is probably the most difficult assignment that can be given to government and yet it is most imperative. If we do not succeed in achieving a satisfactory degree of economic stability, if we do not take the necessary means to avoid inflationary spirals, and, above all, acute depressions, then the present foundation of our democratic society is doomed and we may go through a very dark period before returning to a new situation of stable equilibrium. In the years to come, more than ever before, the essential complementarity existing between private initiative and government action will have to be recognized both in theory and in practice.

GENERAL CONCLUSION

Our forecast concerning the future role of government has several important implications. Two of them, in particular, deserve to be mentioned at least briefly. The first is related to the orientation of federalism in Canada and the second to the problem of bureaucracy.

The political integration effected in Canada in 1867 resulted mainly from the unfavourable impact of the first industrial revolution. A vital role was then assigned to government in the field of long-term economic development, and Confederation was the recognition of the fact that only a central authority could effectively assume those heavy responsibilities. That is why the federal government occupied a dominant position in the Canadian federation until the twenties. After the First World War, the initial objectives of Confederation had been achieved and government intervention in the field of long-term industrial development had ceased to be necessary within the new technological set-up, so that the importance of the federal government was greatly reduced. On the other hand, the rise of the automobile as a new means of transport, the growing importance of natural resources as the foundation of economic development, rapid industrialization and urbanization contributed to establish provincial legislatures in a dominant position. The Great Depression seems to have brought this phase of provincial autonomy to an end. For various reasons, provincial governments did not provide the most basic measures of social security and the federal government took the initiative in this field. This trend will be maintained in the future until the minimum requirements of the main social needs and risks are met. Thus, the federal authorities will continue to assume the most important responsibilities of government in the field of social welfare.

In respect to short-term economic stability, the role that can be played by provincial governments is limited because they have no jurisdiction in the field of international trade and of monetary policy; moreover, their borrowing capacity and their fiscal powers are restricted. In addition, it must also be recognized that a stabilization programme requires a central authority and a unified economic policy. All these factors indicate that the federal government will be obliged to play the dominant role in the collective effort to avoid economic instability. Account should also be taken of its vital responsibilities in respect to national defence. Thus the situation which we are now facing has some analogies with the condition prevailing before Confederation. In 1867, political unification was effected under the leadership of the new federal government and around the objective of long-term industrial development. Now, a new federalism is rising with the federal government still in a dominant position but, this time, derived from the aim of short-term economic stability.

In recent years, the rising power of bureaucracy has been criticized and the demand for the restoration of responsible government has become a favourite theme in some circles. It is interesting to note that very often those criticisms were formulated by people who were themselves bureaucrats of the private enterprise sector. Indeed, bureaucracy is not an institution confined to government. It is also growing in business organizations and in labour unions.

This trend is brought about by many factors. The first and probably the most important is the large-scale proportions attained by our economic, social and political institutions, which has made direct and immediate control almost impossible. A second factor has been the growing complexity of the problem faced by those various organizations. Finally, the progress accomplished by social sciences has given rise to expert and specialized knowledge in this field. As a result of these various evolutions, the reliance on experts has become not only possible but often necessary.

The expansion of bureaucracy certainly creates crucial problems with regard to the democratic control of our private and public institutions. Some people are proposing to solve these difficulties by getting rid of experts. This drastic solution is of course irrational and unrealistic. It is certainly as desirable to be able to rely on specialized advisers in the field of social sciences as it is in the sector of natural sciences. Moreover, this trend toward a certain form of technocracy will almost inevitably be growing; even its critics, if in a responsible position, would not take the risks of refusing expert advice. Thus the society of tomorrow will have to face the problem of bureaucracy. To solve it, it will be necessary to create new methods of democratic control and perhaps also to revise our concept of democracy. A preliminary but essential step in the right direction would consist in getting rid of current prejudices in this regard and in recognizing that the problem is not peculiar to government but that it is also present in business and labour organizations. It may well be that a more enlightened public opinion can provide the only satisfactory and permanent answer to that question, so vital for the future strengthening of our democratic institutions.

THE CHALLENGE TO EDUCATION

Norman A. M. MacKenzie

C. M. G., M. M.,
Q.C., LL.D., F.R.S.C. President, University of British Columbia; member, Royal Commission on The Arts, Letters and Sciences; legal adviser, I.L.O., Geneva, 1925-27; Professor of Law, University of Toronto, 1927-40; Chairman, Wartime Information Board, 1943-45.

THE CHALLENGE TO EDUCATION

THE first thought which occurs to me in examining the prospects for Canadian education in the next fifty years is how really remarkable has been the advance in the last half-century. To name only a few of the achievements: compulsory education has been established as a principle which now everyone takes for granted; almost all Canadian children complete elementary schooling, and a large proportion receive a high-school education; many thousands of formerly autonomous one-school districts have been consolidated into large units which offer increasing opportunities to Canadian rural children; there has been a remarkable proliferation of technical and vocational institutions; university enrolment across the nation has multiplied several times; certain mass media of communication have come into existence as educational influences; and the adult education movement has come into being in many Canadian communities, again as a principle of national growth which has established its claim to continuance. Indeed, it is

155

not too much to say that Canada's educational growth has gone stride by stride with the development of the country itself. Aside from educational advancement, one wonders at times how many of our citizens are fully aware of the transformation in Canada from 1903 to the present day; from colonial to autonomous status within the Commonwealth of nations; from a country primarily agricultural to a country which is one of the important industrial nations of the world; from a country of seven provinces to a country of ten, stretching now from Newfoundland to British Columbia. There is even an element of the miraculous, for example, in how the Canadian West has developed, how the provinces of Saskatchewan and Alberta have come into being, and how these with Manitoba and British Columbia now form an area which is developing not only new mineral and power resources but great new human resources as well. For a Canadian a feeling of inspiration mingled with pride is almost inevitable when he stops to consider that this great western area has developed four important provincial systems of education with their universities, elementary and secondary schools, their training colleges for teachers and adult education and correspondence courses; and three new universities have come into being, each of which can lay claim to an honourable place in the developing story of Canadian higher education. And almost all of this has been within fifty years! Yet that is only part of the story, for in Eastern Canada, too, developments less spectacular but equally noteworthy have taken place.

It is important to remind ourselves of the physical achievements of Canadian education over the past half-century, because many of its critics fail to keep this perspective of expansion and construction in mind. However, in considering the coming fifty years I should like to stress principles rather than statistics, and to examine what *kinds* of educational emphases Canada is going to need in the future. It is no small thing to have provided a great many educational facilities of a reasonably high quality in a new country of the dimensions of Canada. However, we have only to think seriously about the demands and challenges of the next half-century to realize that the *quality* of education for young Canadians cannot in any sense be considered as somehow incidental or peripheral to the great job of establishing what we call "educational opportunity for all". But no one can mention the *quality* of Canadian education without realizing the need of considering the much larger world picture. Perhaps the most remarkable development that has happened to us as a people in the past half-century has been the gradual fusion of our interests with those of the world at large. No modern nation can remain isolated from the great international currents and this fact must colour all our thoughts about the *kind* of education we want for young Canadians for the next half-century.

As a matter of fact, this country has never been cut off from strong international influences. Three great cultural forces, those of France, Britain and the United States, have played and will continue to play important roles in Canadian education. The French tradition has chiefly affected the French-speaking schools and higher institutions of Quebec, and those communities outside Quebec which directly derive their cultural tradition from her. But the mere presence of this influence in so markedly a bi-cultural country has had educational implications deeper for the English-speaking Canadians than many realize; it has been largely an aristocratic and pre-revolutionary influence, but adapted to and coloured by the Canadian scene, and no less excellent simply because it appears unusual and extraneous to much in the other educational traditions.

Britain and the English-speaking educational systems and higher institutions have had a strong curricular influence upon Canadian education, perhaps most evident in a coherent and stabilized core of studies and in a reluctance to experiment

without safeguards. Then beyond these there have been certain
continuing cultural and spiritual essences in the British connection which almost defy definition—influences which have
been steadily fortified across the years by the presence of British
or British-trained teachers and professors in our educational
life, and by Canadian educators who themselves have come
to love much of the British cultural heritage.

From the United States, with which sociologically we Canadians have a close kinship, have come very strong educational
influences, so strong indeed—and frequently constructive—as
to be something of a challenge to the development of our identity
as a separate cultural entity. Perhaps the most striking and
salutary effects of the American tradition have been shown in
the influence of its equalitarian thought upon our educational
practices. However, we have been affected by still other elements
in the American tradition about which many Americans themselves have very mixed feelings, such as a preoccupation with
mechanical and statistical enterprises, and with the misnamed
"democratization" of classroom methods and procedures.

It is from the unique inter-relationships of these cultural
streams as well as from the influence of the country itself that
whatever we mean by "the Canadian mind" emerges, that
mind and spirit which must not only cope with the issues of
Canadian life, but also be influenced deeply by, and contend
with, the restless and fateful currents of world activity. The
individual Canadian, in a word, draws upon the resources
of his educational and indeed all his cultural traditions in
facing the stresses and strains which modern history and modern
technology impose upon him as an individual. This is of
peculiar importance in our time because the challenges to free
and enlightened individualism throughout Western society have
never been so great; and even in what we like to consider a
privileged Western democracy such as Canada the relationship
of education to the survival of individual personality at its

best is so relevant that it is almost certain to be the most crucial test of the fundamental worth of our educational process.

In our own country we have been fortunate to escape the most spectacular and overt challenge to enlightened individualism, namely the establishment of totalitarian political orders with their sombre partners-in-arms, the totalitarian systems of education and cultural dictatorships. This is a fate which has descended not only upon nations like Germany and Italy, which in a real sense brought this upon themselves, but also upon free democracies such as Estonia and Czecho-Slovakia, the latter at least enjoying a conception of liberty and of the freedom of the individual which we like to think of as typically Canadian.

We have been fortunate, too, to have escaped certain of of the more devastating direct effects of the world's ever-surging growth in population: the sudden terrible famines which have devastated whole provinces of India, China and Russia within recent years are unknown to us, and we have only the experiences of the prairie droughts of the 1930's to remind us that even in our economy one can have an area in Canada threatened by economic disaster. Though our housing needs are considerable, we do not know what it means to have millions of people piled in upon one another without proper breathing space, with all the concomitant evils of illiteracy, poverty and disease which such a situation brings. In fact we sometimes forget that there are and will continue to be peoples across the world envious of our considerable prosperity and our great spaces. Yet some students of world economy feel that during the next fifty years the pressure of world population will cause us to lower those living standards which we Canadians properly think of as being essential and basic to our way of life.

This view is supported by such authorities as Professors Burch and Pendell, who assert that even if the "people of the reproductive age groups reduce their net reproduction rate to

10% below 'replacement', the total population of the world would increase in the neighbourhood of 25% during the next fifty years, which would mean a total number of 2,750,000,000 by the year 2000. This increase is likely to intensify world dangers."

Yet even in the face of this possible development, there are optimists among the agricultural scientists who claim that science will continue to find new sources of food for the new world populations, thus making it possible for us to maintain the high standards of living which we have reached in our country.

We as Canadians have also been more fortunate than most in escaping the so-called "psychological pressures" that result inevitably from over-population. Here there is still the feeling of that generous "elbow-room"—of that physical space which our pioneers came in search of. The impingement of the "mass man"—about whom Professor Ortega y Gassett writes so illuminatingly and so despairingly—that impingement upon our cultural consciousness, is surely far less here than it is in many European countries, or even in some parts of the United States. That sense of the overwhelming presence of what Ortega calls "the vertical barbarian" is infinitely lessened in our case by the nature of the spacious country in which we live and by our relatively small and scattered population.

But if the individual Canadian has not personally had to contend with a political dictatorship within his own country, he has had in the past to fight against its extension in the world and—unless I am much mistaken—he will continue to live in a world where totalitarianism will share large areas of control. This will be a world which science has reduced to a large and uneasy neighbourhood, but to which no science, pure, applied or political, will be able to bring in the near future a real social maturity. The result will be that free democracies, semi- and pseudo-democracies, and outright dictatorships will continue to move and act according to their natures and motives. Furthermore, our future Canadian will not be able to rely complacently upon the inviolability of his own democratic life within his own country; eternal vigilance will continue to be the price of liberty and he will need to recognize not only the existence and spread of tyranny in other parts of the world, but also the first signs and threats of authoritarianism within Canada itself.

Again, although relatively free at present from the devastating effects of population pressure and poverty, the individual Canadian is not free from many of the challenges posed by the new techniques devised to influence and control great masses of people; and he is exposed to the stresses and strains which certain aspects of urbanized society impose upon him. The rapid industrialization of the country, the striking shift of population from country to urban centres, and the emergence of one metropolis after another—all these follow a familiar pattern with their interesting implications. We do not need the brilliant essays of Professor Reisman and other sociologists to recognize the liberating effects for the individual of the large urban centre; none the less it is a pattern which, representing the development of standardization in all its phases, including the technological advances in communication, represents a powerful force with which Canadian education must contend. The influence of such mass media is a theme of particular fascination for any observer of Canadian life, because here we are dealing not only with the effects of these great communication agencies upon the individual Canadian's standards and tastes, but, as the *Massey Report* has pointed out, with the effects of the American culture upon our own, and hence upon each one of us. One could reasonably contend that Canadians have to cope with the problem of survival as a distinct cultural identity quite as much as to deal with the continuing problem of safeguarding standards and tastes.

We should, of course, keep in mind the debts we owe to

technological processes, to urbanization, and to the different agencies of mass communication. I do not intend to elaborate here upon the benefits of which we are all conscious, arising out of labour-saving devices, machines which create travel opportunities and save hours in critical emergencies, the wide distribution of medical and nutritional discoveries, advances in public hygiene, and the like. Rather I have in mind the extent to which the growth of urbanization has contributed to the broadening of outlook of many of our people, the decline of the old parochialisms, and the support of larger and better educational enterprises and cultural ventures far beyond the scope of the rural and small town settings. We have developed clusters of nostalgic memories about the pioneer people, but it is important to recall as well the cultural privations and the real limitations of pioneer life. Then again, it would surely be unreasonable to insist that that great mass of information and entertainment which flows through the channels of radio, television, films and publications does not contain much that is truly educative and much that has had a civilizing influence under almost any definition of that phrase.

When all this is taken into account, however, we should remember that education during the next half-century must concern itself most seriously with the stresses and strains which modern mechanized, urbanized living has imposed upon the individual—with those challenges to the identity and integrity of the individual which are presented by all the forces which tend to standardize life, to empty it of its sense of individual worth-whileness and accountability, and to rob it of its feeling of heritage and of having roots. That the stresses and challenges are considerable can be seen in the importance of the role occupied by modern psychiatry, and by the readiness with which great numbers of people subscribe to doctrines and notions which may relieve them of any serious obligation to think seriously and generously.

Does it not seem, therefore, that we ought primarily to be concerned not with the physical apparatus and external framework of education, essential though these are, but rather with the great objectives which should support these institutions?

What are the basic premises, in brief, upon which we are building and ought to build the education of young Canadians, having in mind the special duty of safeguarding the enlightened and responsible individuality of each?

From the elaborate and at times confused listings of educational objectives which I find in many different statements, I should like to stress four which are directly pertinent to the issue as I have defined it. These might be described as follows: (1) The education of a young Canadian should help him to prepare himself to make a living; (2) it should help to prepare him for enlightened citizenship in a democracy; (3) it should help him to refine his emotions, his intellect, and his taste; (4) and it should attempt through him to extend "the rule of love" among all men throughout the world.

In respect of the first objective I am thinking of the teaching of fundamental skills and of work habits, together with a certain amount of vocational guidance as the young person reaches the later years of high school and approaches the time at which he must enter the labour market. This has generally been treated superficially even by those who give serious consideration to the larger implications of education and employment.

A recent study conducted by the Canadian Research Committee on Practical Education (which in turn is sponsored by the Canadian Manufacturers Association and the Canadian Education Association and assisted by a number of organizations representing the agricultural, labour and professional groups of this country) has examined the conditions that exist for young Canadians during the two years after they leave school and are applying what they have learned during their school years. It is a useful study because it cites the views of the young people themselves and also gives glimpses of Canadian foremen and employers, thus bringing into relationship the work of schools on the one hand and the realistic conditions to be found in Canadian employment situations on the other. This is not the place for me to deal with that Report save to say that it is an intelligent attempt at gaining perspective in the matter of educating young people to earn a living.

Let me cite three instances where the implications of this objective run deeper than many of us realize. One is the matter of satisfactory work habits and work attitudes. It is a common criticism that young people entering upon careers in industry and commerce show a lack of thoroughness in their work and an indifference to the success of their firm or co-workers, which in a less fortunate economy or under more adverse conditions could have serious results. No doubt this climate of slipshod work and of lack of loyalty so far as it exists is traceable to many causes other than the basic schooling which these young workers have had. The employers, for example, are themselves by no means blameless. But is it not also possible that in our desire to educate people who will know how to use their leisure time well we have sometimes overlooked the imperative need of educating people who will use their working time well, both for themselves, their employers, and society at large?

This leads me directly to my second point, which is that the satisfactions to be gained from being happily and well placed in one's work, and then performing it well, are of profound importance both for the mental health of the individual and the good health of the whole body politic. Vocational satisfaction will become of greater and greater concern as Canada continues to expand as an industrial nation. It may well be that not merely must we extend our services in vocational counselling for young people while they are still in high school, but we must establish more systematic means of determining the employment potentials in different vocations. We have not hitherto had to face that condition which has existed in some highly-industrialized European countries, of having educated large numbers of intelligent people for whom there is no satisfactory employment, and who then form a dissatisfied and ultimately disintegrating force in the life of the country. As the years pass, however, this problem may have to be faced, and if so, it will best be met by a lively consciousness of the difficulty, and by taking steps to prevent the piling-up of participants in trades and professions already saturated. But, far more sombre than the minimal peril in our society of creating a discontented "intelligentsia", is the tragedy of having large numbers of people whose talents are misdirected and who will lead frustrated and embittered lives, unless through wise guidance they find work suited to their best abilities and aptitudes.

We can almost certainly expect to see an extension of some form of compulsory education. This would have the practical effect of relieving the labour market of large numbers of young and poorly prepared job applicants; yet this is the least positive and fruitful result of such a move. What one would hope is that from the extended training of young Canadians, first through full-time schooling, then through part-time courses, and beyond this, through the expansion of adult education, all of our Canadian people will gain a conception of their work which will cause them to give their highest loyalties to their job, their fellow-workers, and to society at large.

My third point is that Canadian education has a contribution to make toward helping our young people respect the work done by their fellow-citizens in all walks of life. It is a healthy thing for a whole society when there is a sensible recognition by all, of the indispensable roles which all good workers and all good citizens play. Dr. James Bryant Conant has spoken idealistically but effectively to this point in his recent book, *Education in a Divided World*. "We may imagine," he says, "a society in which each citizen, be he a skilled worker, a manager, a storekeeper, a professor, or a farmer, would have the minimum interest in his own or other people's occupational status, the maximum interest in how far his own or other people's conduct approximated the universally recognized ethical ideal. This ideal might be epitomized by such phrases as individual integrity in dealing with other people, human sympathy and moral courage." And he goes on to remark that "all this implies no diminution in the pioneer spirit of adventure and zest for work."

In turning to the second great objective which I have cited as likely to prove of particular value in the coming half-century, namely, *education for enlightened citizenship in a democracy*, I enter an area which has been made obscure by the ubiquitous and slovenly use in educational writing of the words "democracy" and "democratic".

To some people, "democratic living" seems to be synonymous with the *standard* of living found in some of our Western societies, such as "the American Way of Life", or the Canadian, or the British. Perhaps it is too much of a caricature to identify the conception some folk have of democracy with having a television set in the living-room and two cars in every garage; but it is not unkind and it is certainly not untrue to assert that many people seem to have confused democracy with social security, with effective hygiene, with industrial prosperity, and the like.

Then there are others to whom "democratic living" seems to be synonymous with the rule of the majority, and the graceful acceptance by all of that rule—despite the fact that non-conformist groups are most frequently found in enlightened democracies. It is a fact that the political stability of democratic states rests on majority rule, but it is a far cry from this to the conception that everything which is supported by a majority vote is somehow a wise and proper thing.

Still other people see "democracy" always in terms of equalitarianism, as though if only we could rid ourselves of all class distinctions, democratic living would follow as a necessary corollary. This is a respectable doctrine, finding eloquent support in the treatises of great revolutionary writers. But again the *non sequitur* between equalitarianism and true democracy opens a wide gap into which many fine hopes and dreams have fallen, and which has been destructive of many "democratic" plans.

There are others again who appear to use the expression "satisfactory adjustment to the group" interchangeably with "democratic living", without seeing what should be sufficiently evident, that one can have the most satisfactory adjustment to groups within the framework of the most deadly totalitarian systems. To be well adjusted to a maladjusted society is therefore not a democratic virtue but the road to democratic ruin.

The importance of these conceptions or misconceptions can be seen when they are put forward to justify procedures in education which have been considered advanced or "progressive", and which have gained a widespread acceptance in more conservative systems and institutions. For example, the insistence upon the teacher's being only the friendly equal of his students; the assertion that it is better for students to "live democratically" than to study historical content; the doctrine that the pupils should choose the content of certain courses, or choose certain themes or topics by vote, as being "more democratic"; the notion that "traditional discipline" will create "totalitarian personalities", and so on.

Now my concern here is not so much with the extent to which these practices and viewpoints are effective or ineffective, as with the extent to which they are founded upon defensible premises of the word "democracy". The distinguished Head

Master of Manchester Grammar School, Eric James, in a recent series of articles on the theme "What is a Democratic Education?", raises a number of thought-provoking questions on precisely this point. He is happy about the extent to which the individual child in our modern schools is (in his words), "regarded far more as a person and less as one of a class, or as something pliable and amorphous to be moulded and fashioned into some predetermined shape". This change in the schools which "at its best replaces fear by respect and coercion by persuasion" he would count as pure gain. But having made this fundamental statement, James goes on to ask how far educators have in fact confused the meaning of "democracy", and how far, therefore, the concept of freedom, of individual judgment by the pupil, is to be extended? How far is one to go, for example, with democratic self-government among school children? And if the school is speaking with two voices, if it is busily promoting in the child the assumption that his judgment is perfectly valid in many areas which have hitherto been considered those of the adult teacher, while on the other hand it declines, as it almost certainly would, to let the school council abolish arithmetic from the course of studies—if, in short, under such circumstances it imposes "real, if too often unspoken, limitations of their freedom", will not (James asks) the child get the idea that "democracy is something bogus that seeks to give the impression of freedom while actually withholding it"? Furthermore, may not the teacher who is straining to make his teaching "reflect his democratic principles . . . be so afraid of indoctrination, of educating for authoritarianism and not for freedom, that he may be reluctant to express his own views at all"? And, James concludes, "when writing of Dr. Arnold's teaching, his biographer describes 'the black cloud of indignation which passed over his face when speaking of the crimes of Napoleon or of Caesar'. Today, on the contrary, the teacher is sometimes so anxious to leave his pupils free to think for themselves that he is in danger of confusing tolerance with indifference. He may give his pupils the impression that for him every question is an open question. Such an attitude tends to rob teaching of its inspiration and education of its purpose."

It would seem that one of the valuable purposes which education in Canada and elsewhere must perform for itself in preparation for the coming years—years which may well be at times arduous and testing—is to formulate a more sinewy definition of what we mean by "democracy" and "democratic citizenship" than appears at present in general to be the case.

It is because this confusion exists, and yet because the objective itself seems indispensable in our educational processes, that I have chosen to express it in a variation of the customary phrases, namely, "education for enlightened citizenship in a democracy". I have in mind a conception of democracy which leads one directly back to the issue which I have defined as central to this discussion: the significance and responsibility of the individual, and the necessity of helping him to maintain and develop his identity and his integrity. I would suppose that whatever else might enter into one's definition of democracy, the indispensable element for all definitions would be that of "individual liberty", a liberty protected by certain historic safeguards which were not only epoch-making in themselves at the time of their adoption, but which extend and fortify themselves through the subsequent centuries by tradition and custom. I take it that the teaching of these great conflicts, charters, and safeguards is vital: that future citizens must not fall into the trap of assuming that the existence of a democratic "structure"—I mean, a "premier", and "parliament", and apparently "free" elections—is itself democracy. In a word, everything indicates that the next fifty years are going to demand young people who are thoroughly schooled in the heritage of democracy, to whom participation simply in school elections and the like, though necessary, will be no adequate substitute for the clear knowledge of how democracy has evolved and has defended itself throughout the years. To put it in still another way, these future citizens must realize that the forms in which they participate are empty without the knowledge of Cromwell's work and the spirit of Hampden.

But still more than this, the schools must encourage individual self-reliance in opinion, critical dissidence, intelligent nonconformity, the ability at least occasionally to stand aside and stand up for one's own individual beliefs. I do not mean that this kind of thing is not encouraged in good schools, but it is a question here of emphasis, and I feel that more emphasis might be given to this particular phase of training for enlightened citizenship in Canada.

We are quite properly worried about the number of introverted and neurotic people who have been produced by the strain of modern life and who would be better off if in some instances they cheerfully conformed. But there are *other kinds of nonconformists,* and we need more of them. These are the citizens who will not run with the crowd, who will not accept large uniform patterns uncritically simply because those patterns seem to be "normal", and who will not be intimidated by the type of demagogue who at the present time threatens the academic freedom of schools and universities in many countries, and threatens also the freedom of thought and speech of all adult persons. It is not a pleasant spectacle to see whole areas or whole communities in what we consider to be democratic states—that is, states whose fundamental premise is the safeguarding of individual liberty through processes of history and of politics—almost literally subdued by the fear of being thought to vary from some "norm" which has been arbitrarily imposed by the ambitions of demagogues employing the apparatus and sanctions of what they call "democracy" for their own ends. The schools of the Western democracies, including

Canada, must perform the valuable function of instilling in their young people principles and attitudes which will recognize and resist the encroachments of these persons—who are really pseudo-democrats—upon the essential liberties of the State.

When one turns to the third of the four major objectives which I have suggested we have to be concerned about in Canadian education, that is, *"the refining of the emotions, the intellect, and taste"*, it is evident that two developments in our educational and cultural life call for as much reference as possible within the limited scope of this address. One of these is the remarkable growth of the creative arts in Canada— a growth which may be expected to expand and to accelerate as the century continues, due in part to the new sense of political and economic nationalism in our country, in part to the maturing of the earlier pioneer heritage, and in part to the filling-out and enriching of the pattern of races established through the continuing immigration of peoples from other lands. There is a certain spiritual exhilaration in living in a country which is beginning to mature in the creative arts, and yet that very process brings responsibilities with it as well. One of these is to help to create through education in all its aspects a people who will not merely respect the work of the creative artist, but who will have standards of judgment, and an increasing sense of the first-rate in what they see and hear and experience, which will promote the best type of creative activity in its turn. Even the first of these two aspirations, respect for the cultivated life and the creative artist, is not easily accomplished in a new society where we have long associated successful living with mechanical things and physical activity.

Professor Jacques Barzun, in the course of a penetrating essay called "The Educated Man" goes so far as to assert (and I quote): "Modern society is not geared to produce, receive, or respect the educated man, and it is hard to imagine anyone in his senses claiming the title as an honour. The

term is in fact seldom used. 'High-brow' has replaced it.
Nowadays the term is 'egghead'! And since the new word
conveys good-natured contempt, everyone does his best to
prove that his own brow is attractively low—a thin line of
common sense between two hairy hedges denoting common-
manliness. One's intellect or learned profession or habit of
self-cultivation is something to hide or live down, and this is
true even though more and more people are being schooled
and colleged and 'educationed' than ever before." Perhaps
Professor Barzun's lively pen is indulging here in over-statement
in order to add force to his argument; and yet one must
ask whether such an attitude toward the cultured person and
cultured activity does exist in our society. If so, it is a most
serious matter for those concerned with carrying on the educational process. I would draw your attention particularly to
his phrase, "the habit of self-cultivation". Surely the best guarantee that the cultural life of a country will receive the encouragement that it needs, and the best safeguard that it will
grow in the worthiest tradition, is that the people of the country
should be so far as possible cultivated people—people in whom
the habit of self-cultivation has created the capacity to respect
and to admire the cultural activities and attainments of others.

But there is a bigger thing still than helping to create a
national climate in which there will be the needed appreciation
for the arts and for creative artists. There is also the imperative need of helping the young Canadian to develop standards of taste which will recognize and demand the first-rate
among all the varying offerings found in any lively and productive culture. Here again one comes up against the hard
fact of competition from those tireless agents which I mentioned
earlier—the radio, television, the films, newspapers, and magazines. A distinguished Canadian artist has recently stated that
he is far less concerned about the possible effects of so-called
crime films and radio programmes—with, in other words, the

more lurid side of the cheaper mass programmes, which easily catches the attention of public speakers and editorial writers— far less concerned about these than he is about the debilitating effect upon the people's creative activities and taste of the endless streams of mass-produced, standardized, stereotyped movie stories, radio and television melodramas, and the inane appeals of modern hucksters. It is the *inertness* of mind and spirit, the anaesthetizing of those critical faculties which all to some degree possess, which particularly troubles him. The same can be said of many of our practices in reading. If it is true that great numbers of people have been given new areas of information and are constantly given new insights by much of what they read, it is also true that the titles and contents of a great many popular "pocket books", magazines and tabloids reveal levels of taste which must be the serious concern of those who are interested in education.

I am not proposing that everyone should, or can, read the Great Books as his staple fare day by day—and our common sense and sense of humour remind us that this kind of thing is not going to happen, and all things considered, should not happen. However, we might surely insist that if we in Canada are to absorb a derivative culture from the United States, we might at least select critically from the great mass of communicated material, good, bad, and indifferent, which proceeds from that enormously active and richly diversified society. We might even encourage the development of standards which will stimulate the growth of the first-rate at all times and at all points throughout our country in our cultural and mass communication media.

This issue is of particular interest for Canadian education because it is likely to grow in importance, as the twentieth century proceeds; as we Canadians continue to attempt to identify and to preserve a cultural pattern which has distinctive Canadian elements, and as we attempt to have the

development of this pattern influenced by widespread standards
of the first-rate.

How is this recognition of the worth-while and the really
fine achievement in cultural activity to be brought about in
a society where the individual, here as in other spheres of his
life, finds a persistent attack being made upon his integrity as
an individual? Such a question calls for a separate paper in
itself, but perhaps I might leave a suggestion or two. One is
that in Canada we who are concerned with education should
be more alive to the creative possibilities of the media of
communication than we seem to have been up to now. I
am not of course thinking of cultural control by small groups
in the detestable fashion which is the custom in modern
totalitarian states, but of something quite different. My thought
is that we should readily accept these media as great educational
forces which are here, and are going to continue to be here
with us and to grow with our nation across the years. We
should accept this fact realistically, without wasting time in
simply deploring them; and then face the need to get to
work with energy and with imagination to employ them as
fully as we can for the promotion of those better standards
of which I spoke. Fortunately in Canada we are in a better
condition to do this than is possible in some of the other free
democracies which have the same problem. Let me give
one instance of what I mean: I can conceive of the time,
not too far away, when television, which many at present
think about only with foreboding or hostility, may do a
great deal to develop an appreciation for good drama by many
people in all parts of our country—in contrast to the limited
numbers who now appreciate good drama through seeing it
presented in selected urban centres.

My other suggestion has nothing original about it, but it
is one of the old truths which can never bear enough repeating.
That is, that we learn to recognize the first-rate by growing

up with the first-rate. In this I am thinking not only of homes and community agencies and a myriad of cultural enterprises which powerfully affect the taste of the growing child, but more specifically of the content of the curricula of our schools —the need of the child's becoming acquainted in his school studies with great poetry and art, and with the first-rate as seen in good history teaching, and so on. The trouble with many people who have no conception of the difference between the good, bad, and indifferent in the arts and elsewhere in life, between the worthless and the worth while, is that they literally lack taste: culturally speaking, they have never learned good taste from bad—they lack "touch-stones". It is because I believe that we learn to appreciate and want the first-rate by meeting the first-rate that I would be disturbed to see in school purely "practical" work, as it is called, substituted for the opportunities which children of even modest abilities may have to read and discuss some of the best in poetry and the other forms of literature and the other arts. There is a very illuminating comment in the Harvard University Report on *General Education in a Free Society* which says that even those who are demonstrably incapable of appreciating the highest and best in literature and history, none the less need to know that these great things live and move in the world.

Merely to mention this last viewpoint, however, is to risk aggravating that great debate between the two camps in educational thought, roughly identified as the traditionalists and the progressives, a debate which has divided, and one may presume, will continue to divide large numbers of modern educators. It is a discussion which has entered Canadian education, and which is highly pertinent, in the one or two aspects which I can deal with here, to this objective of "refining the emotions, the intellect, and the taste" of our young people. Where are the schools of the coming half-century to place their stress in dealing with the refinement of the personality of the student? Is it to be upon valuable and "insightful" content of the type I have just referred to—emotional and informative experiences through literature, history, the sciences and other subjects, and upon certain traditional relationships between schoolmaster and pupil? Or are they to rely upon the kind of experiences that certain educational psychologists advocate, that is to say, less interest in content, more in what is called "purposeful activities" or "meaningful life experiences", and upon influencing the personality of the child through human inter-relationships which originally derive from procedures recommended in psychological research? In the United States where this last point of view is widespread—particularly among the publicly maintained schools—a strong reaction has developed against it, on the grounds that it leads to a lowering of necessary standards, to superficiality, and to the sacrifice of talents which society urgently needs. Canon Bell, a distinguished critic of progressive school practices, speaks caustically to this point when he insists in a recent essay that American education is producing "at great expense and with the most incongruous self-congratulation, a nation of Henry Aldriches". And when he summarizes his reasons for making this considerable charge, it is seen that he believes that much of present-day education in his country has neglected the basic disciplines; it is turning out graduates who expect the cheap success of reward without labour, who assume that effective thinking requires little effort, who can make things but cannot understand things, who have no real conception of the first-rate through liberal culture because all kinds and sorts of activities have been substituted for liberal learning, and who are not anti-religious but simply illiterate in religious knowledge. Now if these seem extravagant statements, it must be remembered that they are advanced by a responsible observer of the modern scene, and that they are subscribed to in large part by a very considerable body of educated persons—persons who are less concerned about the much-publicized discussion of whether children can spell as effectively as they used to, than they are that their children should share to the fullest extent of their individual capacities in the great cultural traditions which these critics feel are indispensable to the educated, and hence the integrated, life. There are at work in North American education today others who have summarily dismissed the intellectual side of schooling. These educators would almost dispense with the learning of content in some of the traditional studies in favour of all sorts and kinds of activities which are often based upon passing fads and fancies, and which must ultimately create that rootless person, without any real *knowledge* of the sources of his individual liberties, of which I spoke earlier.

But is such a point of view as that of Canon Bell, necessary as it is and perceptive though it is, going to be sufficient in and of itself to carry us through the demands of the social problems and situations we shall find ourselves confronted with in the coming years? President Conant rightly reminds us of still another indispensable aspect of educational need when he points out insistently that education is after all also a "social process". That is to say, one cannot separate public education from its environment, or apply the same standards and aspirations without modification to the public high school of a low-income area in a great city and to an expensive residential school. The past fifty years in public education have been years of difficult transition, of attempting to educate as many of the children of all the people as possible, and the result has been both great achievements and great problems. Let me suggest one area of criticism of our public institutions which shows how far the critics have forgotten the social implications that have to be grappled with. One hears a good deal of criticism of the introduction into courses of study of types of work which the critics claim are actually the responsibility of the home; and no doubt in a sense their criticism is justified. But the difficulty is that the public school is not dealing with a simple or theoretical situation. To ask that the home take on this responsibility is to assume that the home is capable of doing so—but the plain fact is that there are many urban areas on this continent where the home, in the form that the critics are thinking of it, simply does not exist. One might well hope that in time there will be adequate housing and other pertinent social reforms of sufficient scope to make it possible for the homes to assume these tasks, and for the schools to return more fully to the kind of work which many feel is properly theirs. But until that time comes, it seems idle, and even foolish, to berate the schools for attempting to do an essential service which no other community agency in that area is capable of doing.

And then again, the criticism is frequently made that public education over the past two generations has been so concerned with getting as many children as possible into the schools that it has failed to take into account the necessity of educating the leaders which it will always need in order to survive. Once again, one must sympathize with such a criticism and feel the dangers that arise when a democracy gives so much attention to the satisfactory social adjustment, as some call it, of great numbers of young people that it neglects the talents of its intellectually gifted children, whose leadership the State will some day urgently need. But still the point remains, which those critics miss who will not consider the social implications of education, that we live in a society which is prepared to accept leadership if it can be developed, but which is not prepared to accept aristocracy and special privilege. To this extent at least, the equalitarianism which colours all our educational thinking on this continent is based on a realistic social concept which recognizes the aspirations derived from pioneer people. Sociologists have pointed out again and again how the public school among such a people is deeply respected as the vehicle through which it is possible to keep the social lines fluid, to prevent the stratification of social station which inevitably tends to grow as a new society ages. Now this is just the point that some of the traditionalist critics miss, just as many more socially-minded educators persist in under-emphasizing the need to develop the intellectual leadership without which the most amiable and well-intentioned democracy cannot survive.

But beyond this, there is still another great segment of the modern educational problem which is not often enough understood by the "traditionist" critics. That is, the obligation of the public school to explore as far as it can the contributions which psychology and psychiatry may make to that "refining" process which is being considered here. I am thinking especially of the field of the emotions and also of human relations: on the one hand, the need to use every instrument available to help to deal as early as possible with those profound emotional illnesses which cripple the later productive capacity of the adult, robbing life of its fullness both in youth and adulthood; and on the other hand, to use to the utmost in intercultural and inter-personal relationships any new knowledges which may lessen or do away with hostility and prejudice. It is no doubt true that a good deal of damage has been done by educators who have turned away from the priceless benefits of philosophical and historical thought, and from sociology, in order to devote their attention to the psychological approach to almost everything in education. None the less, the harvest of knowledge about human abilities and aptitudes, about interests and conflicts, and the insights into certain phases of personality promises to be so great that it is recognized by some of the leaders in education, including Sir Richard Livingstone, who certainly cannot be accused of neglecting the advantages of a liberal education in the more traditional sense. We must keep in mind that even the high standard of living upon which we Canadians pride ourselves may not be a guarantee of the emotional happiness of our children; so far as psychiatric research can determine, the better-off children are actually as susceptible to the problems of neurosis as their poorer counterparts. In this whole field of mental and emotional health, the school cannot afford to ignore the new frontiers of psychiatry, although it is well advised to share the responsibilities in such an area with properly-staffed, properly-supported, co-ordinating agencies or services rather than to attempt to assume the increasing burden itself.

The great challenge (in this field as throughout the whole area under debate) *of the next half-century in public education is to work out a synthesis of the best features of traditional and progressive thought.*

I come now, and very briefly, to the final objective that I have stated, *"to attempt, through the young person who is being educated, to extend the rule of love among men".* I speak very briefly, because I want here only to suggest a need and propose a study, and otherwise to leave this vast field to the intensive investigation which it deserves and which it must have if the next half-century in education is to bear the fruit that it should. When I speak of "extending the rule of love among men", I have in mind the great Judaic-Christian tradition of which we are the spiritual heirs; but although this to me is indispensable, I am thinking of a context even larger in view of the world stage upon which this drama of the "rule of love" has to be played through. It is with this matter very much as with nationalism at its best: one wants to keep the wonderful lights and insights of one's own nationalism, but one must somehow enter into a higher *inter*nationalism as well, in order to establish the best relations with all men. One thinks in such a connection of the motto of the Cosmopolitan House at Cornell University: "Above all nations is humanity". In a similar way I do not feel myself disloyal to the priceless traditions of the Judaic-Christian tradition in which I was brought up, to say that above all religions, East or West, and above the new pseudo-religions of political doctrine, is the rule of love. How can one transmit this sense of responsibility for all men; this feeling, as Terence put it, that because we are human, everything human is of concern to us? The question is a vital one, because it is not sentimental to say that there are situations and needs which only the intuitive insights and apprehensions of love can solve—situations which intellect and force of character and ordinary good will alone are powerless to unlock. There are, of course, many who find the whole answer within our religious tradition, and who would meet the problem by requiring all the children in this country to be given religious training in the schools; and it is true that much can be accomplished by such training, and that there is much to deplore in any society in which great numbers of students are virtually illiterate in their own religious traditions. But again one has to contend with a demonstrable social fact—that there are many people who are firmly opposed to religious training in the schools, and who, we may presume, will continue to be. And then beyond this, there is still the problem of establishing some sense of what the rule of love can mean for all men among those young people who are not particularly sensitive to ordinary religious things, even when they are well instructed in these things; or among those others who have at least temporarily fallen away from any desire to participate in the formal religious life at all.

What is the solution to be? Is it possible, at least at the college level, that more courses should be introduced than at present exist which will give a panoramic view of the development and value of the great religions, with particular attention to the forgotten emphases in our own tradition? Is it possible that by some means, not least through the sciences, we should attempt to convey to students something of what Schweitzer means when he talks about "reverence for life"—something which one can assume is indistinguishable from the "rule of love"? Have we sufficiently considered how we can enlist the humanities and the sciences, in all their pertinent phases and through all the schooling of the student, including his experience in higher education, in order to bring out the full value of this great concept? However it may be done, one must feel this particular objective indispensable in educating our young people to meet the challenges of the coming years.

If the four major objectives of education which I have selected for emphasis and comment are worth while and are to be achieved, it will be only as a result of the most considered care being given to the instruments which are to carry them out. They will require a fine quality of teaching and this in turn will demand a concept of teacher-training which is concerned not simply with obtaining greater numbers of teachers, important though that is, but most vitally with the quality of the teacher, his abilities, his human interests, his cultural sympathies, and his understanding of the need for spiritual emphases. They will require an extension of educational opportunity in Canada, more particularly by increasing the numbers of older adolescents completing high school, and by providing for other types of education which these young people may well need. One thinks here of a wide variety of vocational institutes, and of as yet undeveloped programmes in adult education. They will require a much greater attention to the education of girls and young women in our society. For although the independent role of women has been technically established, our culture is far from having accommodated itself to the change, and far from developing to the full the talents and contributions of women. They will require a more generous conception of financial support for education throughout our whole economy, not merely through the support furnished by individuals and corporations but through the assistance of all our governments, including our federal government, for Canada's institutions of higher education.

Above all, they will require the conviction on the part of all those having to do with Canadian education that in educating young Canadians they are not only doing something of the first importance for Canada, but also for the world: a conviction that, in what may very well be the dark and difficult years of the next half-century, the Canadian people can provide a hospitable refuge for the victims of world injustice, and can themselves help to alleviate the dangers and illuminate the problems of world discord if they have been educated in the best of human tradition *and* the best of the new disciplines in their schools and universities.

CULTURAL EVOLUTION

Hilda Neatby

M.A., Ph.D., cert. d'Études françaises.
Professor of History, University of Saskatchewan; member, Royal Commission on
The Arts, Letters and Sciences; staff,
University of Minnesota, 1931-33, Toronto, 1944-45; author, *The Administration of Justice under the Quebec Act,*
1937, *So Little for the Mind,* 1953, etc.

CULTURAL EVOLUTION

I. INTRODUCTION

THIS title covers such a wide and ill-defined area that it seems necessary to ask, first, what it means. I suppose that a study of our cultural evolution really calls for an examination of the nature and influence of those forces which have been calculated to keep alive and to develop in us what is essentially human in face of the deadening impact of the forces of materialistic democracy which have been so powerful in the Western World and particularly on our continent during the whole period of our national life. Material wealth and a moral urge toward social equality have their dangers for the good life. An American writer presenting this view asks whether the "good is always the friend of the best", or whether "excellence is not more likely to lose out to mediocrity than it is to mere ignorance or nullity." [1] And in a well-known

---

[1] Joseph Wood Krutch: "Is Our Common Man Too Common?", *Saturday Review*, January 10, 1953. The author finds the "general pro-cultural hoop-la" over which many of his fellow-countrymen are complacent an inadequate substitute for "that deep personal demanding passion for Truth and Beauty which has always been the dynamic force in the production of any genuine culture."

Canadian play an artist emerging from an unhappy encounter with some professional uplifters remarks: "The educated like my work, and the uneducated like it. As for the half-educated —well, we can only pray for them in Canada as elsewhere." [2]

It is the half-educated that are hostile to the creative artist for they tend to be happiest with the mediocre. Not only have they confused quality with quantity; they tend to blur the terms "creative work" and "self-expression" in such fashion that all self-expression somehow rates as creative work—or as something just as good. It seems therefore desirable in a brief survey of this broad subject to go directly to the heart of it, which is the creative artist and his work, and to ask exactly what he does and why his work has value.

The role of the artist in society is simple and essential. Art is communication, the communication of the artist's experience. Art is also creation because the experience communicated is created or brought alive by the artist. Experience, it has been said, consists not in impressions but in making sense. It is the artist's job to make sense, "to render actual new sectors of the inexhaustible field of potential experience." [3] This does not, of course, mean that artists are a race apart or that it is easy or even possible always to identify the original experience of the creative artist. It does mean that civilization lives on the communication of valid experience by the honest artist. Without such communication we may exist but we do not live. We are confined to the objective truth which is the truth of a moment. We fail to enter into our human inheritance.

[2] Robertson Davies: *Fortune, My Foe,* p. 95, Clarke Irwin, 1949. An English critic, discussing quite a different matter, expresses a similar idea. The human race, he says, has never been "more difficult to love . . . it has lost both the guileless spontaneity of the savage and the primitive; and the gaieties and sophistication of upper class culture: and has gained nothing that cannot be obtained in a tin." Emyr Humphreys: "A Protestant View of the Modern Novel", *The Listener,* April 2, 1953.

[3] Erich Heller: "The Hazard of Modern Poetry", *The Listener,* March 12, 1953.

It is often said that artists have a bad time in Canada, but in the twentieth century artists have a bad time everywhere. The chief cause of their frustration lies far deeper than persecution or neglect. Civilized societies live, or have lived, on a general agreement on "the valid morality of experience". A loosening of accepted patterns may for a time stimulate activity and inspire a vigorous period of art. But when the whole pattern is lost in confusion and uncertainty the artist himself is at a loss.[4] He must have liberty, but he must also have a frame of reference. The dilemma of the artist in the twentieth century is that he lives in an age of widespread doubt about the very existence of ultimate truth. If such doubt became certainty the artist would presumably have nothing to say. Even the doubt affects profoundly the capacity to communicate experience. The artists of no other country, perhaps, have been so much affected as those of Canada, for Canadian cultural development has in time paralleled the loosening of patterns, the dissolution of foundations, the general disappearance of the overriding sense of ultimate truth and of any commonly accepted symbols through which the artists' sense of the truth could be conveyed. Artists in older countries had their schools and their traditions founded in an age of greater spiritual and moral security. The Canadian artist began to raise his individual voice against the background of a Western World in process of dissolving its standards and discarding its values. The First World War, for example, so critical in our national and cultural development, has rightly been referred to as "an episode" in "the general breakdown of liberal humanist culture".[5] The general background of our cultural development has not been favourable to a clear and vigorous creative expression.

[4] *Ibid.*

[5] William O. Fennell: "Shapers of the Modern Outlook", *Canadian Forum,* February, 1953, p. 247.

Against this intellectual and philosophic background must be set the familiar material conditions of Canadian life and development. We have had, and we still have, a small population in a very large country. The population is neither concentrated in one part nor evenly distributed over the whole. Rather there is, as the geologists say, a series of deposits of people—one very large one in the area of the Great Lakes and St. Lawrence Valley, and smaller ones in the Maritimes, on the prairies and on the Pacific coast. Moreover, the one large block, although united geographically, is divided within itself by differences of language and of tradition. The artist in Canada, in any communicating of experience to the country as a whole, has encountered not only physical obstacles of space but also more subtle forces of separation: language and modes of thought. The physical obstacles have been overcome in part; other divisive forces have resolved themselves in the growth of two cultural groups each with its own accumulated wealth of inherited experience, each one more or less ready to listen to its own artists but too often unwilling or unable to learn much from those of the other group. It is polite to say that Canada is richer for her two cultures. If we bear in mind that the essence of cultural development is the enrichment of human life by a general appropriation of artistic experience, it must be obvious that no country is the richer only because one-half of the population cannot appropriate the experience of one-half of the artists: a crude mathematical expression of a truth too often ignored. This is not, of course, the whole truth, but it does represent an essential condition of our present situation.

There is one other important condition of Canadian cultural development. Each deposit of population along the Canadian border lives in close and constant contact with communities in the corresponding geographic area of the United States. For English-speaking Canadians the obvious destiny would seem to be to blend their cultural lives with those of neighbours of common language and tradition. To a large extent English-speaking Canadians do do this. That they do not do so altogether is part of the whole paradox of Canadian survival as a national entity.

Canada, it has been suggested, originated with a series of rejected groups: French cut off from France, Loyalists from the former American Colonies, Scots from the Highlands. [6] These groups without having much in common beyond their rejection and their joint habitation of a vast, lonely and mysterious land, have together created, though doubtfully enough and slowly, a national community with autonomous political institutions and an integrated economy. The different groups may be geographically isolated or culturally distinct or both. With all their divisions, however, they have been thrown together by a common determination to survive, a determination which has left its mark on a quiet, cautious, stubborn people.

II. THE CREATIVE ARTIST

The justification of this survival in a separate existence so hardly achieved must be the quality of our common life, a quality which depends largely on the work of our artists and scholars, using the words in their broadest sense. What then has the artist done in Canada and under what conditions? What is his present position, and what is he likely to do in the future? A brief survey of the chief fields of artistic endeavour in Canada—painting, sculpture, architecture, music, literature and drama—suggests some generalizations on the present tendencies; and an examination of the national habits of thought and of feeling expressed in many of the institutions associated with civilized life may give some insight into possible developments in the next half-century.

[6] J. S. M. Careless: "History and Canadian Unity", *Culture,* Vol. 12 (1951), pp. 117-124. Professor Careless quotes Dr. Hugh MacLennan, *Cross Country* (p. 14).

1. Painting

Canadian art [7] in the narrower sense of painting and its related arts and crafts has a long and honourable tradition and has, in modern times, achieved a unique place in the national culture. Craftsmen and artists in French Canada survived the test of isolation which followed the Conquest and developed their own simple and sincere styles, expressing themselves chiefly in domestic crafts and in architecture with the Church as a principal patron. Unhappily it was the crafts and architecture which suffered most acutely from the forces of industrialism and mass production which began to be felt seriously in our country about the middle of the last century. The art of painting, less seriously affected, was practised during the nineteenth century in English-speaking Canada by artists whose works, if not great or original, merited, it is suggested, more attention than they received from the timid and distrustful Canadian public.

It remained, however, for the artists of the twenties known as the Group of Seven to attempt self-conscious national expression through the painting of the Canadian landscape. The clear and brilliant interpretations offered by this group, and by others, of the vast and lonely background which in somewhat sombre fashion seemed to dominate every aspect of national life, made a profound impression on Canadians and attracted attention and interest abroad.[8]

In French Canada generous praise of the work of the School of Seven was combined with a clear and precise analysis of

[7] For a recent account of the fine arts in Canada see Graham McInnes, *Canadian Art*, Macmillan, 1950.

[8] It is pointed out that this development, original and independent in Canada, found its parallel elsewhere in North America where artists were consciously working on techniques new and distinct from those of Europe in order to achieve a truer expression of the nature and quality of the country. Jean Chauvin: "The Arts in Canada", *Canada, Nation on the March*, Clarke Irwin, 1953, p. 180.

its limitations. In the last decade or so a Montreal group which includes English-speaking artists has firmly detached itself from the landscape school. Emphasizing manner rather than matter, with daring and subtlety they have, it is said, restored the balance between subject matter and approach. They have helped revive the great artistic tradition of French-speaking Canada, and, without benefit of gaunt rock or jagged pine, they have maintained and advanced Canada's reputation abroad.[9]

The Canadian painter, in common with painters everywhere, is conscious of artistic paradox. He wants to be widely and even universally known and yet he must work primarily for himself and perhaps for a few others.[10] "Tendencies are toward the expression of driving inner impulses, and the cryptic utterances of self-conscious moods. Many modern statements are artistocratic in character, have no rational communicative force whatever, and arouse only psychic responses in certain sensitively aware minds."[11] In other words, the response of the painter in Canada as elsewhere to democratic equalitarianism and mass mediocrity, is that, defeated by the paradox, he may occasionally be incapable of communicating to any but his fellow-artists. "We must," says Charles Comfort, "encourage the patient to talk himself out." He may at times be baffling but much of his work is "vital and exciting and a reflection of our times."[12]

The future of any or all of the arts depends to some degree, and perhaps to a very large degree, on the incidence and on

---

[9] This group first won recognition at an exhibition arranged by M. Jean Désy in Brazil. It has been noted often as an unhappy factor in our cultural development that we refuse to admire anything of our own until we have received from abroad the necessary permission. See E. McCourt: "Canadian Letters", *Royal Commission Studies*, pp. 70, 74.

[10] Thomas Sperber: "Search for a Miraculous Paradox", *New York Times Book Review*, August 2, 1953.

[11] "Painting", *Royal Commission Studies*, 1951, p. 413.

[12] *Ibid.*

the opportunity of individuals gifted with that special insight which is genius or near to genius. The incidence of the genius is of course unpredictable and uncontrollable, but the opportunities afforded to him for development and for productivity are another matter. In forecasting Canadian performance in any of the arts one can do little more, having noted the present state of development, than consider these opportunities.

The artist in Canada finds his opportunities conditioned by what may be termed problems of maintenance, of publication, and of inspiration and criticism. The three may be distinguished, but can hardly be separated from one another. They affect all artists everywhere; whether or not they are more acute in Canada than elsewhere is an interesting question.

It may, indeed, be difficult for an artist to earn a living in Canada. A Canadian artist and critic, for example, has recently reviewed the work of five young experimental painters in Montreal. All are "spare time" painters; all, he insists, living in Paris, New York, "or some equally receptive centre" would by now have made names for themselves.[13] Canadian painters do not as a rule starve, but it is difficult for them to feed themselves on the returns from their painting, especially if they are doing the experimental work necessary to the life of any art.

"Publication" to the painter is the showing of his works. In Canada there are a number, although an unsufficient number, of galleries and organizations which help to arrange showings. The National Gallery has this year revived the Annual Exhibitions of Canadian Art, started in the enthusiasm of the twenties and renounced during the years of depression and war. These exhibitions are intended to show the best painting of the year, selected by regional committees. Yet, helpful as

13 Michael Forster: *Canadian Art,* IX, 2, pp. 60-65.

these are, they by no means solve a problem which presents a special difficulty in this country.

Inspiration and constructive criticism are also a particularly serious problem in a country where nothing is easier for the artist to find than solitude. The need is partly met by the publication *Canadian Art,* a most useful organ of criticism and information. It is supplemented by notices in the regular press which, it appears, are adequate in French-speaking Canada, but something less than adequate in the rest of the country.[14] Unhappily the helpful intercourse which in painting could so easily go on between English- and French-speaking groups is not always apparent.[15]

2. SCULPTURE

Canadian sculpture flourished early in French-speaking Canada. There the wood-carvers early began the work which achieved its golden age in the late eighteenth and early nineteenth centuries. Examples of the old work are cherished in museums and in churches today. The great tradition was broken by the impact of industrialization, and by the end of the nineteenth century the art was languishing, maintained only by the needs of the church and by the demand for commemorative monuments.

French-Canadian sculpture today, like painting and the decorative arts transformed by a new spirit and new techniques, offers in its simplicity and strength "food for the mind and delight for the eyes".[16] Meanwhile in English-speaking Canada the increasing practice of the art has been reflected in the foundation of the Sculptors Society (1932). Sculptors have

[14] Wilfred Eggleston: "The Press of Canada", *Royal Commission Studies,* p. 52. Donatien Frémont: "La Presse de Langue Française au Canada", *ibid.,* p. 57.

[15] Forster, *loc. cit.*

[16] Gerard Morisset: "Les Arts dans le Province de Québec", *Royal Commission Studies,* p. 401.

been influenced by the work of the Group of Seven and to a certain extent by the international school with its emphasis on abstract shapes. The use of sculpture in public buildings, while creating new opportunities, offers also the problem of integrating the sculpture with the mass of the building.[17]

The economic factor has special significance in sculpture. Tools and materials are expensive, and the sculptor in English-speaking Canada cannot count on ecclesiastical commissions which are so important to his colleague in Quebec. Sculpture in Canada will develop slowly until Canadians realize that it can serve even better for the refreshment of the living than for the commemoration of the dead.

3. ARCHITECTURE

In architecture as in sculpture, a living if not a powerful tradition in the towns and villages of French Canada and pleasant reflections elsewhere of eighteenth-century Europe were smothered by the advent of the factory and the feverish expansion of the mid-nineteenth century. The same thing was happening everywhere, but the Canadian town was particularly small and vulnerable, and there was no firm tradition of "architectural good manners" requiring that the plan of the building be not only pleasing and appropriate in itself but in harmony with its surroundings. The century in which most of our building has been done has been one of architectural uncertainty everywhere, and in Canada speed and cheapness seemed to be of paramount importance. The architect and his art were by-passed in the hurry to get under cover.[18]

We have not, then, developed an architectural style good or bad, although the Quebec country house tradition, the terminal elevators and the railway hotel may be thought of

[17] McInnes, *op. cit.*, pp. 96-97.
[18] Eric Arthur: "Architecture", *Royal Commission Studies,* pp. 419-20.

as Canadian accents.[19] Our deficiency here is an important one. Architectural beauty and harmony must be seen even by those who shun pictures and refuse to open books. Moreover, the work of the architect and the town planner contributes to the enjoyment of all other arts, for it provides the setting for the activities of civilized man; it literally adds urbanity to existence. The current taste for barbarous amusements may be a result as well as a symptom of our failure to provide beautiful and appropriate settings for civilized occupations.

There are, however, hopeful signs for the future. Federal and provincial governments, beginning to assume responsibility for the construction of private dwellings in addition to public buildings, show an increasing awareness of the importance of architects and of town planners. Architects themselves recognize the need to come to terms with the new materials and the new technology. They have a sense of the value at once of practising the "international style" and of developing a healthy regionalism of the kind appearing in British Columbia. Recent awards for plans submitted in national competitions in architecture have been commented on in the press in a manner which suggests renewed public interest.

A development of special significance in the whole field of Canadian art is the use of painting and sculpture in the decoration of public buildings. Here commercial firms have set an example which it is said governments are too slow to follow. Moreover it is urged that in smaller public buildings, schools, post offices, railway stations and apartment houses much more attention should be given to beauty in decoration as well as in design.[20] A French-Canadian critic welcomes the

[19] McInnes, *op. cit.*, p. 101.

[20] Eric Arthur, *op. cit.*, pp. 428-30. "Our town halls are . . . dreary monuments where people would not go except for the payment of taxes and fines; our older post offices can only be described as sordid; our pre-war libraries give the appearance of being gloomy strongholds . . . etc." Most Canadians would agree that the indictment, if in its severity it takes no account of some small fruits of repentance, is not unjust.

recent development in Quebec of all the decorative arts, pointing out that modern art with its emphasis on decorative effects can only gain from a functional association where this is appropriate.[21]

4. LITERATURE AND PUBLISHING

During the last century universal literacy has brought about an immense increase of manufactured literature, with a corresponding decline in the taste of the average reader. Presumably this need have had no more damaging effect on literature as an art than the camera had on the art of painting. It is, however, generally agreed that, although Canadian painting has made at least an appreciable contribution to civilization, Canadian literary output so far might disappear without being greatly missed. This does not mean that literature has no significance in our cultural development. English-speaking Canada is said to have produced "a goodly number of talented writers . . . but . . . not . . . a single writer of the very first rank."[22] French Canada, although it has not produced as yet "any novelist of universal stature" has now a "few novels, which, with a few poems and a few other books, constitute a French-Canadian literature."[23]

Self-conscious nationalism in Canadian literature is older than in painting, finding its roots in Garneau, the great historian of French Canada, and in the English-speaking nature poets of the Confederation era. Literature, however, can afford an escape to nature even less than can painting, and self-conscious nationalism can serve as no more than a temporary stimulant. French- and English-speaking literatures alike have long sought refuge in the landscape, in the quaintness of local

[21] Morisset, *op. cit.*, p. 403.

[22] Desmond Pacey: *Creative Writing in Canada*, p. 191.

[23] Guy Sylvestre: "The Recent Development of the French-Canadian Novel", *University of Toronto Quarterly*, Vol. 21 (1951-52), p. 177. See also Guy Sylvestre: "Réflexions sur notre roman" in *Culture*, Vol. 12 (1951), pp. 228-246, and R. Garneau: "La Littérature", *Royal Commission Studies*, pp. 83-98.

colour, and in historical romance. In the period between
wars both literatures showed signs of increasing maturity. The
significant contribution of English-speaking Canada is in poetry,
now dealing more and more with contemporary human problems although "even yet the landscape tends to overshadow
the people".[24]

In French-speaking Canada also, poetry occupied first place
until recently. Then the shock of the First World War, together with the rapid industrialization of Quebec and the
example of a fresh approach to regionalism offered by *Maria
Chapdelaine,* opened a new era for the novel which has become the most important form of literary expression. It reflects
not only the social and economic problems of Quebec, but
the general philosophic probing of the nature of good and
evil which has become the concern of so many modern novelists.[25] The English novel also is deserting regionalism and
historical romance for a consideration of contemporary life,
but it is doing this slowly and not with entire success. Human
problems are treated with sympathy and concern but with
a philosophical vagueness[26] which is in contrast, it would seem,
with the bolder experimentation of the French-speaking group.
If it is true that great literature often emerges when the traditional bonds of an integrated society are loosened but not
dissolved, French Canada in this age of crisis fulfils the desirable conditions much better than does English-speaking Canada
with its easy-going evolutionary outlook and with no clearly-
defined common creed or philosophy.

In general it may be fair to say that literary expression in
both languages tends more and more to concern itself with

[24] Pacey, *op. cit.,* p. 191.

[25] See Sylvestre, *op. cit.*; W. E. Collin: "Letters in Canada, 1951: French
Canadian Letters", *University of Toronto Quarterly,* Vol. 21 (1951-52),
pp. 387-423, and "Quebec's Changing Literature", *Canadian Forum,* Vol.
31 (1951-52), pp. 274-6; Alan Pryce-Jones: "The Cult of Evil", *The
Listener,* April 16, 1953.

[26] See Pacey, *op. cit.,* especially pp. 179-84.

the traditional task of interpreting human nature. It is permissible to hope that the judgment of one author and critic, "that today in Canada there exists no body of creative writing which reflects adequately or with more than limited insight, the nature of the Canadian people and the historical forces which have made them what they are," [27] may in the next fifty years become untrue.

The problems of the writer have a close family resemblance to those of the painter. No writer in Canada can live on his art, it is generally agreed, with the possible exception of those journalists in French-speaking Canada who are also men of letters. This is undoubtedly a handicap for the serious writer. It is, however, becoming universal. In Britain, we learn, writers who live by writing are a "decreasing class" and in France, it is said, "economic necessity forces most young writers to work eight hours a day at some profession other than literature." [28]

Canadian writers are, then, in this respect not much worse off than many others, and a number of them have found at least a mitigated form of drudgery in university teaching. Writing, however, must be an act of faith, for it is much more difficult to publish a book in Canada than it is to write one. English-speaking Canada is said to be the hardest country in the world in which to sell a book—any book.[29] And the unknown Canadian author has to compete with the best books from the best-known publishing houses in the English-speaking world, for which his own publisher also acts as agent. He does not expect to make money on Canadian books, and his expectations are generally, it seems, fully realized. In spite of this Canadian books are published and do occasionally achieve

[27] E. McCourt quoted in *Massey Report*, p. 222.

[28] *The Listener*, March 19, 1953, p. 460; "The Climate of Fiction", *Times Literary Supplement*, March 20, 1953, p. x.

[29] Simon Paynter: "The Economics of Culture: The Book Trade", *Canadian Forum*, April, 1953.

Canadian best-seller listing. In the view of one Canadian author, publishers have done "all that can reasonably be expected of them to help Canadian literature and especially poetry." [30]

The French-language publishing industry during the war achieved a minor boom and compared with the English is said to be in a relatively prosperous state. The economic consequences of the two languages necessarily weigh heavily on all Canadian writers and publishers.

5. Music

"The music of modern Europe is the one and only art in which are surpassed the achievements of former ages." [31] In this respect Canada does not precisely reflect the tendencies of the modern world for obvious reasons. An art with a difficult and exacting technique, one necessitating considerable outlay in instruments, and one which requires close association among artists can flourish only with difficulty in a country distinguished by isolationism in every form. Canadian music has hardly yet had time to establish its own clear tradition. In French-speaking Canada some who are particularly concerned for the maintenance of cultural traditions urge composers to seek inspiration in folk-songs as painters have sought it in landscape. Canadian composers, however, show signs of a variety of influences from Europe and they also fall strongly under that of the United States.[32] Music, say our young composers, like the other arts has experienced the derivative stage, the self-conscious seeking for a "national" note and, in the natural

[30] E. McCourt, op. cit., p. 73. As has been pointed out (Pacey, op. cit., p. 114) the annual "Letters in Canada" published in the University of Toronto Quarterly since 1935 is a most important and fruitful contribution to the development of Canadian literature.

[31] E. Heller: "The Hazard of Modern Poetry", The Listener, March 5, 1953.

[32] Sir Ernest MacMillan: "Music", Royal Commission Studies, pp. 354-5.

reaction, a sense that "Canadian" music can emerge only through an unself-conscious translation of the composer's experience. A contemporary critic distinguishes in Canada a number of regional groups producing "well-written music in a somewhat limited sense"; and, "three, possibly more composers who compete on an international scale with their contemporaries."[33] The Canadian League of Composers and the Canadian Broadcasting Corporation are endeavouring, not without success, to overcome Canadian distrust of Canadian music.[34]

In music as in drama the performance of the composition is so essential an element in the artistic interpretation of experience that the typical artist's problems of maintenance, publication and criticism are of the first importance. Canadian appreciation of serious music has grown enormously in the past generation, thanks to musical festivals, radio, and the use of recordings. The national radio offers essential support to symphony orchestras, to operas, and to individual musicians. But for this support the leading symphony orchestras would not exist and many musicians would not be here. University schools of music are important centres of instruction and inspiration, and do, in fact, provide congenial occupation and support for a number of Canadian composers. In music, happily, language is no barrier to appreciation and the long-founded tradition of good music and of opera in French-speaking Canada serves not only Quebec but, through radio, the country as a whole. An admirable popularizing influence can be seen in our musical festivals, which in the last thirty years have extended from the prairie provinces, where they originated, to every province in Canada.

[33] Brian H. Taylor: "Canadian Music Today", *Canadian Forum,* February, 1953, p. 250.

[34] One of those responsible for the very successful all-Canadian Concert of the Canadian League of Composers given in Toronto in March, 1952, stated that the promoters were particularly cheered by receiving contributions, some of them quite small ones, from people who could not attend but who wished to show their interest and support.

Nevertheless the musician works under great difficulties. No orchestra can command the full-time services of its members. Individual performers face not only the heavy tax of distances and small audiences, but also the severe competition of the well-organized American concert companies. Facilities for publication are quite inadequate. Canada has no musical periodical, no great library of music, and, although it has several schools of high merit, there is inadequate provision for sound musical education and for assistance to advanced studies.[35] The picture, in short, is full of promise, but fulfilment awaits material support. It is pointed out that nowhere in the world is even the best music self-supporting. The Wurlitzer will pay its way, but the society that desires adequate performance of Beethoven or Mozart, or of its own best music, must be prepared to plan and to provide for its support.

6. Theatre

The theatre resembles music in this, that original composition must be preceded by and cannot be separated from performance. An historian of Canadian literature admits that "legitimate drama in Canada . . . remains a very delicate growth." [36] That interest and capacity are not lacking is shown by the production on the national radio of a series of original Canadian plays in recent years. But as a lover of legitimate theatre points out, radio drama is not the same thing as the theatre, and neither the writer nor the actor can use radio as his sole preparation for the theatre.[37]

Canada has a few professional companies in her largest centres and welcomes to those centres distinguished companies from abroad. The isolations of geography and of language, however, operate harshly. It may be true that the movies have

[35] See Macmillan, *op. cit.*, p. 356 ff.

[36] Pacey, *op. cit.*, p. 195.

[37] Robertson Davies: "The Theatre", *Royal Commission Studies*, p. 388.

in no way affected the taste of that group, never a large one, which asks for first-rate work on the legitimate stage. This group, however, must generally satisfy its taste in the amateur productions, often of real merit, which, encouraged by that notable piece of "private enterprise", the Dominion Drama Festival, are arousing interest even in very small centres of population.[38] Amateurs are further aided by schools of drama which encourage good work in the writing and production of plays.

Amateur drama, excellent and rewarding as it may be, is no more a substitute for professional offerings than is amateur music, or, for that matter, amateur medicine. Amateur drama has served to attract gifted young people who, with training, become competent actors, but, as things are now, if they are to use their gifts and training they cannot remain in Canada. Canada is ready for a professional theatre, "a robust Canadian theatre which would bring forth a large body of Canadian plays, some of them good enough for export." [39] In such a theatre, there should be a practical theatre studio, a centre for the study and practice of all the arts of the theatre. The studio would need some support from public funds, but the theatre which would be founded on it could, it is held, maintain itself. A growing theatre would also provoke informed and helpful criticism. The foundations, however, must be so laid as to provide work of the first quality and for this public support is needed.[40]

Optimism about the future of the theatre in Canada is borne out to some degree by the success of recent ventures, such as the Festival at Stratford of 1953.[41] It is also encouraged by

[38] The Little Theatre of London, Ontario, is another inspiring example.

[39] Robertson Davies, *op. cit.*, p. 389.

[40] *Ibid.*, pp. 390-92. See also Mavor Moore: "The Canadian Theatre", *Canadian Forum*, September, 1950, for a somewhat pessimistic review.

[41] The Toronto Shakespeare Festival has completed its fifth season. See "The Shakespeare Festivals in Canada", *Food for Thought*, May-June, 1953.

the increasing popularity in several parts of Canada of a related
art, the ballet. Canadian ballet is fulfilling the hopes of sup-
porters of the Canadian theatre in the interpretation of the
classics and also, with the help of young Canadian composers,
of Canadian life.

7. A NATIONAL ART?

When the question of "a national art" is raised, painters,
writers and critics are at one in their view that the self-
conscious nationalism of the Maple-leaf-Mountie period can
only be destructive of all sincere artistic expression. It may
have been a necessary stage of adolescent revolt against cultural
colonialism, but it is a stage which most Canadians hope
that we have passed through.[42]

We do not need this awkward Canadian dress because
Canadian artists in all fields are speaking clearly and intelligently
with a Canadian accent which is naturally their own. Canadian painting has its own recognized place. Canadian music
has, it is said, a distinguishable quality reminiscent of the Canadian landscape. And even when one can identify their counterparts elsewhere in North America, Canadian writers have a
distinctive style and approach.[43] As an historian of Canadian

[42] It is not quite certain that we have passed through it yet. The review
of a volume of Saskatchewan poetry, a review published in Toronto, regrets
that there is not more "regional" poetry; the reviewer does not consider
regionalism as a means to freshness and sincerity but, apparently, as an
end in itself. And an article from French-speaking Canada urges musicians
to draw on French-Canadian folk-songs and writers to write new *Maria
Chapdelaine's*. Paul Gouin: "In the Country of Quebec Nothing Must Die
and Nothing Must Change", *Culture*, Vol. 12 (1951), pp. 43-50. See also
on this subject Graham McInnes, *op. cit.*, pp. 111-114, and Marius
Plamondon (in a review of McInnes' work), *Culture*, Vol. 12, 1951, p. 430.

[43] ". . . Moreover, Canadian art as a whole, and more particularly
Canadian literature, has a distinctive conception of man's lot on the earth,
a conception engendered by the peculiar features of the Canadian terrain.
There is a family resemblance between the paintings of Tom Thomson and
Emily Carr, the poems of Duncan Campbell Scott, E. J. Pratt and Earle
Birney, and the novels of de la Roche and Callaghan. In all of them man
is dwarfed by an immensely powerful physical environment which is at once
forbidding and fascinating." Pacey, *op. cit.*, p. 2. McInnes (see fn. 42)
explains the inspiration of Canadian art in very similar terms.

literature suggests, Canadian writers are only now seeing the possibilities before them: "Canadians are slowly wakening to the fact that their country offers immense scope to the writer of realistic fiction, that it is one of the few areas of the civilized world whose life has not been extensively recorded and interpreted." [44]

There are those, however, who warn us that it is a mistake to assume that honest, intelligible speech and a distinctive accent are signs of a mature personality. The documentary or sociological approach, honest and unself-conscious though it may be, is not the way to achieve a great literature. It may even divert the writer from his true task by keeping him on the surface when he should be treating his subjects in depth. Some young French-Canadian critics argue that even the best and wittiest reporting of the local scene, although far removed from self-conscious "quaintness", may delay the development of a great literature.[45] This French group, it is interesting to observe, fears regionalism more than colonialism, and in literature as in other arts believes that French-Canadian culture will benefit most in the long run by maintaining close connections with France.[46]

From English-speaking Canada comes another question: no matter whether our themes be regional or universal, sociological documentation or psychological penetration, have we as a people the qualities necessary for the creation of great works of art? One writer and critic commenting on the fact that our Canadian artists in every field find their great inspiration in Canadian landscape, and preferably a Canadian landscape innocent

[44] Pacey, *op. cit.,*

[45] "Ce qui importe, il me semble, c'est qu'à une certaine tonalité humaine de la voix de nos écrivains, ceux qui naissent, souffrent, jouissent et meurent sous toutes les latitudes, reconnaissent en eux des semblables, des frères." Garneau, *op. cit.,* p. 91.

[46] It is not intended to suggest that this view is universal. French Canada shows the vitality of its culture by the vigour of its cultural debates.

of any sign of Canadian occupation, suggests rather bluntly that we find ourselves appallingly dull, and with good reason. We are pleasant, modest, reticent and unsure of ourselves— "nice" perhaps, but condemned by our very virtues not to inspire the artist, still less to make those heroic acts of dedication and sacrifice from which alone great art can emerge. "Not," adds this critic, "that we expect our writers to starve. But there would be reassurance in the knowledge that some of them were prepared to run the risk." [47]

Comments such as this seem to bear out the contention that Canadians suffer from an inferiority complex. Certainly they remind us that cultural evolution has not the character of inevitability often attributed to biological evolution. Neither political community nor economic self-sufficiency of themselves imply even a high degree of civilization, much less of creative power.

On the other hand, it may be retorted that premature pessimism is a common sign of immaturity. Our proximity to the United States has prolonged our period of colonialism, a period during which we have been rather dazzled by our neighbour's material wealth and power than impressed by the less conspicuous cultural achievements. We have had, so we thought, to devote our efforts to mere survival, and, as a condition of survival, to a co-operation between our two cultures which was confined to surface good manners (with

---

[47] McCourt, *op. cit.*, pp. 75, 76-80. Professor McCourt quotes comments on the Canadian character by B. K. Sandwell, Bruce Hutchison and Frederic Philip Grove. He himself states the truth as he sees it bluntly: "Since the fall of Quebec much of English-speaking Canada has been populated—if somewhat thinly—by a highly literate people, drawn in part from the educated classes of the Old Country, yet in its two hundred years of existence it has produced few good books and not a single great one. What is true of literature is true of all the creative arts. When all possible allowance has been made for the difficulties under which the creative artist in Canada works, it seems strange that no one of outstanding talent has spoken in a voice to catch the ear of the world" (p. 74). The explanation offered by the author is (in part) that "We have been over-awed by the spectacular material achievements of the United States . . ." (p. 75).

occasional outbursts of very bad manners) because we were
afraid to reveal the fundamental differences which lay below
the surface. It seems probable that the next half-century will
see a rapid and fruitful growth of understanding between the
two main groups. International crises as well as national
expansion invite us to see how much more there is to unite
than to divide us. Moreover, the stimulating effect of two
World Wars and of our political and economic maturity on
the creative activity of the artists in each group is drawing
us closer together in sincere admiration for each other's efforts.
It is unfortunate that in Canada people of French and English
speech have so long been content to live side by side un-
moved by, even completely ignorant of, the wealth of their
neighbour's cultural tradition and the level of his cultural
achievement. There is a strong movement for a better understanding with an increasing sense of the need not for a superficial and chatty "bilingualism" but for a genuine mastery
of the two languages, and in the meantime for the erection of
bridges across the cultural gulf, including more translations of
the books written in each language.[48]

Along with the stimulating effect which may be expected
from more frequent cultural exchanges between French and
English groups must be mentioned the significant character of
recent immigration into Canada. English-speaking Canada has
long benefited by the variety of tradition and culture among
the "new Canadians" of the first decade of this century, at
the price of a measure of confusion which has accompanied

---

[48] ". . . It is safe to say that a book such as *Maria Chapdelaine* has done
at least as much as the rhetoric of statesmen to bring about some measure of
understanding between the two great branches of the Canadian community
. . . If the best of French literature—a literature surprisingly rich and
varied—were made available in cheap translations, the rest of Canada
would quickly learn that the arts of Quebec were not confined to rug-
making. Similarly, the translation into French of the best English-Canadian
literature might convince the French Canadian that the attiude of his
neighbour towards him was something less than hostile." McCourt, *op. cit.*,
p. 82.

the wealth.[49] From the advent of the Hitler regime in Germany until the present day, however, there has flowed into this country a thin but significant stream of individuals of distinction in their various callings, many of whom would not have been drawn from the place where their reputations were established by any lesser event. Such tragic migrants, familiar enough in history, traditionally more than repay the hospitality extended to them. It is not unreasonable to regard these newest Canadian citizens as having a significance for our cultural future out of proportion to their numbers.

8. AID TO ARTISTS

It may be said, then, that if we cannot yet predict a distinguished future for the arts in Canada, certainly we must not prematurely deny them any future at all. The incidence of genius is unpredictable and so, I think, is the future development of our still youthful national character. One thing we do know. The arts everywhere and at every time have needed material support, and Canadian conditions make this support particularly necessary. It is certain that, short of some providential intervention, we shall not know the extent of our collective artistic capacity unless we extend further material encouragement to the individuals who possess it. There are a number of sources from which aid may come: the voluntary support of individuals or groups; the wealthy and enlightened individual patron; the commercial firm; the government agency. Each one of these operates in Canada and each has special

[49] It is interesting that almost simultaneously this year there appeared two books dealing with the life and contribution of ethnic groups differing widely in time, place and origin: *Highland Settler* by Charles W. Dunn and *The Ukrainians in Manitoba* by Paul Yuzyk, both published by the University of Toronto Press. *Canadian Art,* Vol. IX, No. 3 (1952), p. 130, contains a notice of a display of over a hundred paintings by new Canadians, most of them recently arrived in Canada and few of them at that period in touch with Canadian exhibiting societies. *University of Toronto Quarterly,* "Letters in Canada" (see fn. 30) reviews "New Canadian Letters". There are, of course, many other sources of information including publications of various ethnic groups.

advantages and limitations which it is impossible to discuss here. In not one of them so far have our exploits been heroic. Our cultural future certainly depends on increased generosity from each one of these sources, with at least a corresponding increase in wisdom in determining the form which generosity shall take. The one is quite as important as the other. Will generosity, with wisdom, be forthcoming? It is impossible to say. Speculations must be based on the nature and quality of intellectual and cultural development in the country. To what sort of people does the Canadian artist offer his communications, and by what means and through what institutions do they receive them?

III. A CIVILIZED SOCIETY

Everything, in fact, depends on the answer to this question. Lone geniuses there may be, but continuous intelligible communication through those aesthetic symbols the creation of which alone "makes men men" [50] is not possible without a rational civilized society engaged in continuous "conversation" in the sense of a continuous exchange of ideas with all that this implies. The absence or, at best, the desultory nature of our intellectual exchanges should be a matter of more immediate concern than the plight of the artists. If "conversation" were going on, if intelligent people were constantly aware of the fact that minds need food and exercise and that those who call on the ends of the earth to satisfy their slightest material needs must also remember that there are things which have been called souls, then there would be no need to worry about the artists. Unfortunately, centres of the kind of conversation which is at once the sign and the source of intellectual life are all too rare.

[50] Mavor Moore: "The Canadian Theatre", *Canadian Forum,* August, 1950.

1. UNIVERSITIES

An obvious place to look for these is in the universities and, indeed, Canadian universities have been practically identified with Canadian intellectual life by one who should be an authority on both.[51] They have, indeed, an almost exclusive monopoly of advanced liberal education. They are very often centres for the study and practice of music, drama and the fine arts. They are almost the only centres of research in the humanities and social sciences, and they are key centres of scientific research. In addition they have a practical monopoly of training for the learned professions, to say nothing of their increasing responsibility for the endless variety of technical instruction which has become a necessity in modern life.

Universities in Canada, like all civilized institutions, have had to struggle against handicaps of poverty and of isolation. They, too, have been obliged to create and maintain their special traditions in difficult times. They have in almost all their activities borne particularly heavy responsibility because in this new country they have been doing what no one else was ready or able to do. In nothing has this been more true than in matters purely intellectual and cultural.

It is in part the very success of the universities that is endangering their intellectual life and therefore, if we are to believe the authority mentioned above, endangering the intellectual life of the nation. The general climate of opinion is, of course, unfavourable to the purely intellectual life. "The intensification of materialism and the dilution of religion have encouraged general apathy or contempt toward matters which cannot be precisely weighed or priced. A good many scholars themselves have become worldly in this sense . . ." says a recent writer on Canadian universities. Worldliness, however,

[51] A. W. Trueman: "Universities and Intellectual Life", *Canada: Nation on the March,* p. 165, Clarke Irwin, 1953.

is pressed upon them. Canadian universities have been regarded by the public and to some degree by themselves
"chiefly as service institutions of a rather narrowly utilitarian
kind, with somewhat grudging tolerance for theoretical studies
normally in the faculty of arts." [52]

This utilitarian approach is not confined to the demand
that the university multiply professional and technical schools
until the organization of its teaching functions comes to be
geared rather to their requirements than to the needs of
those few seeking intellectual enlightenment and cultural development. It is affecting also the work of those who have
achieved very great prestige in intellectual life, research scholars
and scientists. Independent original investigations are one of
the two pillars on which our intellectual life rests, the other
being what has been described as "capacity for and interest
in the adroit communication of knowledge and experience".[53]

In endeavouring to estimate the significance of Canadian
universities as the principal guardians of Canadian intellectual
life, it is important to consider how much of the "research"
that goes on represents investigations truly rewarding in the
purely intellectual sense. It is also desirable to consider how
much teaching is really calculated to nourish and liberate
the mind rather than to convey useful facts and techniques.
It is a nice question whether the intellectual light of the
universities, in becoming diffused over an ever widening area,

[52] J. B. Brebner: *Scholarship for Canada,* Canadian Social Science
Research Council, Ottawa, 1945, pp. 13, 32.

[53] *Ibid.,* p. 27. We now use the name of "research" for a great many
time-consuming, laborious, exhausting, but not very difficult or very intellectual operations. Some of these may be carried on by expert technicians
with a very slight foundation of general learning. They do not provoke
thought; they rather give an excuse for not thinking. They may be
essential, but they are not the same as, and they are no substitute for,
those investigations which require wide and deep learning and the capacity
for original thought. The latter exact from the would-be investigator,
however brilliant he may be, a period of severe and exacting training, and
thereafter willingness to put time and effort into long-term projects with
no certainty of positive results.

may not also be growing correspondingly dim.[54] Until this question is answered there is no certainty that Canadian universities will make as distinguished a contribution to Canadian intellectual life in the next fifty years as they have in the past fifty. Such an investigation is the more important because, although centres of intellectual life and conversation certainly exist outside the universities, it is not certain that such centres could exist independently of university life.

2. LEARNED SOCIETIES

In most countries "learned societies" are key centres of the intellectual "conversations". This is true in Canada, although here again distance lays a heavy tax on intellectual exchanges. The Royal Society, an organization of considerable age and dignity, has received the tribute of harsh criticism from one who feels that it has not fulfilled its original promise. Its annual meetings were intended to give the best Canadian minds the opportunity of fertilizing each other and its transactions were to preserve the highest products of scholarship. "Instead the meetings have been rather drowsy gatherings of pleasant urbanity but little distinction, and the transactions slumber for the most part on library shelves."[55] It may be that the Royal Society, like the universities, suffers from the "specialism" which diverts most scholarly energy to the specialized and professional societies and journals. The latter are increasing in numbers and activity. This in itself is good; what is ominous is that the one intellectual society which embraces both languages and all disciplines should be distinguished by pleasantness and prestige rather than by those

[54] Speaking absolutely no doubt Canadian universities are doing more first-class work than they have ever done. It is the apparent relative decline which is ominous for the future.

[55] Brebner, *op. cit.*, p. 65.

sharp and stimulating exchanges which serve to bring all special insights and experiences to bear on the whole of life.[56]

Apart from the principal learned and professional societies, innumerable other voluntary societies have, by ingenious forms of organization, striven to overcome the problems of isolation and to maintain helpful communication between people of common interests.[57] These receive help of various kinds from universities and from governments provincial and federal.

3. LIBRARIES, GALLERIES, MUSEUMS

Following the example of the Province of Quebec, several of the younger provinces are paying increasing attention to the formation of arts boards or their equivalent,[58] and to the establishment of museums and of archival collections. The most significant recent activities of the federal government have been in the preparation and circulation of documentary films, and in radio and television broadcasting. It has been perhaps the pressure of war and of international crises which has caused these mass media with their direct universal appeal to receive more attention than the older cultural institutions —galleries, museums, archives, and the emerging national library.

The failure until now to provide a national library is perhaps typical of the influence of our neighbour on our cultural development. We have been so freely and so well served by American institutions that it has seemed unnecessary to develop our own. Many of our cultural activities have been nourished by funds from the great American foundations, foundations which find no adequate counterparts in our own

[56] It is particularly unfortunate that in this officially bilingual society members of different languages should meet together regularly only in the relatively neutral scientific sections and not in the pursuit of the arts and humanities which engage the whole man with all his prejudices and emotions.

[57] See *Massey Report*, Chapter VI, Appendix I.

[58] For example, the Cultural Development Boards in Alberta and the Saskatchewan Arts Board.

country where the great era of economic expansion coincides with the era of the income tax. Canada is now wealthy enough to replace or supplement these contributions generously from Canadian funds, public and private. The important question for the future is whether American generosity has in any way dulled in Canadians a sense of responsibility in these matters. A very serious cultural gap and one perhaps not unrelated to our own want of a national library is the inadequacy of library services almost everywhere, but especially in the rural areas. Libraries are ordinarily a municipal responsibility, but regional library services have been started with provincial aid in a few places. The rarity of libraries in the country and of bookstores in all but the largest cities is one of the most depressing aspects of Canadian civilization.

4. NEWSPAPERS AND PERIODICALS

Canadian newspapers and periodicals have to struggle at once with geography, with our two languages, and with American competition. The want of a national newspaper inevitably limits cultural communication. The French daily and weekly press, it is said, devotes even more attention to cultural matters than to politics.[59] Such a charge cannot be made against the English press, which, says an English-speaking journalist bluntly, "may neglect the cultural in favour of the purely sensational in deference to the wishes of the public." [60]

A most important index of the nature of public "conversation" is, of course, the periodical press. Here outside competition is keen. Canada, says a former editor, is the one country in the world whose people read more foreign

[59] Frémont, op. cit., p. 57.

[60] Eggleston, op, cit., p. 50. It is, however, important to observe that the daily press, both French and English, gave great space and prominence to the *Massey Report,* and it may be presumed that this was done because of the editorial conviction that the subject of the report was one of major interest to the Canadian people.

than native periodicals. American competition does not, of course, affect French-speaking Canada directly. In English-speaking Canada, in spite of the competition, periodicals have in the past thirty years greatly increased "in numbers, circulation, wealth, influence and coverage".[61] On the other hand, amalgamation has eliminated small regional publications, and with them much good semi-amateur writing. The principal cultural periodicals in Canada are sponsored by universities, another indication of the university colouring of our intellectual life. There are, however, one or two encouraging exceptions to this rule, which give some indications of an increasing demand for serious periodical reading, and therefore offer hope for the future.

5. BROADCASTING

There are no agencies of greater significance in Canadian intellectual life than the so-called mass media of radio and television. Our experience of the latter is still limited, but it may reasonably be regarded as having an impact similar to radio but probably much more powerful. These media are both at present organized as a national service under the central control of the Canadian Broadcasting Corporation. The national radio service, created with much difficulty and expense, has served in the twentieth century as railways did in the nineteenth, to maintain the east-west communications essential to national unity among patches of population often remote from each other but relatively near to their southern neighbour.

The national radio has also served as a most important instrument of general education and culture. In a new country with no strong and settled tradition of intellectual life, and poor, as has been seen, in cultural amenities such as libraries, picture galleries, music and the theatre, it has rendered in-

[61] *Ibid.*, p. 51.

valuable service. It has brought music of all kinds, plays, books, and even, indirectly, pictures to many who by this means have maintained former interests and acquired new capacity for enjoyment. An American authority on radio refers to the "signal service" to the rural population of "one of the largest listening group projects in the world".[62]

Nevertheless, if broadcasting is considered as a just reflection of the vigour and intensity of our national intellectual life, there is no encouragement for complacency. The service may reach high levels of excellence; our best "talks", for example, may be comparable to those heard over the BBC, but we do not produce such talks either consistently or at any time in great quantity. It is probably safe to assume that Canada does not provide a sufficient audience to justify many talks of "third programme" quality. Probably scientific talks at this level might be adequately appreciated, for our considerable group of highly trained scientists does seem to constitute the kind of intellectual society capable of maintaining a continuing "conversation". On more general matters, however, the "third programme" speech seems to require more knowledge and concentration than we are prepared to give. We have not the constant pooling of knowledge and ideas, the steady analysis of problems of current interest, the joint search for solutions, all of which must result in that continuous stimulating intellectual conversation which the "third programme" talk feeds and inspires. We simply have not enough people who find their chief recreation in intellectual pursuits. It is possible, however, that the officials of the national system, too conscious of this fact, occasionally make the error of underestimating public capacity.

On the other hand, they are accused by representatives of commercial elements in the system of overrating public capacity and public taste. It is argued in the name of democracy

[62] Charles A. Siepmann, quoted in *Massey Report.* p. 30.

that radio should be used not for education but exclusively for "entertainment"; such limited entertainment as, it is conceived, may be acceptable to "the humble and the little educated".[63]

Our future cultural development must depend to a very great extent on the use made of radio and of television. A Canadian professor considering whether broadcasting in a democracy should be publicly or privately controlled describes the attitude of the public as "apathetic and acquiescent . . . dominated by the more immediate considerations that neglect the great power which the radio may exercise over men's minds".[64] If this is true it is a grim comment on the probable future of intellectual life in Canada.

6. RELIGION

Canada is nominally a Christian country; that is, her public institutions recognize the Christian faith and observe Christian forms of worship on numerous public and formal occasions. It is probable, too, that the vast majority of Canadians have some kind of affiliation with a Christian church even though the church attendance of most of these may be, to say the least, perfunctory, and the attachment of many confined to participation in the rites of baptism, marriage and burial.

In Canada as elsewhere in the Western World, this situation has been accepted with approval by many intellectuals. The conflict between dogmatic Christianity, with its insistence on the reality of sin and the need for personal salvation, and rational humanism, admitting human frailty but seeing hope

[63] Joseph Sedgwick: "The Massey Report and Television", *Saturday Night,* February 28, 1953, p. 30.

[64] Alexander Brady: *Democracy and the Dominions,* p. 568. See also H. Innis: *The Bias of Communication,* and "Shapers of the Modern Outlook (Harold A. Innis)", *Canadian Forum,* January, 1953, pp. 224-5; Albert Shea: "Mass Communications", *Canadian Forum,* January, 1951 (review article on Charles A. Siepmann: *Radio, Television and Society*); "Consumers' Choice", *Times Literary Supplement,* July 24, 1953, p. 477.

only in faithful and tolerant human striving, has existed through-out the greater part of our history. Here as elsewhere it has been tempered by a common ethic and by a large measure of toleration, or of indifference, on both sides.

In recent years the positions of both parties have been threatened by materialistic totalitarianism, and each group has been compelled to redefine its position. Without touching on philosophic differences it may be said that many humanists believe that if "the basic issue behind today's problems is the struggle for moral authority",[65] the remedy must be found in such a new synthesis of humane and scientific studies as may introduce a new sense of values in social affairs. The hope for humanity is seen in a new dedication to the search for truth and to the discipline which the search imposes.

There are humanists who, renouncing any compromise with materialism, see "a very real basis of compromise between those who accept supernatural authority and those who accept only the authority of man, since both believe in the worth and dignity of the individual." [66] Others feel that Christian dogma with its debilitating doctrine of sin and of the need for supernatural grace has little if anything to contribute to the work of a healthy and vigorous humanism.[67]

On the other hand, there are numerous signs of an increase of energy and enthusiasm among those who depend for moral and even intellectual security on the work of grace as well as on the operations of human intelligence. Books, periodical articles, radio programmes and everyday conversation reflect a growing interest in Christian dogma and an increasing sense

[65] M. Long: "The Issues Behind Today's Problems", *Food for Thought*, November, 1952, p. 16. See also R. A. Cameron: "The Source of Moral Authority", *ibid.*, pp. 30-32.

[66] Long, *ibid.*

[67] See, for example, F. H. Underhill: "Shaw", *Canadian Forum*, December, 1950, p. 194.

of its relevance to the affairs of this world.[68] This interest is a matter of comment among those who regret the tendency as well as among those who welcome it.

There can be no question of its significance in Canadian cultural development. It is impossible to say whether a culture can develop without being centred in a religious faith of some sort; it is a fact that such a thing never has happened. Considering Western civilization alone, even the unhappy results of bigotry and narrow puritanism must be regarded only as the necessary defects of virtue in view of the cultural role of the Christian church as a whole.

Moreover, the modern movement is, in Canada as elsewhere, very much a movement of intellectuals. It is the response of many thoughtful minds to the terrifying revelations of human capacity for wickedness two centuries after the "enlightenment"; a response which finds a curious contemporary counterpart in the search for purity through the cult of evil.[69] In twentieth-century Canada we have not yet found our

[68] See, for example, articles in *Dalhousie Review,* and especially Vol. 31, No. 4, 1951, F. Hilton Page, "Religion and Psychology Today". This article contains a discussion of the modern and useful relationship between religion and psychology although the author maintains that religion is not just another kind of psychology and that it may not always subserve the purposes of mental hygiene. *The Listener,* July 9, 1953, publishes a talk which might serve as an interesting footnote to Professor Page's article, "Daily Paper Pantheon", by Alan McGlachon who suggests that "in the comic strip may lie concealed the indestructible germ of natural religion" (p. 66). In the past year there has been a series of articles in *Food for Thought;* M. V. C. Jeffreys' "The Democratic Paradox and the Humanist Somersault", May-June, 1953, argues that "democracy in fact assumes the Christian view of reality and the nature of man rather than that of progressive perfection of the social order by human reason." The article on "Philosophy" by George P. Grant in *Royal Commission Studies,* 1951, states that "the practice of philosophy (and . . . all the arts of civilization) will depend on a prior condition, namely the intensity and concentration of one's faith in God" (p. 132). This article was selected for special and favourable comment by more than one "secular" reviewer. Professor Grant's philosophic assumptions have, however, received severe criticism from a senior Canadian philosopher, Professor Fulton S. Anderson. See *Philosophy in Canada, a Symposium,* pp. 3-4. See also Eugene Enman: "Reading, Writing and Religion", *Harper's Magazine,* May, 1953, pp. 84-90, for a review of a situation which must find some parallel in Canada.

[69] Pryce-Jones, *op. cit.*

Methodist Movement, but there is some evidence that Augustine is becoming to the Protestants what Aquinas is to the Roman Catholics.[70]

One aspect of the general revival of religious interest in the Western World, the oecumenical movement, is of particular importance in Canada. Religious and philosophic differences among ourselves have accentuated our cultural isolation and have divided most deeply from each other many with an earnest concern for the non-material values of life. There are increasing signs of a certain drawing together among Christian groups in Canada, not with any idea of eliminating doctrinal differences but rather in the hope of exploring and opening the common ground that obviously exists. This is not the place to discuss the religious significance of such moves or their probable outcome, but the possibility of such bridges between French- and English-speaking groups must interest anyone concerned with our cultural future.[71]

IV. CONCLUSION

When one is asked to peer fifty years into the future the instinct is first to look back fifty years into the past.

The last half-century with two major wars, the unexampled period of the depression, and the present unexampled accession of power and prosperity have seen an amazingly rapid rate of economic and constitutional development. In intellectual and cultural matters there has also been remarkable growth.

[70] For example, the Trinitarian Society of Canada, which has for its purpose serious theological study and research, includes members lay and clerical of various denominations throughout the country. Meetings are held in Toronto and papers published from time to time.

[71] Two examples of such meetings are the Hazen Conference of 1952, when French-speaking Roman Catholics and English-speaking Protestants spent four days discussing questions connected with religion and education in universities, each person speaking in his own language; and, a permanent group, the Montreal Council on Christian Social Order, composed of all Christian groups. There must be many other instances.

It could hardly be otherwise in a period during which not only has Canadian destiny but the destiny of our whole world seemed often in doubt. Only a completely insensitive people could fail to be moved by the universal sense of crisis. The First World War was followed in Canada by a self-conscious effort at national self-expression. The second one has been followed by a more mature self-examination. Have we anything to say, and how are we saying it? This has led to important considerations on the difficult lot of the artist and of the scholar, their need for help, the proper means of securing it, and the inevitable suggestions that artists and their like be allowed to find their own level.

Our concern, kindly or patronizing or critical, with the future of the artist may in more ways than one provide the key to an understanding of our future. We should ask, not so much what we are going to do with the artist, but what we are going to do with ourselves. The true artist has vision and insight; by definition he is a seer. He conveys the truth by which, literally, men and nations live. He shows what life is in all its aspects. Man cannot exercise his faculty of refusing the evil and of choosing the good unless he knows, and that means unless he has been shown, what these are. It is not a question of what we are to do with struggling artists, a question asked in the same tone as we ask what we are to do with the victims of poverty, disease and vice. It is a question of what we want to do, of what we should do, with and for ourselves. Do we want to get below the surface of the obvious and the material in order to penetrate into those mysteries which, even though they may sometimes be dark and difficult, yield life as distinguished from existence? Or do we want rather to use the wealth which we have gained from the achievements of reason and the fruits of toil to bury ourselves in material satisfactions?

We have the elements of a national culture in those who

have given themselves over to the values of religion, philosophy, scholarship, art, music, literature, but we have not a coherent whole. Cultural evolution is not organic evolution. In a democratic society it must represent a conscious dedication to the good life, a genuine worship of the truth that makes the good life for the community. If in Canada we can secure that dedication and worship, there is every hope that we shall not lack artists, philosophers, and scholars to interpret to us in their various ways the aspects of truth that they have seen. If on the other hand we refuse to give to our hearts and minds the thought and care that we lavish on our physical needs we may very easily use our wealth only to demonstrate a premature decadence and a relapse into barbarism.

CANADA IN THE WORLD

Donald Grant Creighton

M.A., LL.D., F.R.S.C.
Professor of History, University of Toronto; Guggenheim Foundation Fellowship, 1940-41; Rockefeller Fellowship,
1944-45; Nuffield Fellowship, 1951-52;
Royal Society of Canada Tyrrell Medal,
1951; author, *John A. Macdonald; The
Young Politician,* 1952, etc.

CANADA IN THE WORLD

I

"So MANY Canadians, speaking or writing about their country," declared a reviewer in an English weekly recently, "have been modest to the point of apology that one might pardonably have taken diffidence to be a national characteristic." Diffidence, in a person or a nation, is the reflection of uncertainty and inexperience; and, on the basis of a good deal of evidence, it might very well be claimed that the period between the two World Wars was Canada's age of diffidence in international affairs. It was also, of course, the age of Canada's Mackenzie King; and however comically inappropriate to Mr. King's character and career as a whole the word "diffident" may be, it can certainly be used to describe the hesitations, ambiguities, and silences of his foreign policy. "To put the day of decision off—and off—and off," Lytton Strachey wrote of Queen Elizabeth I, "it seemed her only object, and

227

her life passed in a passion of postponement." It is perhaps
as difficult to associate Mr. Mackenzie King with passion of
any kind, as it is to think of him in the same category as
Queen Elizabeth I; but at any rate we can all agree that
postponement became with him a settled habit of mind. He
united a grey colourlessness of style, a grey ambiguity of
thought, and a grey neutrality of action. He became an
acknowledged expert in the difficult business of qualifying,
toning down, smoothing out, and explaining away. He re-
served judgment, avoided commitments, delayed action, and
escaped responsibility. He was all these things, and did all
these things, not against the protests of his fellow-citizens,
but with their firm if unenthusiastic support. With his squat,
solid, unremarkable presence, and his earnest, rather whining
voice, he became the veritable embodiment of the uncertainties,
the mental conflicts, the parochial terrors of the Canadian
people between the wars.

This period in our career in international affairs has passed
away. Fifty years from now it will have become a part of
an already remote past. But, if we are to make reasonable
guesses about our future in world politics, we ought to know
why this phase came about and why it is unlikely to return.
Diplomatic and military power depends on human and material
resources and the ability to use them effectively. It depends
largely on physical factors; but not on them alone. It may
also be in part the consequence of a nation's self-knowledge
and self-confidence, of the wisdom of its leadership, and the
variety and depth of its experience. In 1919, when Canada's
career in international society may be said to have begun,
it lacked these sources of intellectual and moral strength.
The Canadian people were profoundly ignorant and unaware
of the outside world. They were not any too sure of
themselves. And in so far as their country could have been
said to have had a foreign policy at all in the past, that policy

had been directed to the attainment of two basic, essential objectives, without which a Canadian political existence in its own right would have been impossible. Canadians had aspired to establish a new and important nation state, autonomous within the British Empire, and separate and distinct on the North American Continent. The second of these objectives—the maintenance of an independent existence in North America, despite the continental imperialism of the United States—was obviously the more important of the two and for a long time was given priority. But early in the twentieth century, after a fairly long period of peace, the Canadians began to feel less apprehensive and more secure in North America; and since the world, including the United States, seemed willing to accept the fact of their separate political existence, they shifted their attention to the second objective of their nationalist programme. The achievement of complete autonomy inside the British Empire was now advanced to a position of absolute priority; and the country set off in an eager pursuit of status, of an acknowledged position in the international world, a pursuit which ended successfully in the resounding declarations of the Balfour Report of 1926, and the Statute of Westminster of 1931. The changes of these years, so far as they concerned Canada's control of her own internal affairs, were almost purely formal, mere regularizations of existing practice. But in the matter of the foreign policy of the British Empire a real revolution undoubtedly took place. Up to that point, the diplomatic unity of the Empire had continued unimpaired. Now it ceased to exist. During the 1920's Canada clearly and emphatically indicated that she was going to formulate and implement her own foreign policy separately from the United Kingdom; and the Report of the Imperial Conference of 1926 endorsed without qualification the theory upon which this declaration was made.

Mr. Mackenzie King, in Philip Guedalla's phrase, was an

arriviste who had arrived. He was a pilgrim who had eventually got to Mecca, and the Canadian people were the children of Israel who had at length been brought into the Promised Land. What were they to do now that they had got there? Mr. King had no very ready answer to this question. The personnel of the Department of External Affairs, which Sir Wilfrid Laurier had founded in 1909, was slightly increased in number. The first three Canadian legations were established at Washington, Paris and Tokyo. But, after this promising beginning, an abrupt halt was called to the development of Canadian representation abroad; and all over the rest of the world Canadians remained dependent upon the diplomatic and consular services of the United Kingdom—in flat contradiction to Mr. King's declared principle of Canadian autonomy. It began to look as if the title, not the reality, of status was what had really been desired. A separate foreign policy was all very well in theory. But what, Canadians asked themselves apprehensively, was it going to mean in practice? Canada began to discover that moving out of one's parents' house and setting up for oneself in high international society was a highly complicated, extremely expensive, and possibly dangerous move. Canadians, in short, had made good their claim at a time when they were still inhibited by a limited experience and a colonial past.

II

In this difficulty, Canada instinctively fell back upon the old habits of colonialism. Attendance at conferences and other such diplomatic gestures were occasionally necessary to justify our position in international society; but in the company of our political peers we could be as inconspicuous, unobtrusive, and self-effacing as possible. We could squeeze into the smallest corner of the back seat while somebody else drove. We could stand about in corners and by doors while other people monopolized the conversation. This air of diffidence, which was really falsified by our own claims, this habit of pleading inexperience, unconcern, and incapacity became perhaps the distinguishing characteristic of this first phase of our career in international affairs. These were the years in which Canadian politicians loved to dilate, not on Canada's strength and great potential influence, but upon its regional and cultural divisions, its geographic and economic strains and stresses, its utterly unparalleled difficulties as a North American nation on the one hand, and a member of the Commonwealth and the League of Nations on the other. Canada would unquestionably wait upon the leadership of others. Its foreign policy would certainly be derivative, imitative, and lacking in conviction. But whom should it follow? What should it imitate? The answer was simple. The fashionable model for Canadian imitation in the inter-war years was the United States.

During the nineteenth century, while annexation by the United States had been the greatest peril, Canada had relied heavily upon the diplomatic and military support of Great Britain. During the nineteenth century, while the diplomatic unity of the British Empire remained intact, Canadians had thrilled with British diplomatic triumphs and raged or sorrowed at British diplomatic defeats. This intimate sense of comradeship was only gradually weakened; but once the attainment of separate national status became Canada's first objective, there was bound to be a significant shift of emphasis from the old world to the new. The importance of Canada's membership in the British Commonwealth was now deliberately minimized. People made the remarkable discovery that Canada was a North American nation, and all sorts of astounding conclusions were deduced from this hitherto unrecognized fact. A whole new generation of politicians, publicists, journalists and professors—the professional Canadian nationalists of the 1930's

—arose to extol the sufficiency and normality of our North Americanism. It was pointed out on numerous occasions and with the greatest possible complacency that the Canadian now played baseball, ate dry cereals, chewed gum, smoked blended cigarettes, drank rye whiskey and lager beer; and it was intimated hopefully that if he only persevered in these respectable American activities for a sufficiently long time, he would eventually realize his true personality in the image of his great neighbour the United States.

The United States was a good neighbour. Canada was a good neighbour. The North American continent was God's continent. In North America, we were all "just folks"—we were all one great, big, happy family—innocent, peace-loving, virtuous, full of the highest possible ideals, and breathing good will for all mankind at every pore. On the other hand, Europe, including Great Britain, was an alien and sinister world, crowded with a deplorable collection of snobs, decadents, incompetents, agitators, communists, militarists, imperialists, and trouble-makers generally, with whom, obviously, we should have as little as possible to do. War was really a European disease. North America, healthy with peace, was immune to it. And immunity could be prolonged indefinitely by the simple process of reducing our contaminating contacts with the outside world. Canada, it was generally agreed, should cut its commitments in the League of Nations, just as it had already cut its commitments inside the British Commonwealth. The League of Nations was all right so long as it remained a judicious compromise between a service club and a debating forum; but, once it became clear, after the Italo-Abyssinian affair, that the League was not going to be a very successful Rotary Convention, Mr. King turned his back upon it with cheerful resignation. As 1939 drew nearer, Canada burrowed deeper and deeper into the dark comfortable recesses of North American isolationism and irresponsibility.

In the meantime, the world, in its odd incorrigible way, had gone on. Other leaders were quite ready to make commitments, if Mr. King was not. Other nations were prepared to take decisions and begin crusades, if Canada was unwilling. The international crisis was followed by a desperate war, the desperate war ended in an uneasy peace; and for ten years, Mr. King and Mr. King's Canada went through an attrition of experience such as only centuries could have brought before. The little Canadian crusades of the past seemed buried under vast accumulations of history. To a new generation, the great struggle for Dominion status seemed as remote as the Wars of the Roses. The old British Empire, with its vast holdings in the Far East, had vanished as utterly as England's half-forgotten medieval Kingdom in France. The aeroplane and the bomb had annihilated distance and jeopardized security; the complacent, self-satisfied parochialism of North America had no longer any basis in reality; and the United States, abandoning its old insularity, had rushed off in all directions to save the world from Communism. Canadians knew now that mere absence of commitments would not necessarily prevent war. That had been proved by the events of 1939. But ten years later, in 1949, another, and a very different lesson had also been driven home. Canadians had come to realize that collective security, as embodied in the United Nations, would not necessarily save the peace.

In the meantime, while experience and knowledge were coming in the most terrible of all schools, Canada rapidly expanded its diplomatic system over the greater part of the world and built up a Civil Service which was to become the admiration and envy of many other nations. As the world contracted with the development of air power, our position, at the heart of the English-speaking world, became more and more strategically important; and, at a time when the resources of other nations were showing signs of use, if not of actual depletion, Canada suddenly discovered itself the possessor of enormous quantities of the key materials of power. Exactly thirty-five years ago, in the autumn of 1918, we were seeking admission, on terms of equality with Belgium and Serbia, to the Peace Conference which was about to assemble at Paris. Thirty-five, fifty years from now, what will be our position in the world? In 1919, we succeeded, against the doubts and objections of the United States and France, in establishing our claim to a place, in our own right, in the Assembly of the League of Nations. A quarter-century later, at a conference which met in San Francisco to create a new international organization, Canada was no longer satisfied with a seat in the Assembly and the right of election to the Council. Our representatives insisted at San Francisco that there was a group of so-called "middle powers"—of which Canada was demonstrably one—which, because of their position and their ability to perform the duties of the organization, ought to enjoy a decided preference over smaller powers in elections to the non-permanent seats in the Security Council. Fifty years from now will Canada still be pressing the claims of the middle powers? Or will another and a more important task be expected of her?

Power is relative. Though there are several Central and South American republics with populations larger than that of Canada, they do not show many signs of playing an influential part in world affairs. In Africa, apart from the European countries which are represented by their colonies, there is no nation, existing or potential, which is likely in the next half-century to wield an international influence at all comparable to that of Canada. It is from the heartland, the great central land mass of Eurasia, that power and leadership have come in the past, and from which they will likely continue to come in the future. The economic and political decline of what we are now beginning to think of as the "peninsula" of Europe has gone a long way since 1939. But, even so, this small, densely populated region, the homeland of Western culture, will continue to be a great source of human ability and industrial power for any foreseeable future. Its future political organization is still obscured by the consequences of the War and the pressures of the Cold War. France, like Italy, may fail to hold its place in the ranks of the Great Powers; but Great Britain will maintain the influential position which it has enjoyed in the post-war world; and Germany, either in its own right or as a part of some West-European political or military organization, will, for better or worse, recover fairly rapidly at least a part of her past authority. In Asia, three nations, China, India, Japan, may reach or regain the stature of great powers. These half-dozen Asian and European states exist on a plane distinctly inferior to that of the towering super-powers, the United States and the Soviet Union. But, within their own sphere, they may exercise a secondary leadership of great importance. It is to their company that Canada might aspire. She is not of their stature yet. But, in fifty years time, how far away will she be from it? Power may become multiple again, and this would encourage the rise of new states to eminence. Power is at present dual—the prerogative of the United States and Russia. And this duality is prolonged and strengthened by the fact of the Cold War.

III

Anyone who tries to speculate about Canada's future external relationships and Canada's future place in world affairs is confronted, at the very beginning, with the fact of the Cold War. The Cold War has now gripped almost the entire world, delaying its peace, postponing its recovery, stiffening it into hard, unyielding attitudes of suspicion and truculence.

Of course, this unnatural state of congealed defiance may not be transitory at all, but permanent or semi-permanent; and if so we can inform ourselves fairly accurately about the future by the simple process of taking a good look at the present. Or the Cold War may prove itself transitory, in a sense disastrous to humanity by turning abruptly into a hot war; and if this should happen, ordinary speculation about the future would be beside the point, for the whole subject would have to be turned over to a major prophet of the school of Jeremiah. Yet there is a second way, fortunate for humanity, in which the Cold War might prove transitory. It might stop. It might thaw out into a real peace. And the signs are accumulating that the peoples of the world, despite what their governments may say, are sustained not so much by the rival political slogans of the period as by a secret irrepressible hope that peace will come.

The world is divided into two great hostile camps. So thoroughly divided indeed that it seems like two worlds instead of one. We call the division we inhabit the "West", though it includes both middle-eastern and far-eastern sympathizers. We like rather complacently to refer to it as the "free" world though, in fact, it happens to contain large areas which are not politically "free" at all, in any normal usage of the word. We have simplified and dramatized the contest in which we are engaged as a struggle between free enterprise and Communism, between Christianity and irreligious determinism, or more grandly and vaguely, between two conflicting "ways of life". It may be difficult to define the rival ideologies accurately; but there can be no doubt about the composition and the leadership of the two groups. The opposing sides are led and directed by two super-powers, the Soviet Union and the United States, and it is their titanic rivalry which now dominates world politics. Neither one of the rivals is a "have-not" power, in the sense in which Germany, Japan, and Italy claimed to be "have-not" powers in the inter-war years. Each has enormous resources and enormous areas for expansion; they are separated from each other by what in the old days would have seemed enormous distances. But, as Arnold Toynbee has said, the world shrank to the dimensions of a duelling-ground once the discovery of the atom bomb was made. The two super-powers now face each other, at point-blank range, with the deepest fear and the deepest suspicion; and for the last half-dozen years each adversary has tried to bring as large a part of the world as possible into its own armed camp.

By the spring of 1947 the Cold War was already developing the pattern which has characterized it ever since. The Soviet Union systematically tightened its hold upon the satellite countries on its western frontier by brutally extinguishing all groups or individuals who might oppose Communist orthodoxy. In this campaign the one really significant failure was in Yugoslavia. The greatest success—a success which shocked and frightened the Western World—was in the much-respected democratic republic of Czechoslovakia. In the meantime, the United States, suddenly extending, in an enormous jump, its financial and military influence to the Mediterranean and the Bosphorus, announced the Truman doctrine of help to Greece and Turkey. Marshall Aid, offered to and rejected by Russia, became the means by which the United States identified itself more and more closely with the economic fortunes of western Europe; and on its part, western Europe—the Benelux countries, France and Great Britain—showed unmistakably, in the Brussels Treaty of 1948, that in the case of a crisis they were prepared to take sides with the United States. The climax of this defensive movement of economic and political collaboration between the two great divisions of the West European-North American society was the establishment of the North Atlantic Treaty Organization in the spring of 1949. In Europe, the year 1949 brought a great diplomatic triumph for the forces led by the United States. In Asia, on the other hand, the same year witnessed a great victory for Communism in the triumph of the Chinese People's Republic. Since then the two sides have remained in a state of uneasy and perilous balance. Already they had almost come to blows over the issue of the Berlin corridor; and then the conflict in Korea brought a new and more dangerous threat that the Cold War would be suddenly transformed into open fighting on a world scale. Canada, the United Kingdom and the other nations of the Commonwealth regarded the Korean War as a defence against military aggression as such; but there were very important sections of opinion in the United States which looked upon it rather as a crucial episode in the struggle against world Communism. At times, the fight in Korea threatened to broaden out into a global encounter; and even now, though the truce has at length been won, the chances of such a development are not ended.

In the meantime, however, certain nations, including Canada, have come to a better understanding of the justification of the Cold War and the purpose of the engagements they have contracted during it. We should be under no delusion now. The defensive arrangements which the Western World has made during the past six years are no permanent solution to our problem at all. These defences were, and are, terribly necessary. But it was terribly unfortunate that we had to make them, and in themselves they have only a negative contribution to make to a fair peace. The North Atlantic Treaty Organization is a military alliance—certainly nothing less, and, as yet, nothing much more. It is true that, at the time the Treaty was being signed, the governments concerned, including Canada, solemnly protested that it was not what they called an "old-fashioned military alliance". But whether these protestations were well-intentioned or not, we had, and have, no particular reason for accepting them too literally. Modern demo-

cratic governments have the habit of treating their electorates,
and their electorates' legitimate demands for accurate information, with just about as little consideration as the most unscrupulous dictatorships of history. The official hand-outs that emanate
from conferences at Ottawa, London and Washington closely
resemble the kind of unctuously misleading statement that
might have been made by a heavy mid-Victorian father if
his six-year-old mid-Victorian son had indelicately enquired
about the facts of life. If the Roman authorities had issued
an official communiqué, couched in modern terms, about the
crucifixion of Our Lord, it might have run somewhat as follows:
"Governor Pilate has had a friendly and helpful exchange of
views with Jewish representatives on the subject of the recent
ideological disturbances in Judaea; and with respect to the
agitator Jesus, the apparent instigator of the disturbances, he
has decided that the democratically ascertained wishes of the
Jewish people should be carried out." Modern diplomats either
talk like spinster aunts of uncertain years, or else they bellow
at each other like gangsters in the vulgar slanging-matches
that go on in the Assembly of the United Nations. The world
has never given up secret diplomacy; and for six years now
it has been back at the old game of power politics. Fear
and the will to survive have dictated almost all that has been
done.

IV

If we assume that this state of affairs is transitory, if we
try to cross the frozen waste of the Cold War into the country
of the future, there is one great feature of the new landscape
which will confront us immediately. The most important
occurrence of our post-war world, the occurrence which will
certainly have a most potent influence over the events of the
next fifty years, is the revolution that has taken place in Asia.

It is perhaps the greatest single event of our time. The establishment of the Indonesian Republic, the emergence of four successor states—India, Pakistan, Ceylon and Burma—from the old British Empire in India, the ejection of the American-supported Kuomintang from the Chinese mainland by the armies of the People's Republic, and the protracted and difficult struggle which the French have carried on to maintain their hold on Indo-China—are all significant aspects of a great general movement. It is a revolution which has brought, and will bring, profound changes in the governments, the social relationships, and the economic systems of those different nations. But its meaning does not stop here. It has also resulted in a great and permanent alteration in the relations of these eastern countries with the West.

These relations, of course, go back a very long time. They have been almost uniformly unfortunate. But the West has hit the East harder and far more frequently than the East has hit the West. It is true that very far back, in the first decades of the eighth century, Islam almost overwhelmed the infant civilization of the West by a gigantic double invasion across the Bosphorus and across the Straits of Gibraltar. Over seven hundred years later the Ottoman Turks arrived to renew the attempts at invasion. In 1453, exactly five hundred years ago, Constantinople was captured and the Eastern Empire fell; and as late as 1683 the advancing warrior Turks were hammering for the second time at the gates of Vienna. But these attacks subsided. They have not so far been renewed. And in the meantime, the West has again, again, and again returned to the invasion, conquest, and exploitation of Asia. Our violent intervention in the Near East goes back to the first Crusade, launched soon after the Norman conquest of England. Our armed exploitation of the Far East begins with the appearance of the first adventurous Portuguese traders in the Indian Ocean and the China Sea at the beginning of the sixteenth century. There is scarcely a single important Western nation that has not taken its part in the plunder of Asia. Spain, Portugal, the Netherlands, France, Great Britain and the United States have all annexed larger or smaller empires in India, South-East Asia, and the islands of the South Pacific. Great Britain, France and the United States co-operated during the nineteenth century, with a mixture of commercial cunning, diplomatic pressure, and brute force, in what is euphemistically described as the "opening up" of China and Japan for Western trade. In the past four centuries Russia has been four times invaded from the West—by Poland in 1610, by Sweden in 1709, by France in 1812 and by Germany in 1941.

It is in the light of these centuries of Western intervention and aggression that the meaning of the revolution in Asia can be best understood. It is, in a very large measure, a gigantic effort on the part of the East to free itself from Western control. For this great encounter the East has armed itself with two powerful weapons, one material, and one spiritual, but both equally Western in origin. The first is Western technology and the second is Communism, a Western heresy, worked out by a German Jew, on the basis of the economic and social development of Western Europe and the United Kingdom. Peter the Great of Russia was the first great Asian ruler to realize that the only way to defeat Western technical superiority was through the wholesale adoption of Western technology; and his successful experiment was followed less than two centuries later by Japan which, in the few decades after 1867, was transformed from an agricultural and feudal society into a modern industrial power. Since the Revolution of 1917, Russia has made another giant effort—Mr. Arnold Toynbee calls it a "forced march"—to bring itself abreast once more of Western technical advance. Her example will now almost certainly be followed by China; and the next fifty years may very well witness an economic and social revolution in China comparable in importance to that which has taken place in Russia during the half-century that has just passed.

The other great weapon in the armoury of the Asia revolutionaries is the Western heresy, Communism. Communism is regarded as a brutal, stultifying, and mistaken philosophy of life by the great majority of the people in Europe and the Americas. But this judgment does not satisfy a small minority of Westerners. They look upon Communism as wholly evil, and believe that any compromise with it is morally impossible. It is a very human, long-established habit to identify one's enemy with evil and to decide that it is morally righteous to destroy him. There were a great many good conservative people in the late eighteenth and early nineteenth centuries who looked upon the American and French revolutionaries of the period as unnatural and wicked beings. First Robespierre and then Napoleon was enthusiastically nominated for the position of Antichrist. The war against the French Republic and the Empire became, for a great many people, a holy crusade; and even after the final overthrow of Napoleon, Alexander I of Russia, who might be regarded as an early-nineteenth-century General MacArthur, showed himself almost embarrassingly eager to destroy democracy by force wherever it reared its ugly head in Europe. The Conservatives of those days were terrified lest the Revolution should spread, either through the triumph of revolutionary armies, or by the infiltration of the revolutionary ideas of democracy and republicanism. It is precisely for these reasons that the West fears Communism at the present time. We are frightened that our society may be directly or indirectly destroyed. We believe Communism to be inherently and ineradicably aggressive.

The truth, as we Westerners certainly have the best of reasons for knowing, is that every revolutionary philosophy is aggressive, particularly in the first difficult years or decades which precede and follow its establishment in the constitution of a State.

Revolutionary doctrine is composed of abstract ideas, timeless and universal abstract ideas, which are assumed, as an article of faith, to be equally valid for all countries and all ages. All revolutionaries earnestly believe that it is their first duty to spread these ideas for the benefit of a suffering humanity. The contraction of the world as a result of changes in transport and communications may have made the Communist aims more realizable and hence more frightening than those of their predecessors; but in all such movements the fundamental purpose is the conversion of the world as a whole. The revolutionary State is by its very nature a missionary state; and of this truth the American Republic and the first French Republic supply examples which are as good as those furnished by the Soviet Union. The first French Republic surrounded itself with a string of minor revolutionary states. The United States, by adopting the Monroe Doctrine, and resisting European intervention in the Americas, assisted the colonies of South and Central America to win their independence, and thus created a group of satellite republics which still faithfully follow American foreign policy in the Assembly of the United Nations.

Revolutionary objectives have not altered greatly from one century to another. Revolutionary methods, despite the horror with which Marxist tactics are contemplated, have not changed as much as we like to think. Revolutionaries have never been very squeamish about the methods they employ. If propaganda will do the trick, well and good; if not, no objection whatever is made to force. The dissemination of revolutionary ideas, the establishment of revolutionary cells, the movement of large numbers of revolutionary civilians into the area to be conquered, the local revolution which is given external support, the appeal for annexation to the parent revolutionary State, are all devices which have been employed by republican France as well as by republican America. It was in the large-scale movement of American citizens into Texas that the United States found a justification for annexing the region; and it was by force, after propaganda had dismally failed, that the Thirteen Colonies tried in 1775 to drag the old province of Quebec into the American Revolution. During a large part of the nineteenth century, Americans continued to believe that Canadians were an "oppressed people", who ought to be "liberated" for their own good, whether they liked it or not. The Canadian rebellion of 1837, in itself a negligible affair, was kept alive for over a year by efforts chiefly of the citizens of New York State, who not only furnished the few Canadian rebels with arms and supplies, but who also themselves repeatedly invaded Canadian territory in considerable numbers.

V

Will the new revolutionary movement, Communism, continue to spread in Asia by means of these characteristic, aggressive, revolutionary tactics? The future, it must be admitted, is terribly uncertain. The one great hope of the Western World lies in the little group of successor states, and particularly in the greatest of them, the Indian Union, which emerged from the voluntary liquidation of the British Empire. India occupies a position in the Asian world which is, in some respects, curiously analogous to the place which Canada has managed to keep in the Americas. Canada resisted the tide of republicanism which swept North and South America; Canada maintained vital and sympathetic links with Europe. India similarly has so far resisted Communism and has kept her contacts with our "free world". She has borrowed from the West, but in her own fashion, a fashion very different from that of nineteenth-century Japan or twentieth-century Russia. While Russia and Japan sought merely to gain the power of Western technology, India acquired Western education and Western political and administrative systems. She took—or at least, a small educated minority of her people took—the best of the arts of peace which the West had to offer; and her friendship, the friendship of a quarter of the world's population, is a priceless advantage which the West must strive earnestly to keep.

Can it be kept? In India, as in most other parts of the Far East, the pressure of the enormous population on the means of subsistence is extreme. This appalling social distress may help to give Communism its chance, or its victory, throughout East Asia. Communism will probably gain some additional popularity precisely because it is a Western heresy, because Western orthodoxy and the native regimes and foreign nations which have stood for it in the East, have now become so discredited or disliked. At present Japan is governed under the military jurisdiction of the United States; her previous rulers were a set of native military imperialists who brought upon their country the most catastrophic defeat in her entire history. In China another westernizing regime, the Kuomintang, which ruled corruptly and inefficiently and which at the same time relied heavily upon the financial and military support of the United States, has been driven completely from the Asian mainland, and the Chinese quarter of the world's population has gone over to Communism. It may be that the triumph of the People's Republic meant the inevitable alienation of China from the West. But whatever chances the West had of keeping the friendship of the Chinese people were wrecked, and the principal responsibility for that destruction must be borne by the United States. The United States put itself and kept itself in that most odious of all political roles, the role of the wealthy foreigner who supports the hated counter-revolution. The prolonged American intervention in the politics of the Far East enabled the Communists to enlist the potent force of Asian nationalism on their side and to hold up the United States as the last and worst of the foreign imperialist oppressors. After the American Revolution, the United States insisted with increasing emphasis and increasing success, that the Americas were for Americans. It has now insured, by the calamitous failure of its policy in the Far East, that Asia will appropriate the same slogan and turn it resentfully against the West. "Asia for the Asians" will be a potent rallying-cry in the East for as far as we can see into the future.

The West has therefore got off to a very bad start in its approach to the Communist revolution in Asia. That revolution is the great new fact of the modern world. Upon it international politics will probably turn for the next half-century at least. Inevitably the first feeling which it inspired in the West was one of apprehension; the West's first instinctive reaction was defensive. In so far as the Cold War has prompted European and American countries to strengthen their defences, and to prove, as in the case of Korea, that they will resist aggression to the uttermost, the dreadful tension of the last six years has been beneficial. But, at the same time, it has been in part prejudicial, for it has helped to create a mood of hysterical dogmatism; it has encouraged large groups of Westerners to identify Communism with moral evil, and to dream of what Professor Butterfield calls "a war of righteousness"— a great holy crusade for the "liberation" of the peoples of Communist-controlled countries. These dreams are nightmares from which we must pray for deliverance. Our real task, once we have built up our defences and proved that we are ready to resist attack, is to accept the unquestionable fact that Communism is the established system in a large part of Asia, and to build an international order in which we and Communist countries may live side by side in peace.

The question of the recognition of the People's Republic of China and of its admission to the morally vacant place on the Security Council, is a particular example of the general problem

which confronts Canada and other Western countries. His-
torically, diplomatic recognition is nothing more than the
admission of a fact in world affairs. It is, as a recent speaker
in the British House of Commons suggested, exactly like
admitting that Everest is a high mountain, or that yesterday
was a rainy day. But a good many people in the United
States and some in Canada have apparently come to believe
that recognition implies moral approval, that it is the diplomatic equivalent of a testimonial from the local clergyman,
or an avuncular pat on the head for a deserving small boy.
Communist countries will not be greatly interested in these
condescending Sunday School prizes, and no nation should
pharisaically assume that it has the right to distribute them.
Standards of international conduct which we ourselves impose
—and break and alter when it suits our convenience to do so—
will not bear very close scrutiny in the light either of past history
or present conditions. In our circumstances ideological diplomacy will be only less fatal than ideological warfare. The
last thing we should try to do, in any negotiation, is to adopt
a superior moral attitude, to do everything to save democratic
face, to bargain for small points of ideological honour.

VI

In this task, which is the great international task of the
next decades, what contribution is Canada likely to make?
One thing at least we have learned to do, and that is to
abandon our complacent, parochial North Americanism. Back
in the 1920's and 1930's, when the Canadian government was
in hot pursuit of Dominion status and quick retreat from
European entanglements, North America seemed in itself the
perfect answer to any question in external relations that Canada
could possibly ask. Canadian-American relations were the only
relations that really mattered; Canadian-American defence was

the only effective defence; and so long as Canada and the
United States maintained a solidly united front, then all would
be well in the best of all possible worlds. Mr. King had always
publicly insisted that his government would make no commitments—above all, no permanent commitments—in external
affairs, without the previous concurrence of the Canadian
Parliament. But in 1940 Canadians discovered that North
America was apparently a specially excepted area in which
these promises had no binding effect whatever. In August
of that year Mr. King made a purely executive agreement
with the government of the United States for the establishment of what was openly described as a Permanent Joint
Board on Defence. Parliament did not make this permanent
commitment. Mr. King and his cabinet did; and they made
it apparently on the assumption of the inevitable political
solidarity of the North American continent. Mere geographic
proximity meant absolute and eternal identity of interest. It
was unthinkable that Canada should ever differ fundamentally
from the United States on any important question of world
politics. For a country that had just finished its climb out
of colonialism by the achievement of Dominion status, this
was a very curious assumption indeed. Did it mean that Canada
was in fact becoming a colony of the United States, that it
was accepting a position not very different from that of Panama
or Cuba, that it was, in short, becoming a kind of northern
"banana republic"?

The post-war period has seen the end of the myth of the
impregnable security of North America and the myth of the
infallible wisdom of the United States. Good relations with
the republic must continue to be a most important objective
of our foreign policy; but good Canadian-American relations
will not necessarily enable Canada to make its own contribution
to the solution of the world's crisis, and may actually prevent it
from doing so. In the past Mr. King used to argue very earnestly

that a British Commonwealth *bloc* would excite resentful opposition throughout the world; in our present critical situation a North and South American *bloc* might have even more unfortunate consequences. A monolithic union of the Americas would simply strengthen that opposition of continents which it ought to be our first task to break down. Canada, like India, cannot accept the doctrine that mere geographical position implies submission to a continental political solidarity. India's refusal to be intimidated by the displeasure of the super-powers has enabled it to play a creative part in the affairs of the postwar world; and, during the last few years, Canada has similarly been acquiring that habit of independent judgment which is the first attribute of political maturity. The second phase of our colonialism, the period of our tutelage to North America, is over; and during the next half-century Canada will show an increasing self-reliance in the making and stating of its views on world affairs.

Canada has outgrown North American solidarity as an end in itself. It is also unlikely that she will find final satisfaction even in her association with that much more comprehensive body, West European-American civilization as a whole. In these days of the North Atlantic Treaty Organization, it is very fashionable to assume the cultural and political unity of North America and West Europe, and to talk, with erudite enthusiasm, about the "North Atlantic Community". Twenty-five years ago the intellectual vogue in Canada ran in exactly the opposite direction. Then it was comically out-of-date to argue that Europe was the centre from which the culture of the Americas had migrated. To be really fashionable in those days it was necessary to believe that all that was best and most beautiful in North American life had come, not from Europe at all, but from the point in North America furthest removed from Europe, that is, the Western Frontier. The "frontier theory", as it was called, was the intellectual expression of our self-satisfied North American parochialism; the idea of the "North Atlantic Community", which is all the rage at the moment, is the ideological accompaniment of our present need for unity in the defence of West Europe and America. And it is highly entertaining to notice that some of the Canadians who used to be so hot for the uniqueness and separateness of our North American way of life, are now rushing off enthusiastically to proclaim our cultural and moral identity with Europe.

The cultural unity of West Europe and the Americas was a fact long before anybody thought of N.A.T.O. And we can only hope that it will remain a fact long after N.A.T.O. has ceased to have any reason for existence. Europe is, without any qualification whatever, the heart of Western civilization. If Europe were destroyed it would mean the death of the heart, the heart of the whole West, and the consequent dissolution of the original form of our North American civilization. The North Atlantic Treaty Organization is an affair of the utmost necessity in the circumstances of the moment. But we should be very unwise if we tried to use these circumstances as a whip of terror to drive Westerners prematurely into unwanted unions, or if we attempted to build too heavy a political and military superstructure upon a cultural foundation which up till now we have largely taken for granted. One of the greatest glories of Western culture is the richness of its variety, the endless complexity of the different cultural threads that have been woven together to make its texture. It is very easy for North Americans, and very hard for Europeans, to forget these differences. At present, in the eyes of many in the New World, the age-old rivalries of Europe have been reduced to insignificance by the giant diplomatic encounter which we call the Cold War. The Cold War has been promoted by all the devices of twentieth-century journalism. The old rivalries and historic ambitions of the European peoples have little news value at the moment. Yet they still exist. And it would be dangerous for us to press too hard for a political or military organization in Western Europe which might bring a temporary advantage in the Cold War and yet do permanent harm to European welfare. It is perfectly obvious that there are important groups and interests in Western Europe which are sceptical of the wisdom of the European Defence Community scheme, or actively opposed to it. These doubts and reservations are worthy of respect. Canada will continue to be deeply concerned in the affairs of Europe, for her ties with Great Britain and the continent are close; but Canadians should not assume that Western Europe will be easily federalized, or that a North Atlantic super-state is a probable, or even a desirable, creation. It may be very unwise, in our obsession with the Cold War, to create too many institutions which harden and perpetuate its divisions. Despite the size and variety of the North Atlantic community, it is still limited and exclusive; and for a future of peace, our need is for organizations which transcend cultural barriers and cut across the great blocks of power into which the world is at present divided.

One such organization is the Commonwealth. Some time ago, during what might be referred to as the "North American phase" of Mr. King's multiple existence, the disparagement of the Commonwealth became a pious exercise in which all right-minded Canadian nationalists felt they ought to take part. They used to go around muttering darkly about "British imperialism" and "power politics", like a lot of old women trying, with mumbled incantations, to evoke the horrible hobgoblins of the past. The Commonwealth has politely given the lie to these insinuations by the simple facts of its recent development. "British imperialism" has meant, not the concentration, but the distribution of power. During the post-war years, Great Britain has done in the Far East what no other European or American power has been able to do. She has successfully promoted the cause of the "free world" in Asia, and has made friends, rather than enemies, in the process. She has at one and the same time co-operated with Asian nationalism and has helped to found great Asian democracies. The emergence of India and the other successor-states proved in the twentieth century what the emergence of Canada had proved in the nineteenth, that membership in the British Empire is essentially a training in the art of free government. And the subsequent agreement of 1949, which permitted these new Asian nations, whether as realms or republics, to retain their historic affiliation, revealed the Commonwealth once again as the greatest living example of the free association of diverse peoples. Twenty years ago, its future was very uncertain. But it has continued to exist in a state so flourishing as to surprise its old friends as well as its old enemies. And there is every indication that its members will continue during the next half-century to rely upon the benefits of their old association, as they themselves develop individually in political power. No treaty or executive agreement binds these friendly nations together; they have no written commitments one to another; in an age distinguished above all others for power politics, they do not form a solid power *bloc*. Above all—and this is perhaps its greatest benefit for the age in which we live—the Commonwealth is a truly cosmopolitan organization. It unites contrasted cultures, it bridges rival continents.

Only one other organization will be able to carry out this act of reconciliation more effectively, because more completely, than the Commonwealth, and that is the United Nations. Many people today are disillusioned with the United Nations; and some at least are disillusioned because they held too extravagant, or too self-interested, views of what it would become. The new organization was simply another effort at collective security, very much like its predecessor, the League of Nations, with a new constitution whose wisdom had yet to be proved, and with potentialities for good which could be realized only by skill and patience. Unfortunately the new organization never had a chance of growing up in favourable circumstances. It was plunged almost immediately into the stultifying atmosphere of the Cold War. It had no opportunity of developing habits of co-operation. It could not even work out the security arrangements which were indicated in the Charter, and organize its own international army. And so, when the crisis in Korea came, and the Security Council, in the absence of Russia, decided to intervene, it could think of nothing to do but to hand the whole control of its own war over to the United States of America.

Armed aggression is the crucial test of any international organization. It may fail to meet the test. And experience has taught us now that failure may come either because the organization does too little or because it tries to do too much. The League of Nations destroyed its prestige by its inaction in the Italo-Abyssinian affair; the United Nations endangered its authority almost equally seriously by plunging into action in Korea. The Cold War was on, but the United Nations could not take sides in the Cold War. It was, and can only be, ideologically neutral; and its intervention in Korea was not to start a crusade against Communism but to stop armed aggression. This was the single, legitimate purpose of its decision; but during the three long years of the war, the single purpose of the United Nations was often in danger of becoming the double purpose which seemed at times to determine the policies of the United States. The United States complicated the Security Council's original decision by making its own private decision about Formosa. It complicated the conduct of the war by indulging in recurrent impulses to broaden its scope and character. And it complicated the peace by making a private agreement, outside the guarantees of the United Nations, with the government of Mr. Syngman Rhee.

The embarrassment of the United Nations was, and remains, extreme. For a long time it looked as if it could win the war only by giving up its own integrity and losing the peace into the bargain. Yet, in a difficult and uncertain fashion, it has so far won through. It has kept to its original purpose. It has successfully repelled the aggressor and proved that aggression does not pay; and it now may be coming close to the position in which it can initiate comprehensive settlements in the principal troubled areas. Its organization will for a long time to come be very imperfect. But any impatient effort to remedy these defects, in accordance with the demands of one of the super-powers, ought to be strongly opposed by Canada. It is true that, as long as the five privileged powers retain their veto, the organization will probably remain a loose confederacy of states; and as a result, its members, including Canada, can expect only limited and disappointing progress for some years to come. This is the price we shall likely have to go on paying for the universality of the United Nations. It is a big price: but the substitution of an anti-Communist alliance for a universal society would entail an even greater sacrifice—a sacrifice which we should be prepared to make only in the event of a global aggression.

AN OUTSIDER LOOKING IN

Denis William Brogan

M.A., LL.D., D. ès Lettres,
Chevalier de la Légion d'Honneur. Brit-
ish political scientist, now Professor of
Political Science and Fellow, Peterhouse,
University of Cambridge; Director,
Hamish Hamilton, Ltd., formerly Lec-
turer, University College, London, Lon-
don School of Economics, Fellow and
Tutor, Corpus Christi College, Oxford;
author, *The Development of Modern
France,* 1940; *American Themes,* 1948;
French Personalities and Problems, 1946;
Politics and Law in the United States,
1941; *The English People,* 1943; *The
Free State,* 1945; *American Political
System,* 1933, and others.

AN OUTSIDER LOOKING IN

THE French have a saying that some things go without saying, but they have also a saying that some things that go without saying had better be said. And, although it goes without saying that I am honoured to be invited to this conference and delighted to be in this venerable, romantic and dramatic city of Quebec, I shall say it. It is a great honour, indeed, to be invited to comment on a stocktaking of a great and exuberantly growing country. It is a pleasure to be asked to do this in a city so renowned, a city whose history, in outline at any rate, I have known since childhood.

It also goes without saying, but I am going to say it all the same, that I am very ill-equipped for my task. I have long been a careful and interested student of Canadian history and Canadian problems. Naturally enough, pondering the way they do things south of the border, I have, from time to time, contemplated with a certain British nostalgia the somewhat less dramatic, ebullient and versatile way they do them north of the border. The parallels, resemblances and differences between the experience of the United States and the experience of Canada make a fertile subject of reflection. Yet reflection, interest, study are no substitute for first-hand knowledge and of that I have little. Before I flew out on this trip, I had, indeed, seen Quebec from the sea and from the land, but I had never set foot in it. Nor, though this is less serious, had I (nor have I) set foot in Toronto or Winnipeg. So the views on the present and future of Canada that I am going to inflict on you come from one absurdly incompetent to give them and may have only the interest that a tolerant aunt or uncle displays at the babblings of a promising but not very articulate child. I won't pretend that I am inarticulate, but that my views will strike you as childish is only too likely. Comforting myself with the text of Holy Writ that praises the utterances of babes and sucklings, I shall plunge ahead.

I have, of course, an advantage that it is hard to overestimate. I have been permitted to see in advance the papers read to this Conference and, as you will see and the authors will see even more clearly, I have been quite an unscrupulous pillager. If any views or any information should strike you as particularly sound or original or both, you may be pretty certain that I have stolen the views and simply copied the information.

Before I move on to the main theme, I should like to insist on one aspect of these papers that struck me very forcibly. That aspect was the absence, almost the excessive absence, of the booster spirit. The readers of the papers were not anxious to put Canada's best foot forward. They noted, without complacency, the sudden upsurge in Canadian fortunes, the sudden increased weight of the Canadian impact on the world. But in no paper, whether it dealt with the duties of Canadian business or the limitations of Canadian culture, was there any naïve or even sophisticated complacency, no slackening of moral

or intellectual fibre, no disposition to rejoice that the lines are
at last fallen to the Canadians in pleasant places—and no
visible sign of any inward conviction that this indisputable
fact proves anything about Canadian deserts. Indeed, even an
ignoramus like myself can see inconsistencies in these sober,
calm, highly critical assessments. If they were all the truth
we should not be meeting here. So I enter a mild protest
against so much modesty. If it were ironical or if it were
mock modesty, I should have nothing to say. But it seems
to be genuine and I want to talk you out of it—a little. I
want to talk you out of it in small details and in great matters.
I am willing to believe Professor Creighton when he tells us
in his most admirable book on young John Macdonald, of
the magnificence of the city hall that Kingston built when it
still hoped to be the capital of Canada and I suggest that he
take the matter of the alleged uniform drabness of nineteenth-
century Canadian public buildings up with his colleagues. On
the other hand, later on, I shall take up with Professor Creighton
what I think to be his undue depreciation of the role of Canada
between the two wars or even later. A lack of *panache,* of
extravagant self-esteem, of the *mere* booster spirit, is all to the
good. There is enough of that for all North America on constant tap south of the border, though even Colonel McCormick
has had tremors, or so he has told us, as he contemplated
the Canadian threat to Fort Dearborn, I mean Chicago. But
it can be overdone; there is a danger that the modest man or
the modest nation may be taken at the face value of the words.
And a nation like Canada which, unlike the victim of a
celebrated jest, has little to be modest about might, from
time to time, speak up in meetings, domestic or international,
and with good manners, call attention to certain Canadian
qualities which the world badly needs. If you don't, I will.

   It is half a century since a great Canadian, Sir Wilfrid
Laurier, announced that this was to be the Canadian century.

That, at the time, may have been an example of the booster spirit of which I have been talking. It was a bold call to action, to faith, to gambling in futures. If it seemed, at times, a ludicrously inept prediction, the fault was not mainly, or, perhaps, in any serious degree at all, Canada's fault. The world in which Sir Wilfrid Laurier saw Canada as one of the great expanding beneficiaries of the natural world economy, committed suicide in the First World War and not the most rabid partisan will pretend that Canada could have done anything to prevent that war or to change the world in which that war was inevitable. It is true, and it is often repeated, that the First World War made Canada a nation, a nation in the diplomatic and international sense, a nation in that the war accelerated the industrial and financial autonomy of Canada. But the war had bad results for Canada, internal and external, and delayed rather than fostered the fulfilment of Laurier's prophecy.

Today, after a Second World War, the spirit if not the letter of Laurier's prophecy is coming true. It is so evident that even the most deliberately pessimistic, the most determined touchers of wood in the panel of the Conference have not been able, like Dr. Johnson's would-be philosophic friend, to keep from letting cheerfulness come creeping in. But there is, all the same, in most of the papers an uneasiness that is perhaps natural. On the whole Canada has, from the days of Champlain, had it hard. Everything has had to be fought for and worked for. Compared to the United States, even to Australia, there have been, till recent times, no windfalls in Canada. You have thus escaped the temptations (which affect nations as well as individuals) of behaving like "Coal Oil Johnny", to quote a representative figure from United States mythology. You have not been tempted like Dr. Johnson's young man to "show the spirit of an heir". And even if there had been fewer people of Norman and Caledonian origin in the Canadian population, this would have been true. Even the Irish-Canadians submit, I am told, to the genius of the country and display a moderation that would strike oddly in Dublin—or in Belfast.

But this long training in thrift, in industry, in prudence has, in recent years, been threatened by the sudden good fortune that has made what used to be considered the great, useless, empty northern space of Canada, one of the treasure-houses of Canada and of the world. You seem to me to be rather like a family that has come into a fortune and doubts the truth of the lawyer's letter or, to use an analogy more true to modern British life, like one of those winners of a hundred thousand pounds in a football pool who announces that he's going to work as usual next morning and won't let his good fortune change the tenor of his life. After a few months, when he discovers that it *is* true, he *does* change the tenor of his life. So I think, and hope, will you. Some of the pessimistic things said about culture, the fine arts, the state of basic scientific research, the general conditions of education in Canada will change for the better when the reality, the permanence of your good fortune, really soaks into your minds.

But before you can spend your new fortune wisely, generously and joyously, you will have to put away the idea that there is something immoral in luck. There isn't. A great deal of the power and wealth of the United States is due to luck. Luck put the iron in Minnesota as it put it in Labrador; luck put the oil in Pennsylvania and California as it has put it in Alberta and British Columbia. Luck gave Quebec a magnificent winter climate to exploit ski-mad citizens of the United States with, as it gave California a climate fit for the making of movies when that was still an economic asset. It is not being lucky that is immoral or dangerous; it is folly or timidity in using the goods the gods provide you. And, remember, in this terrible modern world, no nation is really lucky unless the rest of the world, in some form or other, shares that luck. But as the papers show, especially Mr. Ambridge's paper, that lesson need hardly be insisted on. We all know, today, that no matter for whom the bell tolls, it tolls for us.

There is one last comment I should like to make on the tone of the papers, the magnanimity of the references to the United States. Magnanimity in politics, said Burke, is truest wisdom, but it is not a quality that politics, national or international, readily breeds. It is gratifying, then, to see it displayed here. More than one of the members of the panel has pointed out the importance, for Canada and the world, of the fact that as the Paley report made plain, the United States is now a deficit economy, and is, whether the average American knows it or not, bound by the needs of the American economy to deal on equal terms with countries like Canada for which, indeed, the average American has long felt nothing but kindness, but which he has not been accustomed to treating as an equal "high contracting party". That has changed; more and more Americans are beginning to learn the facts of life in the second half of the century which, if it is not yet the Canadian century, is certainly not as exclusively the American century as it was, in North America at least, as recently as twenty years ago. The United States now has to bargain, now has to ask where it could, in the past, take a more *de haut en bas* attitude. It would have been human for Canadians not only to rejoice politely in this changed state of affairs (I suspect they do, very politely), but to let memory of past attitudes colour current policy. I was interested and delighted to note that none of the previous speakers did so.

There were some hesitations, expressed in one paper, at the unlimited export of irreplaceable natural resources like natural gas. For if Canada is a treasure-house, it is a treasure-house first of all for Canadians, and, while a better conservation policy can restore land and forest, it cannot in any measurable time restore resources like natural gas. But there was also a determined refusal to exploit Canadian resources to create artificial processing industries, a realization of the duty, as well as the wisdom, of keeping Canadian resources of this kind available to the world. Where the export of an important raw material does little or nothing to sustain life or health in the exporting province, as it has been suggested is sometimes the case, then mere *laissez-faire* is not enough. If the gypsum of Nova Scotia does not notably help the life of Nova Scotia merely by being exported, it is not beyond the wit of man to ensure that some of the profits of the export of gypsum remain in Nova Scotia (or in any other province or region) in ways that promote the good life in the province or the region. If we think of Canada as the prudent and well-behaved son, this generosity to the Prodigal excels what we learn of brotherly love in the parable for, if I remember aright, the Prodigal's elder brother thought that husks and the company of swine were quite good enough for the younger brother who had wasted his inheritance. And, again a characteristic Canadian note, there was no attempt to pretend that the fact that Canadian resources had not been dissipated, as American resources have been, was due to special Canadian merits. It was due, it was said more than once, to the isolation of some of these resources, to ignorance of their existence, to the retardation of Canadian economic expansion. Canada has these resources, it was implied, for the same reason that a small boy who cannot reach the top shelf cannot steal the jam that his elder brother can gorge himself on with ease. (This parallel, I hasten to say is mine; it is not borrowed from my predecessors.) But, and this is the Canadian note, this view does, in fact, underestimate the degree to which that great virtue, prudence, has been at work. When all is said about the defects of conservation policy in Canada, about the neglect of fundamental scientific research that, in the not very long run, will be paid for in an obsolescent technology, it still remains true that, compared with American practice, Canadian exploitation of natural resources is cautious, only affected by as much of the gambling spirit as is healthy, is socially-minded. In short, Alberta and Oklahoma are very different societies and for solidity, if not for liveliness, Alberta is better.

It is time to turn from these complaints of Canadian modesty to the more difficult task of giving my own view on the present and future of Canada. I have expatiated enough on my insufficiency; I can only say that I am doing my best. And I shall begin, boldly, by calling attention to the importance in the free world of the role of Canada as an intermediary, a role important today and, as far as I can see, likely to remain important for the foreseeable future. I know that stressing this role often annoys Canadians, and for good reason. There is no ground for believing that Frenchmen were particularly pleased when Macaulay (I think it was) said that the chief function of France was to interpret England to the continent. So I can fully understand the irritation felt by Canadians at being treated as mere accessories, as a kind of glorified Berlitz teacher or Cook's interpreter. Nevertheless, the function of a *trait d'union,* the function of providing a common meeting-ground, is important—and it is more and more important as Canada grows in power and consequently in responsibility. It is one thing to be a minor kinsman tactfully soothing two irascible grown-ups. It is quite another thing to be an adult to whom both irascible grown-ups are, in various ways, indebted and whom both find, in different ways, to be indispensable. The power of mediation, the power of independent leadership is a function of Canadian economic power and it is the character of that power that I now wish to deal with.

I have dismissed already the theory that Canadian prosperity is merely a matter of luck and suggested that, even if it were, luck is a fact to be noted, not deplored. But obviously it is not merely luck that accounts for the mainly Canadian development of Canadian resources. Welcome as American capital is to Canada, welcome as American know-how is, the basic source of Canadian prosperity is in the character of the Canadians and of their civilization. It is this that makes the international role of Canada so important. She is a giver, not a taker or even a merely neutral solvent but, by choice or necessity, actually an important member of the international community. It is not only because Canada has been so generous to Britain (a generosity, I fear, not nearly well enough publicized in Britain), that Canadian economic strength is welcomed. It is welcomed because Canadian strength is, for the world, an intrinsically good thing, especially if it is used, as it has been and as I believe it will be, intelligently, prudently and generously.

But Canadian economic strength has another aspect that Canadians may not assess at its true value. I shall begin by saying that I am an incorrigible pro-American. I think that most European criticisms of the United States are ill-informed, when they are not malignant as well as ill-informed. But even I, very ready to "be to her faults a little blind", can see that there are some blemishes on the generally magnificent record of the United States in the past dozen years. And those blemishes have been stressed (more often in malice than it is comforting to think) almost to the exclusion of the more attractive and much more numerous aspects of the American character to which they and their friends can point with great pride. But that there are aspects of American life that are not, to a European or an Indian, automatically attractive, must be admitted, and those are the aspects of American life that its enemies naturally delight to dwell on. This, they say or imply, is the price paid for the much-vaunted standard of living, this is the price of know-how; it is to barbarians like these that so much undeserved power has fallen!

It is, therefore, an advantage to the whole world that Canada, the other nation which has a very high standard of living, that is a master (or mistress) of know-how, is not seen in the same unfavourable light. I can sympathize with many of Miss Neatby's complaints at the present state of the arts in Canada, but it is not all to Canada's disadvantage that her contribution to the graphic arts is not represented for many millions by Dick Tracy, to literature by Mr. Mickey Spillane and, in still the most popular of all visual arts, by Miss Marilyn Monroe. Canada may not be giving an adequate impression of her present or future, but she is not travestied as is the United States by her most universally acceptable cultural exports. It is a very important service to the world at this moment to show that the highest potentialities of modern technology are attainable without violence, disorder, cultural savagery. As I have said, I, for my part, think that these charges against the United States are deliberate attempts to avoid seeing the forest by concentrating on some trees. But be that as it may, no one sees in the modern development of Canada what the critics profess to see in the modern development of the United States, the purchase of mere material wealth at the price of barbarism.

That is one service that is rendered, but there is another. We live in a world in which problems of economic recovery, difficult enough in any case, are made more serious and less soluble by all kinds of nationalist follies. We can see even in Europe highly promising experiments, like Benelux and the steel and coal pool of the Schuman plan, continually under fire because of the survival of naïve mercantilist views of the nature of international trade. I wish I could say that, in Britain, we were setting the good example that should be expected from the traditional nation of shopkeepers. I fear that we are not. It is Canada, with her combination of great wealth and productivity and her need for export markets, that talks and practises good sense. These truths have more than once been firmly stated by leaders in Canadian academic life, in business and in politics. They were reaffirmed a few weeks ago by your Prime Minister; they represent the policy of Canada. It is true that it is to your interest to preach and practise the extension of international trade, the lowering of trade barriers. I do not assert that Canada is moved entirely, or perhaps at all, by a sense of the service she is rendering to the free world. It is primarily, possibly exclusively, the pursuit of a policy based on enlightened self-interest. But how rare today is the nation that pursues a policy based on enlightened self-interest! How common is the suicidal pursuit of unenlightened self-interest! I do not expect to see any nation governed by, let us say, the equivalent of St. Francis of Assisi. The world will not be perfect till all men are perfect, which will not be this long time; so St. Thomas More said and he called his ideal commonwealth, Utopia, "nowhere". I, for one, am very willing to settle for enlightened self-interest, and Canada, by her example and by her great and increasing economic role, does a great service in setting us a good example. True, Canadians would have to be very stupid not to see their interest in an increase of foreign trade, but many nations *are* very stupid and Canada's example shines like a good deed in a naughty and stupid world.

But there is another example of the Canadian pursuit of enlightened self-interest that is of special interest, not only because of its immediate results, but because of the light it throws on one of the successes of Canadian political organization. More than one of the papers stresses the importance for Canada of increasing the population rapidly. It is unnecessary to stress, in the capital of the Province of Quebec, the importance of one way of doing this. But there is another way, the encouragement of immigration. It was a commonplace in old and backward days that immigration was a good thing for an undeveloped country, that certain types of immigration were good things for even a highly developed country. (An ounce of Huguenot blood is worth a thousand a year, Lord Keynes used to quote, a view that is plausible, although it may, in his case, have been influenced by his own ancestry.) But be that as it may, the need for immigrants is a commonplace of the old political economy, now neglected if not refuted. An immigrant represents considerable capital expenditure in his native land given free to the country that receives him. At no time, nevertheless, has the desirability of what I may call the exporting countries being able to export some of their population been more evident. To send their sons and daughters where they can, not only in the old and possibly obsolescent phrase "better themselves", but, by doing so, add to the economic strength of the free world, is a relief and an aid to many European countries. And, as has been pointed out, there is a connection between the relative populations of Canada and the United States that is affected not only by immigration, immigration from Europe, immigration from the United States (as in the case of Mr. Howe and others) but, and this is not with you a matter for rejoicing, emigration from Canada to the United States. (The emigration to the United Kingdom represented by Lord Beaverbrook, Mr. Beverley Baxter, Mr. Braden and others is a separate topic.) But the increase in Canadian wealth, creating a demand for population and, at the same time, increasing the power of Canada to retain her own sons and daughters, is, again, a good thing for more than Canada.

To move on, I cannot but think that Canadian hospitality (in some contrast with the eye-of-a-needle policy now pursued south of the border) owes something to the dual nature of Canadian society. It may be (I dispute this and will return to it later), that the existence, side by side in Canada, of two different though closely related cultures, is an impediment to the growth of the arts, but it has one good political effect. Canadians know the sterility of attempting to impose cultural uniformity. To make of mere uniformity a fetish can lead to absurdities and worse than absurdities. It can lead to denial, to everybody, of a freedom of choice and expression that may be dangerous in the hands of a small minority. Again, I wish to remind you that I do not accept the absurd picture of an intellectual reign of terror painted by fools or knaves or dupes in Europe. But there is a kinship between Senators McCarran and McCarthy. It is the good fortune of Canada, that "un-Canadianism", as a crime, is difficult to define, because Canadianism involves at least two cultures which, as I say, though kin are far from identical. It is not being fanciful to suggest that the generosity, as well as the wisdom, of Canadian immigration policy owes something to the lessons that Canadians have taught each other for the last hundred and fifty years.

And it is necessary to mention, briefly, the lesson in practical federal politics that Canada gives to the nations of Europe who are desperately seeking some way to exorcize hates and suspicions well enough grounded in the past, but fatal in the present and future. Of course, the Canadian example will be all the more effective if Canada solves some of the problems of creating a genuine Canadian culture, not unified in the sense of creating a synthetic least-common-denominator or highest-common-multiple tradition, but in the sense that the two great cultural groups can each express not only its own vision of Canadian life, but share that vision with its neighbour. Here I am less pessimistic than perhaps Canadians are. I am very far from being a blind optimist about the automatic effects of education at any level. I am, after all, a teacher and the father of four children. But at the stage which the

Canadian economy has reached (I don't mean only in wealth, but in communications, in distribution of population and the like), there are greater possibilities of creating a cross-fertilized culture than existed in the past. It requires wealth, sagacity and will. All are available if tapped.

There is obviously a danger, one from which, indeed, the Canadian contributors have shrunk, of rejoicing too uncritically in Canadian progress, and claiming that contemporary deeds justify the faith of the founders. Canada is not out of the wood, not only because no nation can be out of the wood in these umbrageous days, but because there are a number of problems facing Canada that have not been solved and cannot be solved easily. They are not insoluble; they are, compared with the problems facing some countries, problems of the second degree of difficulty and urgency, but they are real problems all the same. Two of these are closely linked and I shall stress them not only because of their importance but because I am a little more competent to deal with them than I am with some others.

The two linked problems spring from the same general problem. Is there a Canadian people apart from the fact of the existence of a state, and a powerful state, called Canada? If Canada is, as yet, only imperfectly a nation, how can it be made one?

It is as well, I think, to begin by admitting that there is an apparent anomaly in the existence of Canada in its present form. The border between Canada and the United States is one of the most artificial in the world and in some regions, not only in the St. Lawrence Valley, it is not only arbitrary but absurd and, as the controversy over the Seaway shows, a nuisance. That the nuisance is being committed by the more powerful of the two states does not make it any less a nuisance; indeed it makes it more a nuisance, for the power to annoy increases with size, as any parent knows. It would be possible to give other instances: the border between the oil and gas fields of Alberta and British Columbia pipelines and the natural market (in the non-political sense) provided by the states of Washington and Oregon.

But there is a deeper problem involved than the artificial character of the border whether that is visible at Rouse's Point, Bellingham (Washington), or Eastport, Maine. Artificial boundaries of that kind are not confined to Canada. The border between Mexico and the United States is also artificial and, as we know, often violated. Europe is full of artificial borders, of historical accidents. If Napoleon had died on Elba, the Saar would still be part of France and not a problem. If the House of Orange had not run so markedly to females, Luxembourg might be part of the Netherlands and musical comedy would have lost a subject. It is not the artificiality of the Canadian border that is odd, nor even its unarmed character. Some of the European borders are for all practical purposes unarmed; even the border between Mexico and the United States is only lightly held from a military point of view. No, what is strange, at first sight, about the border between the United States and Canada is that it divides two cultures that in language, institutions, tastes, religious coloration and the material way of life are very closely alike; in some things so closely alike that it is hard to distinguish between them. It is not a mere matter, as it is in parts of Europe, of where the frontier runs, west of Saarbrücken or east of Entschede that is important; it is the existence of a frontier at all. There had to be a frontier between France and Germany, between the Netherlands and Germany. There is no such evident necessity for a frontier between Seattle and Vancouver, between Winnipeg and Minneapolis, between Toronto and Cleveland. Many if not all of the differences between "Canadians" and "Americans" are not justifications of the border, they are results of it. I have no desire to minimize the historical reasons why the border exists in the form that it does, or to decry the heroism and toughness of the United Empire Loyalists or of the later groups who determined in the nineteenth century that Canada should be "British". But modern historical research has shown (in great part it is modern Canadian research) that in the formative years of Upper Canada, people moved to and fro across the border with much less difficulty and much less sense of making a choice than they could do today. Good soil and good timber, as much as republican or monarchical institutions, were the decisive factor for many thousands whose more numerous descendants do not realize how politically footloose their ancestors were.

I do not know of any real parallel to this situation, in which two countries have had so much in common without becoming identical, indeed while accepting more and more resolutely the fact that they are apart. Neither in Canada nor, except in the lunatic fringe in the United States, is there now any movement for political fusion, whatever there may be in the way of common effort and planning for defence. Yet this acceptance of the political division is accompanied by a very high degree of parallel if not quite identical ways of doing things. As I have said, I don't think that there is more identity of this kind than there was in the past. I think there is less, for as Canada has grown in strength and wealth and as the direct role of government has increased in both countries, the differences arising from the increased power of independent economic action in Canada and from different governmental policies have increased. Yet, to be repetitious, the "cultures" of Canada and the United States, using the word in a general and possibly too materialistic sense, are very close indeed. In part this is, of course, merely the result of the general spread of the modern technological, and if you like, materialistic culture that dominates all the Western World and is invading the Eastern World with frightening speed. If Coca Cola is competing successfully with wine in France, ice hockey, I am told, is threatening the allegiance of the Scots to their national game. (I don't mean curling; I mean Association Football.)

It is not a question in Canada of imitating some American ways of doing things. Canada is (with an important exception that I shall come to in a few minutes) part of the North American culture in most aspects of daily life. I can remember my first visit to Canada, one of a few hours nearly thirty years ago. To my then untutored eye, the only visible differences were the red coats of the police, the royal monograms and the advertisements for English chocolate. I know better now; but that first impression was not totally false. And there is, consequently, for an outsider like myself a permanent shock arising from the fact that Canada is so like the United States and another from the fact that being so alike she is not identical. Faced with the first shock, one is inclined to ask whether being Canadian has any assessable meaning that is not summed up in political separation from the United States; whether in fact, a view that I advance even as a speculation with great diffidence, the only real Canadians are the Canadian politicians, government servants and members of the armed services. If this view can be defended, then "Canadianism" is, I fear, too thin an idea to bear much strain. Defending Canada from the Americans, from Benedict Arnold to Champ Clark or an occasional congressman, is not an adequate programme today for a State so rich, so powerful in the world, attempting to plot its future. The very fact that the old annexationist ambitions of many Americans are now held by few, and none of the few important, makes the problem more urgent. For if it is possible to keep a state going, to keep it on the way to nationhood by such a negative policy when that nation was an infant, it is no longer possible when it is a lusty young adult. To see Canadianism in terms of anti-Americanism is an irrelevant programme today. To see it in terms of un-Americanism is,

today, a more sensible but not a much more adequate programme.

The other formative force in the development of Canadian
nationality is also negative, though not so emptily negative as
anti-Americanism or non-Americanism has been in recent times.
For the movement from colonialism to nationalism has been
a movement from a recognizable status to another, not a
continuous vigilance against what was often a highly problem-
atical danger. No Canadian leaders since the days of the
Family Compact, even if then, thought that the legal and
practical connection between Canada and Britain was of no
importance or had found a perfect solution. So the various
stages of development from the Durham Report to the Statute
of Westminster were stages in a real progress (I am using
the term as neutrally as possible). In the course of that
progress real Canadian problems were dealt with, well or ill,
and Canadian ways of doing things were learned and became
habits. But that progress, that evolution has now reached a
terminus. I, at any rate, cannot see what further contribution
to the development of a Canadian nation can be made
by a mere extension of the "liberation" from the leading strings
of the Mother Country. I suspect, I can't do more than suspect,
that younger Canadians hardly know or care what the old con-
troversies were about; they are "old, forgotten, far-off things".
I question whether anybody today would manage to raise his
or her temperature two or three degrees by reading Kipling's
once resented line, "Daughter in her mother's house, mistress
in her own" except, possibly, to reflect that in these days of
an ageing population, the daughter is often mistress in her
mother's house as well, the mother, a dependent, grateful,
more or less, for the daughter's bounty! I don't say, for a
moment, that that is how a young Canadian sees the relationship today, but it is, I think, possibly the most natural way
for him to see it.

What I am more concerned to point out is that the basic Canadian relationship is not either with the United States or with the United Kingdom, but with the world of the hydrogen bomb. The very fact that Canada is now one of the treasure-houses of the world makes the naïve isolationism of the inter-war years, of which Professor Creighton complained, impossible. A uranium-producing country cannot be neutral. I don't think that Canada was any more peccant between the wars than Britain or the United States. But the world has certainly grown too small and dangerous for even venial sins of that type to be permissible today. They may still be committed but, in a double sense, they are mortal.

Times have indeed changed since Canada, in 1919, fought to be admitted as a signatory to the Treaty of Versailles on the same footing as Serbia. Now, willy-nilly, Canada is immensely more powerful than Serbia or its successor and, in all probability, not a whit less vulnerable. I know how much has been done to educate the Canadian public to its new role, its new duties, its new necessities. But I do not know how successful that education has been among the Canadian masses, how far they understand that Canadianism must have a positive and burdensome content. It was possible for Canada, in 1939, to debate its entry into the Second World War, and that debate was carried on at a high level. I read it at the time and was deeply impressed by it, and this is perhaps an appropriate place to pay tribute to the brilliant son of this province, Ernest Lapointe, who so shone in that debate. But it is not enough to be proud that Canada entered the war openly and consciously, did not enter sideways and with one eye shut. It is more useful to think of what changes in Canadian life, political, economic, cultural are imposed by the fact that Canada will not again have the time or the chance to choose.

The most she can hope to have is what the French call

"une voix au chapitre" and the weight of that voice will depend on the weight of the Canadian contribution to the power, the mere power, of the Western World. I know how great it is; I fear it will have to be greater. And I hope I may be permitted to describe a difference in temper between Canada and the United States that struck me last year when I went for a few days from Seattle to Vancouver. In Seattle, the impact of the Korean War was very evident, the wounded came in every week; the draft was continuously at work; the streets were full of soldiers and sailors; the air full of planes. And, an unfortunate but natural result, the atmosphere in Seattle was tense, the political campaign was overshadowed by war. It was a relief to come to Vancouver, to a calmer atmosphere. I have no doubt that, in any circumstances, Vancouver would have been calmer. But some of the calm came from the fact that the tempers of the inhabitants of Vancouver were not being tried in the same way, that the immunity from what was called American hysteria had admirable causes—and others that were simply the result of the different ways in which the Korean crisis affected the two countries. Canadians, perhaps, took too much credit for their emotional stability when they had far less to be unstable about than had the Americans. A continuation of this attitude (assuming that I am right in believing that there is or was such an attitude) will diminish the weight, the due weight of Canada in the world. For in this age of armed truce, those on whom the greatest burdens fall will always call the tune. It will, therefore, be one of the problems of Canadian leadership in the next few years not only to think out Canadian policies that are not simply the policies of the honest broker, but policies that the great powers do not, for whatever reason, think out or propose. But it will not be enough to propose a policy, it will be necessary to put behind it the weight of an enlightened country.

How is it to be enlightened, and how united? It can be enlightened by efforts like this, by the bringing together of Canadians of very different tastes, views, aspirations. It can be done by press, radio, schools, colleges, churches; by the continual insistence by all who have any teaching function, in the widest sense, of never concealing the painful truth and of insisting, at appropriate times, on the necessity of expensive and distasteful courses of action that the position and status of Canada now call for. I would have to know your country much better before having any opinion on possible concrete action worth putting before you.

But there is one course of action, called for in any case, that can also be a useful course of action in solving the general problem of giving the concept of "Canada" a positive, not a negative, content. That is the fostering of specifically Canadian aspects of North American culture and the fostering of the double culture of Canada in the sense of making the two great cultural groups far more conscious of what each other stands for and what each group has to give and to receive.

This task is important; for the creation or the strengthening of a Canadian nationality it is fundamental. The position of Canada in North America is unique in that its national life, its culture, is based on two different linguistic groups. It is a long way from the Durham Report; and John A. Macdonald was a better prophet than Durham when he bet on the survival of Jean Baptiste. That survival is a basic fact of Canadian history, of the Canadian present and of the Canadian future. No realist view of the Canadian problem is possible without the acceptance of this fact. It is easy to point out the inconveniences of this fact; the costs of a bilingual federal government, the division within what *might* have been a more unified Canadian culture, which has its roots in this fact. But there it is;

" 'Tis true there's better booze than brine
But he that drowns must drink it."

So the poet says. But I should like to go further than
insisting on the necessities of the case and insist on the advantages of the case, and they are very great.

But before going on to argue this point, I should say in
passing that I have been a little surprised and more amused,
in the past, when I have heard Canadians descanting on the
internal strains in Canada. From a European standpoint how
mild, how little impressive are those strains! The divisions
inside many European countries, not to speak of the external
pressures and hostilities, are such that the troubles of Canada
seem quite negligible. In how many European countries is
there blood and recent blood between parties, groups, religions,
classes! I shall not begin, that is to say, by taking this internal,
cultural division inside Canada too seriously.

I should rather stress the possibilities of a bilingual culture
which are open to Canadians and to stress the advantages, for
Canadians, that would flow from a far greater interchange
of ideas, of arts, of personalities between the two cultural groups.
I have already stressed the fact that the problem of resisting
"Americanization" is common to the whole world, including
the United States, if, by Americanization, we mean the excessive
confidence in gadgets (and there can be spiritual gadgets as
well as mechanical gadgets), the excessive exaltation of the
contemporary, the comparative neglect of hindsight as well as
of foresight. This is a problem for the whole free world and
the United States is merely the most prominent, not the only
sinner.

Nor can I put much hope in the exclusion of these dangers
to Canadian culture, some would say to any real culture, by
political, by legal methods. For good or ill, we are in this
world where a mixture of standards is even more dangerous

than a candid and philistine contempt for standards. Canadian culture will survive this onslaught by its own intrinsic merits and its own utility for Canadians, or it will be swamped by it. No tariffs, no censorship will do the trick, here, in Ireland, anywhere. This world is too much with us, but here it is.

It is because this assault is going on and will continue to go on, that it is important that the double cultural tradition of Canada should be exploited. This I know is not a novel idea. But it has often been advanced in what, I think, is a self-defeating way. Thus French culture in Canada has been defended as a natural barrier against American barbarism as the last stronghold of the classical virtues. That it is a barrier and will remain a barrier I do not doubt. But as Quebec and other areas of French culture in Canada become more and more industrialized, the "Canadiens" will be subject to the assaults of this new machine culture as are the French, the Italians, the Irish. The idea that these attacks can only succeed if they are delivered in English, ignores a now old European experience. French, Irish, even Basque will not be barriers if the way of life invites invasion. Comics, be-bop, the worst inanities of radio and television can cross any linguistic barrier; this is the new republic of illiteracy, as universal as the republic of letters in the Middle Ages or the seventeenth century.

But there is a special opportunity open to the culture of French Canada, arising from the comparative lateness of the entry of French Canada into the world of modern industry. The innocent optimism of a generation ago, which afflicted and blinded so many in the English-speaking world, is no longer permissible. We know too much of what mere industrialization can do. On the other hand, we know how sterile and how self-defeating is a blind and uncritical clinging to traditions that the economic and social structure are undermining. There is no future and not much life in "la culture folkloristique", to use a rather barbarous French phrase. What is possible is the prudent, yet critical, preparation of a traditional culture, like that of French Canada, for this encounter with the modern world. For that encounter not to end in an easy victory for the modern world, that world must be understood. That modern world is not by any means the enemy of the good life in all things; its essential gains, which are real, can be preserved and developed. But its dangerous tendencies which are also real, its degradations which are also real, can only be fought if its strength and weakness are objectively assessed. It is an old story; and history has been with men like St. Thomas, who did not merely cry "Wolf" when Aristotle invaded Christian Europe, but examined, adapted and used the Philospher for the good of the *respublica christiana*.

Obviously no one can call up St. Thomases on order, but his spirit, a bold and adventurous spirit, is more easily commanded. For better or worse, French Canada is now part of that modern world and must either come to terms with it, French Canada's terms with it, or be, not very slowly, submerged in it. It will not be a very great reward, for more than three centuries of heroic defence of a way of life, if the mere shell of the language survives and the contents are the same as those of any other society equally invaded by a mechanistic and levelling spirit.

French Canada has so far escaped the worst of the levelling spirit, the confusion of the view that "a man's a man for a' that" with the less justifiable view that all men are not merely equal, but identical, that basic problems, in learning or the arts, can be settled by majority vote. It has already been said and it needs to be repeated, that original minds are few and the wind bloweth where it listeth. That means, of course, that many non-original minds will benefit by the tolerance and support provided for the truly original minds; but that cannot be helped. But to repeat myself, French Canada which has not, as far as I know, yet submitted to the more naïve and destructive forms of egalitarianism, may contribute a great deal by its entry into the modern world. It may contribute (and this is an important service), to the illustration, for France, of the possibility of a fusion between the most valuable gains of the modern world and the most permanent and valuable acquisitions of the old, now endangered, way of life. For in France there is, alas, an almost complete barrier between the traditional French culture and the New World in which France, like Canada, has to live. If French Canada can show France a way round that barrier, that will be a great service indeed to a world that still looks so often to France for leadership.

But what is to be the contribution of the other half of Canadian culture? Again, the English-speaking Canadians will have to make up their minds what things in that culture mark Canada off from the United States *positively*. They will also have to make up their minds what things they can contribute which are not only indubitably Canadian (which is something), but which have a value for the whole Western World, not only for Canada. And that, again, means a candid stocktaking. Not only will many things be identical on each side of the border: there is no reason why they shouldn't be. To go out looking for a specifically Canadian way of doing things, merely because it is Canadian, even if it is manifestly inferior to the American or British way of doing things, is to be as silly as are the childish nationalists of Europe or Asia. I seem to be arguing against the recent drift of Canadian opinion, but whatever one may think of the specific recommendations of the *Massey Report,* the mere stocktaking itself is of great value.

It would be impertinent in me, given my limited knowledge, to comment in detail on the characteristic marks of Canadian culture. But I should not worry too much, or too early, about

the absence of or the limitations of specifically Canadian contributions to music and painting. A national musical culture
is a rare enough thing; it is only in quite modern times that
England has begun to acquire one. All the world, as far
as visual art goes, has been going to school to the "school
of Paris" for three generations now. In music, in the visual
arts, it is more important to make available the existing highest
art forms than to concentrate on local talent in local terms.
Local talent will learn more from the masters than from other
local talent. Even in literature, in the theatre for instance, the
contemplation of the work of the masters has a tonic, not
depressing, effect. Stratford, Ontario, may have done more for
the theatre in Canada by producing Shakespeare than by
searching the highways and by-ways for a local Shakespeare
or even a local Ben Jonson. But, and this is an important
but, artists of any kind in a country like Canada are handi-
capped by the comparative rarity of examples of work of the
first class. So it was in the United States less than two
generations ago. I never protest when a picture or a rare
book or even a first-class artist is exported to America or
Australia. I don't subscribe to the funds to keep them at
home, although I have, once or twice, been tempted to contribute to a fund to send some of these treasures away.

And the future Canadian culture of the English-speaking
half will not only gain a great deal from the flow of immigrants
from non-English cultures, it will gain a great deal—and
give a great deal—if both the French and English variants
of Canadian culture are encouraged, almost coerced, to know
each other better. If the situation of mutual ignorance and
misunderstanding is as Miss Neatby describes it, it is disgraceful
and remediable. Canada should not be above learning from
other nations with similar problems and possibilities. There
is a great deal to be said for the Swiss system by which students
from *la Suisse romande* spend a year in a German-speaking

university and vice versa, for the interest with which a paper like the *Neue Zürcher Zeitung* watches and reports on cultural life in Lausanne and the *Gazette de Lausanne* returns the compliment. The great newspapers of Canada of both languages could do as much, could keep Toronto and Montreal informed of the achievements, even of the failures and follies, of the intellectual life in the other city. Even Glasgow and Edinburgh are ceasing to ignore each other, so surely there is hope for Canada! But speaking very seriously, this cross-fertilization is necessary and, I should have thought, required only three things, an appreciation of its necessity, mutual good will and money. If all three can't be provided, then the problem is insoluble, but that I refuse to believe. Let students from Toronto and Hamilton go to Montréal and Québec; let students from Trois Rivières and Montréal go to London and Vancouver. Let students from all these places go to Antigonish and learn a new *lingua franca,* Gaelic.

I have talked quite long enough; the details of such a purposeful cross-fertilization out of which, I believe, will come not an identical Canadian culture but a common Canadian culture, are not for me to discuss even had I the time. Of course all this will cost effort, will mean the breaking down of old habits on both sides, and will mean money. Especially it will mean money. But that can and will be found. There is an old verse once recited in my native land that describes the remarkable phenomenon that girls with portions always get husbands:

> "Pit a lass on Tinto Tap
> Gin she hae some siller.
> Tho' she be as black as night
> The wind'll blaw a laddie till her."

Money is not, I know well, an infallible means of getting a desirable life, national or individual. But in a nation like

Canada, faced with great and expensive problems, it is a help to have it and a privilege to use it to help to create a more united and more nationally conscious people.

I have taken up your time and have not, I fear, done much more than that. But I should like to end on a note of confidence—and of warning. The confidence is based on what Canadians have achieved and what they are visibly achieving. That achievement is not only material. In a world rent by warring ideologies and with nations torn within themselves by faction and by carefully cultivated traditions of hostility, the example of Canada is refreshing and inspiring. Your politicians have wisely eschewed the temptations of intellectual symmetry, have cultivated what Cavour thought the greatest of statesmanlike qualities, "le tact des choses possibles". May they continue to do so. But they and the Canadian people must realize, will realize, that the range of possibility is now immensely greater for Canada than it was even fifteen, even ten years ago. They must and will realize that in this age it is necessary to be bold, and boldness is often the only real prudence.

I can very well understand the irritation that many Canadians must feel as they contemplate their deserved good fortune and yet realize the kind of world it is that they are fortunate in. I was once told by a great scholar that the most formidable of Chinese imprecations on an enemy is "May you live in interesting times". You live, we all live, in very interesting times. I wish we didn't, but there it is. But the whole history of Canada for over three hundred years has been one of tenacity and boldness from the desperate survival of New France to the reckless boldness that brought about Confederation and laid the foundations of a new and great nation. Canada is the heir of the two great formative traditions of Western Europe: it is her pride and her opportunity to develop both. And I am sure that all in Europe who know anything of this country will repeat, with necessary emendations, the bold and prophetic words of Lord Carnarvon during the passing of the British North America Act, "We honestly and sincerely have fostered your growth, recognizing in it the conditions of our own greatness".

DIGEST OF DISCUSSION

DIGEST OF DISCUSSION

The Conference was intended to provide representative Canadians from many walks of life, in government, business and industry, education, labour groups and the professions, with the opportunity to hear in abbreviated form the eight papers here printed in full, and to discuss them briefly. The interest shown by the entire group was such that it would do less than justice to the idea and the atmosphere of the Conference were the discussion to be forgotten. A digest cannot include the by-play that enlivened the sessions, but can suggest how opinions varied. In a sense, it makes this volume a book plus brief critical reviews of its contents.

The programme was so arranged that the first four were presented on Friday, two each in the morning and afternoon, with a coffee break after the first and third papers, and in the same way the second four papers were presented on Saturday. Throughout, the endeavour was to secure the participation of people from various interest groups and from both French-speaking and English-speaking Canadians.

THE CONFERENCE OPENING

Words of welcome were spoken by DR. HENRI BEAUPRÉ, an alderman of the City of Quebec, who, as Acting Mayor, represented His Worship Mayor Lucien Borne, absent through illness. His opening remarks in French, like those of the Chairman, were a reminder that the Conference was being held in Canada's oldest city and in the heart of Canada's French culture.

HERBERT H. ROGGE, President of the Canadian Westinghouse Company Limited, who the preceding day had received from Laval University the honorary degree Doctor of Economics, then welcomed the assembly, saying in part:

"Before us we are happy to have a good cross-section of the kind of people who have helped to make the country what it is today, and who will continue to contribute to the progressive enrichment of Canadian life. On the platform will be discerning people, who have taken time to look at the shape of things to come, to study it under the strict discipline of experience, yet with some promptings of inspiration and, one hopes, a little clairvoyance. What they are going to tell you I do not know myself, and I am looking forward to their expositions with as much interest as yourselves. But before we hear them, you may be interested in knowing why the Canadian Westinghouse Company Limited has sponsored this Conference.

"More than two years ago, some of us were reminded that 1953 would mark the fiftieth anniversary of our founding. The fiftieth anniversary of a manufacturing company is ordinarily of little interest to people outside the company. But to those in daily contact with it, who work for and with it, such an occasion can be one of inspiration. Incidentally, to a management harassed by the innumerable problems that beset a modern industrial company, a fiftieth anniversary seems much more than an organizational birthday; it has some characteristics of a miracle! Companies can die just like people, and many do pass away every year, some after a long and useful life, others after a few years or months of existence.

"When employees began to take an interest in our fiftieth anniversary, we asked several of our more imaginative people to collect ideas for celebrating the event. In due course, a memorandum was placed on my desk, which was, I understand, the result of several conferences among our people. 'It is proposed,' began this memorandum, 'that Canadian Westinghouse Company organize and sponsor an integrated study of Canada's development in the next fifty years, and make the results public in an appropriate way, as part of the Company's observation of its fiftieth anniversary.' 'The general idea,' I continue to quote, 'is to bring together some of the country's leading scientists, sociologists, engineers, educators and industrialists to look at the growth and organization of Canada during its next half-century, and to bring out from their studies and speculations a body of integrated data, projections and ideas which will be of real value to government, industry and the public'."

After explaining how preliminary consultation had met with widespread approval, and had led to the appointment of the Chairman and the Committee, Dr. Rogge continued:

"At this point the Company as an institution stepped out of the picture. Our only suggestion to the Committee was to examine the forces and institutions that have made Canada what she is, and then to gaze as far as possible into the future, with a view to helping all Canadians gain a better understanding of our country and thus contribute more effectively to her future development. The Committee took us at our word. I have not seen any of those papers in advance, and it is with great interest that I anticipate the two days' proceedings.

"We have often been asked why our Company has undertaken sponsorship of such a project. It is not an easy question to answer, especially when the questioner is a so-called 'practical man', because we do not expect to gain any commercial or promotional advantage from this project. But I am sure that, in a deeper sense, we have much to gain. As we see this country, impelled by powerful forces, rushing swiftly toward some sort of destiny, we wonder. Is it not wise for us to pause and take stock of where we are, and where we are going? If we cannot be exactly like an architect, who blueprints his plans before he turns the builders loose on the job, should we not at least take a look at the direction of our progress and gain what understanding of it we can? If, in today's fast-moving events, we cannot be sure of our destiny, at least we can be enlightened passengers on the national express train. Some of the knowledge turned up by this effort to explore the future may serve to guard our country against dangers at present unknown, or help her and her people to surer success, greater prosperity and more lasting happiness.

"In any event, we feel that that is what we may gain from these proceedings, along with all the rest of the industrial and commercial companies, the organizations, associations, institutions, governments and people of Canada."

THE DISCUSSION OF THE PAPERS

The following is a digest of the discussion from the floor or in later invited correspondence.

THE CANADIAN PEOPLE

WATSON KIRKCONNELL (President, Acadia University) disagreed with Dr. Sandwell's hopeful conclusions about population increase through immigration, recapitulating the experience of 1871 to 1931, and arguing that our greatest source of population increase has actually been "the cradle rather than the port."

"The continental percentage figures given by Dr. Sandwell tend to conceal our catastrophic experience in the past. In the decade 1871-81, our immigration doubled, but only one immigrant in five remained in Canada. In 1881-91, the immigration increased two-and-a-half times, but only one in nine remained. In 1891-1901, six out of every ten immigrants left Canada.

In our most phenomenal period of influx, 1901-11, some 1,848,000 entered Canada, but the emigration was around 1,000,000. Between 1921 and 1931, we received 1,500,000 new citizens but lost 1,250,00. During the whole period from 1851 to 1931, we lost 6,110,000 people to the United States, of whom 1,740,000 were native Canadians and 4,370,000 were immigrants who had found it impossible to get a foothold in our economic life. As the late M. C. MacLean of the Dominion Bureau of Statistics has pointed out, if there had been neither immigration nor emigration during these eighty years, Canada's population in 1931 would have been at least as large as it turned out to be."

He expressed doubts that the discovery of added mineral resources would necessarily lead to an increase in population, unless processing in Canada provides employment, illustrating by reference to the few men required to extract gypsum in Nova Scotia for shipment to the United States, and anticipating a similar situation in Labrador if extraction were done in Canada and processing abroad, a condition more likely to exist as United States ore resources dwindle. If Canada continues to use up natural resources faster than they can be replaced, the situation is further worsened. Even an increased Canadian population might not correct the disadvantages of the Maritime Provinces. Nova Scotia "lost by Confederation two-thirds of its revenue", has declined in population status from 10.51% in 1867 to 4.58% now, and has lost half its fertile soil through erosion. "The Maritime cranium" is therefore less likely to profit than is "the waistline of the Central Provinces".

D. C. MASTERS (Bishop's University) pointed out that immigration, formerly most numerous in periods when new land was readily available, could be expected to continue if capital investment and industrialization expand. But a shrinking in natural resources would set up again the emigration cycle that came between Confederation and 1896. As to the theme of cradle vs. port, he hesitated to say that natural increase would bring sufficient numbers, because birth-rates have a way of levelling off.

WALLACE GOFORTH (Gilbert Jackson and Associates, Toronto) deplored any discussion based on blind economic forces and reference to past events, insisting on a philosophic approach and on emphasis on vision as a condition of progress. Canada, certainly in the minds of the Fathers of Confederation, is not to be defined as the tail attached to the North American dog, nor have Canadians been content so to regard themselves. Emphasis on mere muscle as having been the basis of our growth is wrong, since the will to use muscle in the service of an ideal, the self-reliance of men, and the instinctive practice of thrift, have been more significant and are more enduring. Our material heritage sets maximum limits on numbers but not on quality. Following the visions and faith of the past might well give us a population of 40,000,000 fifty years hence: but a loss of resources and of inner resources in the interval might mean an impoverished population half that size.

J. ROBY KIDD (Director, Canadian Association for Adult Education) expressed the hope that Dr. Sandwell would deliver another paper at a later time, dealing not with figures but with the quality of people, because swift urbanization and industrialization raise psychological and social problems that cannot be analysed on the basis of figures alone.

R. G. ROBERTSON (Deputy Minister of Resources and Development, Ottawa) questioned the emphasis on Canada's population as a fairly constant fraction of the population of the continent, except as the general climate of the continent has its effect. To tie Canadian to continental population may be misleading, since the availability of resources such as hydro-electric energy must be given more emphasis. Nor do Dr. Kirkconnell's figures on provincial population indicate a necessarily continuing pattern, since Ontario in 1901 had 41% and now has about 30% of the total. "It seems to me of much greater consequence that the factors in Canada are becoming and will become considerably different from the factors in the United States," especially because the cost factor must be reckoned in the availability of resources.

B. K. SANDWELL, in reply, denied having based any argument on immigration and emigration in quoting census statistics, admitted that large immigration has been needed to counterbalance emigration of Canadians to the United States, but insisted that Canadian emigration in the next quarter-century would be reduced, as differences in opportunity between the two nations change in Canada's favour. He reiterated that Canada's population totals can change only very slowly the proportion they bear to the continental total. Canada, if not the tail, is a part of the North American animal and must share its blood-stream. Again, urbanization holds the key to numbers. The amount of food that can be consumed in Canada is limited and the number of food producers not likely to increase greatly, but the consumption of manufactured articles can increase indefinitely. Disliking many of the effects of urbanization on national character, he had to accept the facts and hoped that means would be devised to minimize the unfortunate results.

CANADA'S NATURAL RESOURCES

K. W. NEATBY (Director, Administration Division, Department of Agriculture, Ottawa) admitted that his duty was to disagree with the paper, and began by challenging the speaker's optimism about renewable natural resources and the importance of their export. Today, Canada consumes 80% or 85% of its total food production, including agriculture and fisheries, and any increase in population must be accompanied by an increase in food production if there is to be any exportable surplus.

"Agricultural production can be increased, and references have been made by Mr. Mackenzie to the fact that large areas of untapped potential agricultural land are available.

That is quite true. Leahey estimates that our total arable land amounts to about 130 million acres. Of this area about 85 million are cultivated, including improved pasture. Development of the remaining 45 million acres will involve the destruction of nearly 40 million acres of forest. Moreover, the best farmland, in these regions, will commonly be the best forest sites. Cost of transportation facilities, clearing and improving the land, as most of it is comparatively infertile, will be great; but it does constitute a very valuable reserve. Improved varieties of crops, better management and hydroponics will increase food supplies, but against this must be remembered the annual loss of thousands of acres of farmland for cities, airports, roads and industries."

Similarly, although forest growth now approximates annual depletion, there is little reason for optimism, and "I think we can run short", the theoretical possibility of forest increments being less than that of agricultural increments.

"Perhaps I have said enough about renewable resources to explain why I feel that statements such as 'Huge timberlands, large areas of potential farmlands' and 'Estimates of the population that this country can support vary a great deal, but few of the experts would put the minimum below three or four times the present population' should be examined rather carefully. Of course, if by 'support' we mean a couple of thousand calories per day, half or three-quarters of which might be derived from *Chlorella pyrenoidosa*, the experts may be right.

"It is hardly necessary to remember that world population is increasing at the rate of about 25 million per year in order to regard the speaker's attitude toward renewable resources as over-optimistic. Respecting non-renewable resources, it was said that 'Even under the most optimistic estimates of future population there seems little fear of there not being enough —for our own use.' So far as I am concerned, no reasonable estimates promote optimism.

"Finally, I wonder if the plea for private enterprise in the use of natural resources may be somewhat overdone. For example, surely the forest industries must be quite highly competitive. If so, there must be a tendency to harvest readily accessible stands before more remote mature or over-mature stands. I am told that logging roads cost not less than $6,000 per mile. Over-mature stands deteriorate rapidly and sometimes are hazards to neighbouring forests. I would certainly not advocate the nationalization of the forest industry, but I suspect that governments may be forced to exercise more control and perhaps to co-operate with industries in road building.

"Surely, in more general terms, it is going too far to say that '. . . the function of government is to regulate and stimulate . . . not to operate', and that 'governments are not likely to have the skill, the know-how or in fact the power of decision necessary to manage a business in a competitive world.' Surely several governments have shown that they can build and maintain roads, power plants, telephone systems, and operate railways and airways quite successfully."

MAJOR-GENERAL HOWARD KENNEDY (Chairman, Eastern Rockies Forest Conservation Board) agreed that some competitor countries enjoy rates of forest growth much greater than ours, but held that similar silvacultural treatment of our better areas would produce much greater growth here than at present. Canadian statistics include areas barren or over-mature or of poor quality, whereas "conifer growth on pine plantations in Ontario and many coastal areas in British Columbia exceeds one hundred cubic feet per acre per annum, which is something very few countries can touch." The claim that operators are practising sustained yield is open to question, since "many operators are harvesting only five or six cubic feet of conifers per acre per annum from limits capable of yielding four or five times that amount", and harvesting on our best growing sites in Eastern Canada still results in many of these areas reverting to "silvacultural slums", a major problem discussed recently by the Canadian Institute of Forestry. Agreeing that "the role of government is to stimulate and regulate", he felt that the claim that "sound forest management is the responsibility of the operators and is most likely to thrive best under large independent operators" needs to be qualified.

"Government regulation of operations on Crown lands is still very necessary and upwards of 90% of our forest lands still belongs to the provinces. Nova Scotia, with only a small fraction of its forests held by the government, has suffered just as great if not greater ravages from individual operations than the Crown lands of other provinces. Whether we like it or not, I believe we are not going to get rid of government regulations."

L. D. JACKSON (Mayor of Hamilton) questioned both Mr. Mackenzie's views on the merits of an all-Canada pipeline for gas, having regard to costs and "long-term issues at stake", and his opinion that the prospect for wheat was clearer than for other foodstuffs because of Canada's economic advantage in its production. In view of the present huge pile-up of wheat in Canada and the decreasing proportion of wheat flour in the dietary of all nations, he asked for elaboration on the position of wheat in our economy.

M. W. MACKENZIE, concluding the discussion, admitted that to answer Mayor Jackson would take considerable time, but stated that his opinion on gas distribution was based on the difference of a few cents per thousand feet estimated as between the rival plans and the advantages of flexibility in the distribution of energy, which could be likened to the results of our building of a transcontinental railroad. Looking ahead even less than fifty years, the difference in present construction costs would be negligible as compared to the value of a complete Canadian distribution system for energy, including gas. He held that Dr. Neatby had not denied that an increase in food production sufficient to maintain an export programme was possible. Wheat is now in a surplus position, but there have been previous surpluses and the problem, however serious, is a short-term one. In the long run, wheat consumption will rise with increased population. Even so, we shall still be in the export business, but the problem of marketing may be a more serious one. He professed to have learned much since leaving government service as to the possession and use of know-how.

To the discussion, later additions were made as follows:

C. E. REYNOLDS (Chairman, Ontario Northland Transportation Commission) disagreed with any suggestion that an increased Canadian population would remove Canada from the list of food exporters, citing Holland and Denmark as thickly-populated areas now maintaining high living standards and exporting large quantities of food. Intensive cultivation and the full use of idle land in Canada would correct our present concentration on wheat in the Prairies, but mining of the soil must cease. Irrigation may well provide the answer to the problem of recurrent drought, the extensive garden lands of the West could support large canneries, and the "frozen north" could be further cultivated. The better use of land would justify the return to forest cover in poorer areas, thus preventing erosion, raising the water-table and increasing yield on good land properly cultivated. The Great Clay Belt of Northern Ontario could alone sustain over 6,000,000 people and could supply large quantities of vegetables, honey, etc.

Further, while the "illimitable forest" idea must be abandoned, the existence of forest nurseries, the silvacultural policies of large operators and improved methods of fighting fire and insects justify the hope that better forests will exist, and that the result will be more wood, not less, especially as inaccessible areas become accessible. Logging roads will make clearing and agriculture possible in new areas, thus improving the economic balance and providing better protection for forests. The utilization of wood waste, the reforestation of uneconomic farmlands, plantings to prevent erosion and floods, are hopeful methods; and, although no return to early conditions is possible, regeneration of forests is already taking place. The policy of criminal waste having continued until this century, there has been incalculable loss, but that policy is now gone, and scientific control of forests is coming into its own.

ROBERT F. LEGGETT (Director, Division of Building Research, National Research Council) expressed disappointment with the paper, and emphasized the high duty of husbanding natural resources. He referred to his published views in his Wallberg Lecture of 1953 (*Resources for Tomorrow, The Engineer's Stewardship,* University of Toronto Press), in which he had said:

"Consider, if you will, the distinct probability that, within the lifetime of many in this room, the United States will be deficient, by the equivalent of one-third, of her present production, and may have to import most of this (much of it as raw materials) from other countries, not the least of which will be Canada, and you will realize something of the international aspects of the matter. It is true that, at the moment, our own country is very favourably situated with regard to its non-renewable resources: we are probably still a long way from that 'point of no return' so recently passed by our neighbour country to the south. But surely that should make us the more anxious to use well all that we have and to eliminate all possible waste in the use of materials which can never be replaced. Surely too, this good fortune should itself be one of the greatest incentives to ensure that everything possible is done to protect and conserve the natural resources which are renewable, and upon the continued supply of which all other development ultimately depends."

THE CHALLENGE TO SCIENCE

O. M. SOLANDT (Chairman, Defence Research Board, Ottawa) deplored the tendency in previous papers to regard Canada as "an ill-defined portion of the United States dog, living and trading in a world very much like the world of today", whereas fifty years from now the world will not be the same, and many current social and economic problems will not exist. He argued against the tendency to measure progress in terms of population numbers, volume of expenditures and numbers of bath tubs. Since Canada is now set in the perspective of the globe and global activities, Canadian scientists can be influential as citizens of the world.

"We must remain strong, if we are to remain free and prevent the outbreak of a world war which would break up all the plans we have been discussing; but we should recognize that the mere prevention of war is not our ultimate goal or an end in itself. We want to try to prevent the causes of war while we are evolving a means for the settlement of international disputes, and here I think science and scientists can be even more helpful.

"It seems to me that one of the greatest contributions science has made and will make is to improve communications, and by improving the means of travel we shall ultimately, if national difficulties can be eliminated, make the world into a neighbourhood in which everybody understands the problems of the others.

"The introduction of atomic power which has been mentioned will, I am sure, do a lot to improve productivity in various parts of the world which are suffering from a power deficiency. One of the ways that science can help is to bring the food and resources of the world into balance with the population. This will certainly do something to remove the causes of war, and there are many scientific discoveries now working toward this end.

"Finally, we must give social science and social scientists a better chance, and here the physical scientists have to lead. They have done a lot to reduce the public esteem of the social scientist by sneering at the inexactness of his methods and the difficulties he encounters. I think some physical scientists should try joining with the social scientists and find out how difficult their field really is.

"It seems to me that we in Canada must remember that

we are not just a small prosperous nation with a rosy future. We are one of the most favoured nations in the world, favoured with natural resources, with a good political and racial heritage, with good government, with good and powerful neighbours and with a good position in the Commonwealth. We represent not only ourselves but the aspirations of the whole free world. If we fail to make a success of the future, I am sure people all over the world will feel there is no hope for our democratic way of life."

K. F. TUPPER (Dean of Applied Science, University of Toronto) pointed out that the challenge is to the scientist rather than to science, and that the distinguishing mark of the scientist is intellectual honesty. Science is international, as a recital of the names of scientists concerned with atomic energy makes plain: German, Italian, Danish, English, American and others. Canada's Tomorrow will be just as international as science. Science is strictly neutral, and scientific forces can destroy or construct with equally scientific accuracy. But the scientist must not be morally or socially neutral, and must take responsibility for social results as well as for brilliant research. Just as uranium has leaped into prominence as a source of energy, other sources may well become available for the needs of growing population, in food, shelter, clothing. These basic needs are far more important than are powerful cars and TV sets so far as human happiness is concerned, and we are still far short of supplying these needs.

R. F. LEGGETT (Director, Division of Building Research, National Research Council) agreed with Dean Tupper's distinction between the neutrality of science and the responsibility of scientists. If science can be classified as pure and applied, and the development of materials taken as the end of scientific work, without raising larger questions of intellectual values, the development of the material side of Canada has been the work of applied scientists using the discoveries of pure scientists. "Science falsely so-called", a New Testament phrase coined in face of a different situation, can be used today as a warning against the prostitution of science. "There is a great danger and challenge to scientists in so-called world science."

J. A. CORRY (Vice-Principal, Queen's University), speaking as a social scientist, underlined Dr. Stratford's emphasis on the social effects of scientific developments. The breakdown of habit and custom by the accelerating pace of change is serious, and although the almost automatic increase in government activity in the past fifty years may be deplored, it is the sign of "human society trying to protect itself against that too rapid pace of social change". If we are not careful of human society, "the kind of human society that can support science may very well disappear". He quoted:

> "What boots it that my noble steed,
> Chosen so carefully, the field outran:
> I did not reckon on the bookie's speed.
> The proper study of mankind is man."

R. K. STRATFORD denied having a "bath tub philosophy", and agreed with the suggestions made in discussion, reserving judgment on the too simple classification of science as either pure or applied but thoroughly agreeing that the challenge is to scientists rather than to science, which is only the product of scientists. With Dr. Corry, he emphasized the need for more attention and support in the field of social science.

THE CONTRIBUTION OF INDUSTRY

W. A. MACKINTOSH (Principal, Queen's University) admitted that it would be unfair to criticize Mr. Ambridge for the many topics necessarily omitted from his paper, and admired "the bold thesis that we cannot build and defend an island of prosperity in this country or on this continent unless we take positive action to transport and supply this industrial knowledge to less favoured countries." Were exact prediction possible, there would be no need for industrialists, since government could readily set up commissions to carry out the predictions.

"But there are some things we have to deal with, and one of the facts which needs to be kept in our minds in these discussions is that it is not likely that in the next fifty years we shall have departed at all seriously from the pattern in this country, in which we combine small amounts of expensive labour with very large amounts of energy and capital equipment to produce goods at competitive world prices. If we do depart from it, because labour becomes plentiful or energy scarce or if world markets are closed to us, we shall be a poorer people in the year 2003 than we are at present or hope to be.

"My second point is this: In any talk of industry, in any talk of private enterprise, the key word is 'enterprise'. The great contribution of industry as we know it has been its dynamic quality, and if industry, without accurate prediction for fifty years ahead, can maintain the great quality of dynamic strength, then it will have served us well in the next fifty years. If you think in terms of what is static, of what is clearly defined, of what is a simple unit or division, then all the stresses of social and economic life are greatly increased and any solution becomes almost impossible."

D. A. MacGibbon (Professor of Political Economy, McMaster University) questioned Mr. Ambridge's thesis that raising the standard of living abroad would tend to check the birth-rate, since the first effect of a rising standard of living is to increase population, if only through a decline in the death-rate. The truth of the proposal is highly speculative and can be proved only after a long interval, during which the question of population increase might become very acute. The example of Japan throws some doubt on the well-intentioned idea of branch industries abroad.

Jean Marchand (Secretary, Canadian Catholic Confederation of Labour) agreed entirely that a shared vision, such as produced miraculous results in Canada during the war, was the secret of industrial success, but suggested that the paper would have been more pointed had it taken more account of the necessity to share the vision widely. He regretted the omission, however necessary within the limits of the paper, of a suggested plan for the maintenance of industrial peace.

"Once the standard of living of the Canadian population is settled or presumed to be settled, I think there are a lot of other problems to be solved here in Canada. I refer particularly to the integration of the different parties in enterprise, in social and even in political life, in the broad sense of the word."

This is the more necessary because the impression still exists that industry is more interested in profits than in mutual benefits to all, and such a condition gives rise to trouble within the nation and among nations.

E. V. HUGGINS (Vice-President, Westinghouse Electric Corporation), who was invited to speak as one of the relatively few guests from the United States, was sure that Canada was not thought of as the tail of the American dog, but that a common blood-stream made the two countries mutually dependent, as seen in the common defence programme. But much larger goals lie beyond this. What we are doing is essential but not an end in itself. As to tariffs, they are both necessary and baffling.

"I think it can be relatively easily proved that, but for the fact that tariff preferentials in a number of industrial countries in the world, including our own, had been of the calibre they were, the supplies of the free countries would not have been built up and we would not be here today. This country and the United States would be run by Germany. It was only because United States and Canadian industry were developed and administered behind adequate tariff walls that we had the productive facilities to carry on through the last war.

"Trying to look a little bit into Canada's future, I cannot believe that fifty years hence Canada—and a strong Canada

—will not include a very substantial manufacturing industry, not just extractive industry of raw materials but those which use the materials to make the end products for use here and throughout the world.

"In the United States both the individual companies and the nation as a whole have been trying to grapple with the problems Mr. Ambridge has been talking about here, trying to improve the economic forces of the country. The problems are present and acute across a broad field. They are certainly not limited to a profit. I think that the industrialist today, when he talks, proves he is talking about more than a dollar sign, because he realizes far more than he used to that the dollar sign is attached to the welfare of his workers, the welfare of the community and of the country, and now, to an increasing degree, the welfare of the world.

"If we are all going to contribute to the welfare of the world, we must be strong, each in his own unit. We in the United States have our own particular role to play. We are continually being told that the great strength of the free world lies in a sound and prosperous United States. To an increasing degree that will involve your country, and we look forward to working with you."

J. G. NOTMAN (President, Canadair Limited, Montreal) spoke in support of Mr. Ambridge's theory by recalling the expressed opinion of Dr. Loo, when he was purchasing agent for China in Washington, that the only solution for China's economic problem lay in industrialization, since in his country an acre of land was often the source of income for a whole family. But such a development could not come quickly, and the problem of population would continue to exist in the necessarily long interval.

D. W. AMBRIDGE begged off from a discussion of population problems, claiming that population statisticians disagree, but insisted afresh that the least favoured nations were those with the problems of high birth-rates and high death-rates. His own experience had included Mexico and Latin America, and he felt that in industry lay the only solution. Moreover, where ignorance and economic distress exist, dangerous ideas find the readiest acceptance. Raising the standard of living would make population problems more tolerable even if population did increase, and the best protection for ourselves lies in raising the level of prosperity among less favoured peoples. His omission of reference to labour had been deliberate, his aim being to discuss nations as entities rather than to draw sectional distinctions within a single paper. Further, since tariffs had been mentioned without definite suggestions, he would attempt none.

A general comment on the first four papers was added later by K. W. TAYLOR (Deputy Minister of Finance, Ottawa) who suggested, as a proviso to the hopeful views expressed, which he shares, the following:

"It would be unwise to ignore certain possibilities, which are perhaps unlikely in an extreme form, but which we may have to face recurringly in varying degrees.

"Our wealth, our welfare, and our capacity to support a rapidly increasing population enjoying rising levels of consumption, depend very heavily upon the kind of world in which we shall be living. Our prosperity is closely linked with that of the United States and Western Europe. American prosperity is closely linked with that of Western Europe, South America and other areas. The economic health of Western Europe is directly affected by events in Asia and Africa. It is hard to see a viable Japanese economy without a substantial two-way trade with China. Prosperity is in a very real sense indivisible. There are cushions and buffers of varying degrees of resilience between us and the remoter areas which can absorb minor shocks, but major and prolonged economic difficulties in any important area are bound to be transmitted to us.

"Short of a cataclysm that results in the mutual destruction of the effective power of both Russia and the NATO group and thus leaves the next century or two in the hands of Asia, we are likely to be among the most prosperous areas of the world. But this could be highly relative, and our absolute level could be very far below our present expectations. It may, of course, be higher. If all goes well throughout the world, we can look forward to several generations of expanding wealth and welfare. But things could go wrong.

"A prolonged major depression may be improbable; I am sure it does not need to happen, but it could. It could happen as a result of our own unwisdom, or as a result of circumstances over which we have little or no control. It is both dangerous and arrogant to slip into the state of mind that it can't happen here, or again. Canada has a balanced self-sufficiency in very few things. For most important commodities we have a large export surplus or a heavy import requirement, and this is likely long to remain. Hence, multilateralism in economic relations is a major Canadian national interest, and we are naturally disposed to raise it to the status of a universal and self-evident truth. We should realize, however, that many other countries do not regard this policy as being quite so self-evident. If we want them to accept this idea of multilateralism and freer trade, we shall have to work hard to help to create the kind of world in which they will find such policies to be in their national interest."

The Role of Government

Floyd S. Chalmers (President, Maclean-Hunter Publishing Co., Toronto) based his remarks on three forecasts he found in the paper: first, that government will have the task of maintaining the proper climate in a new age of industrial development which will be dominated by private initiative, because Canada's many "excursions into the field of public ownership have not been the result of anyone preaching any particular ideology", and are not proof that we are socialist in our approach; secondly, that government will be concerned with short-term economic stability; and thirdly, that there will be a growing role for government in the field of welfare activities, until a certain minimum standard is reached. He added:

"On these three points there are the questions of how that is going to be done without building up powerful permanent organizations behind the government, or how it can be done by governments of any political colour elected by the people themselves. Is there not a possibility that we are building up in Canada an official bureaucracy which could become a non-elected, non-removable government, carrying on the same policies regardless of the political party; and is this not a grave challenge to our democracy?"

MISS PAULINE JEWETT (Ottawa) questioned the theory of equilibrium, and suggested that there had been an under-estimation of "the importance of ideas in determining the role of government, the accepted roles of both government and private initiative at any given time and in any given country." The fact that Marx worked in the British Museum gave his ideas a tremendous impact on England in the late nineteenth century, through such channels as the Fabian Society.

"His ideas have been a very powerful force in most countries. The suggestion that we have found them unfit for Canadian consumption leads to no argument here, though it seems to me they have had a much greater influence on the role of government than is suggested in the functional theory. For example, one surely could say that, had Lord Keynes lived a little earlier or departed from orthodoxy earlier than he did, the ideas that he might have developed would have had a tremendous influence in the early thirties on the problem of short-term economic stability. They certainly have had, since then and today; but they might have had then, had they been brought out a little earlier than they were.

"Finally, in this country, the impact of American ideas may be much stronger and possibly contrary to what we would like to have them here. Even in our own country such ideas as social credit might change very much the role of government in the future."

EUGENE FORSEY (Director of Research, Canadian Congress of Labour, Ottawa) raised three questions. First, may not the "certain period" of government's role in social welfare be indefinitely lengthened, as education, housing and health become increasingly expensive? Secondly, will people prefer to spend their money themselves rather than pay more taxes, even though the pooling of resources might result in a real or supposed saving? Thirdly, does not the economic function of government in Canada, as the preserver of short-term economic stability by monetary policy, international trade policy, fiscal policy and public debt management, need to be enlarged through public investment and enterprise? The role of government may not be so small, restricted and modest as anticipated.

R. M. FOWLER (President, Canadian Pulp and Paper Association, Montreal) agreed that we actually have in Canada a kindly relationship in economic matters between private enterprise and government institutions and that we are likely to go on having it. It is of great importance that there is this absence from friction in "the common mixture", because Canada depends largely on international agreement, which is the role of government.

"I think as businessmen we should recognize and keep this working partnership that now exists, fortunately, in Canada between government and business. We are extraordinarily well served by our Civil Servants, and I think we do not always remember that in this kind of collaboration between government and business we have something that is probably unique in the world. It is not matched in the United States, I believe. I doubt very much if it is matched in the United Kingdom.

"This is the only point on which I would criticize the paper, and I consider it a most important point. I do not think he emphasized at all that it is something that could be lost, that as we grow in Canada in size and complexity, the easy interchange of ideas of which Mr. Ambridge spoke yesterday will become more difficult. It seems to me that as we get away from war-time experiences we can easily lose this technique of partnership. All I am suggesting is that it would be wiser for us to watch ourselves and see to it that we do not lose something which is of great value, this working friendly partnership between government and business."

MAURICE LAMONTAGNE, in replying, suggested that the problem of bureaucracy is not peculiar to government, but exists equally in business, as a result of growing institutions. How this is to be related to democracy is a continuing problem. His apparent under-estimation of ideas was not intended, the point being that Canadians have not indulged in extreme ideologies but have evolved a relationship between private enterprise and public intervention. As for social welfare, government action may well increase, but more slowly than before, even though the minimum standard in covering social risks and needs rises with general standards. These, once reached, cannot easily be reduced, as is evident from old-age pensions. Investment, mentioned as a weapon to maintain stability, he had included in his definition of fiscal policy.

THE CHALLENGE TO EDUCATION

F. C. A. JEANNERET (Principal, University College, Toronto) dealt with the cultural influence of France on French-Canadian education, and the evaluation of progressive educational methods. Of the first, he said in part:

"He speaks of the great cultural influence of France on French-Canadian education as 'largely an aristocratic and pre-revolutionary influence'. Yes and no. This is what it was, of course, until 1760, and naturally there was relatively little direct exchange of ideas between France and Canada for almost a century; but there was a tremendous carry-over throughout this period, for which the clergy and the teaching orders were

responsible—that important element of the population that
did not elect to return to France after the *cession,* but remained
to minister to and educate the flock of 65,000 *Canadiens.*

"In addition, for over a century now the intellectual interchange between France and French Canada has been very
much greater than suggested by President MacKenzie. Roman-
ticist France exercised a tremendous influence on Crémazie,
Fréchette and the intellectual and cultural development of
French Canada from early in the last century, and the great
number of young French Canadians who have gone to France
to complete their education have continued this French influence. French-Canadian literature and French-Canadian education have been, are, and for a long time will be very much
more directly influenced by the literature and the educational
programme of France than have English-Canadian literature
and education by the literature and educational practice of
England. Visiting professors from France and text-books used
in French schools have had a tremendous impact on French-
Canadian schools. French literary models have served French-
Canadian writers well from Philippe-Aubert de Gaspé right
down to Robert Charbonneau, Gabrielle Roy, and Lemelin,
whether they realize it or not."

That he did not share the speaker's optimism about progressive thought in education, to be judiciously combined with
traditional learning, was plain, as follows:

"Surely good and evil cannot mix any more than can oil and
water. While not denying that there was and is much bad
teaching even in the strongholds of the traditionalists, I would
find it infinitely easier to locate the proverbial needle than to
discover any good, let alone the best, features in the Progressivist's philosophy of education.

"About the last person I would ever accuse of muddy thinking
would be Larry MacKenzie. The so-called Progressive educa-
tionist, on the other hand, does nothing else. My great worry
when I became an educational administrator a few years ago
was that I too should go down this primrose path which

apparently becomes so fiendishly attractive to the teacher turned administrator. As a brake to prevent me from slipping too fast, I insisted on continuing to teach a certain number of classes, and this, I think, should be prescribed for every educational administrator, perhaps even with a year back into teaching for every five of administration. Educational administration seems to do something to the mind and should have some such corrective.

"One of President MacKenzie's magnificent objectives of education is 'the refining of the emotions, the intellect, and taste'. He speaks of the 'imperative need of helping the young Canadian to develop standards of taste which will recognize and demand the first-rate', and admits the great damage that 'has been done by educators who have turned away from the priceless benefits of philosophical and historical thought'.

"I have heard one of the Progressivist false prophets say 'I am suspicious of all knowledge.' He said that the important thing, the one thing that counted in education, was that teachers should be dynamic. It didn't seem to matter whether they had anything to teach, whether or not they had anything to be dynamic about, just so long as they were dynamic. This well-known Progressivist was equally contemptuous of all educational discipline.

"For a man to admit that he is 'suspicious of all knowledge' is but to proclaim that he is proud of his ignorance, that he is fair game for charlatans of every variety, anti-democratic propagandists, quacks and fanatics in every domain, political, scientific, and religious.

"The mob spirit spreads rapidly in any climate not conditioned by sound learning and scholarship, the recorded wisdom of the experience of mankind. As we project our educational programme fifty years into the future, let us remember that human culture is a cumulative achievement. Only by critical evaluation of the heritage of the past can we hope to gain insight into the evolution of concepts, pass objective judgment on political and philosophical doctrines of the moment, or cope intelligently with proposals for our future well-being. Plato, Aristotle, Dante, Descartes, though they wrote many centuries ago, are still very much alive, of immediate and vital significance for the man who would understand the contemporary scene or predict the future. Imagine if you can the educational programme of fifty years hence of the Progressivist prophet who is 'suspicious of all knowledge'."

LÉON LORTIE (Director of Extension, University of Montreal) recalled that those who will be the enlightened industrialists and statesmen of the next fifty years are now in school or are not yet born. Calling for increased respect for the teaching profession in order to restore the self-confidence of teachers, and emphasizing the enrichment of Canada from the French influence ("I belong to such a group, and this group believes in absolute truth and regards clear and logical thinking as the supreme attainment of democracy"), he warned against a false idea of democracy, saying:

"Teaching and learning are seldom labours of love. They, on the contrary, imply a love of labour. No durable results can be achieved without a constant effort and I doubt if the progressive school can prepare our youth to use, in President MacKenzie's own words, 'their working time well', because this school does not teach how to work. We need leadership, but how can this school train for leadership when nobody wants to be led?

"A sense of the hierarchy's position should be developed. To give respect and expect respect is surely a basis for building up aristocracy. There is, I think, a natural subordination between a master and a pupil. The master has something to teach and the pupil has something to learn. Now if the child is to be respected, as he should be, I think then the teacher is entitled also to the same degree of respect."

D. C. MASTERS (Bishop's University) pointed out that the fundamental educational problem is philosophical. Issues are not to be decided by public opinion polls but by loyalty to unchanging moral and spiritual values and their interpretation in relation to changing conditions. His own group, like Dr. Lortie's and many others, believed in stressing unchanging values.

N. A. M. MacKenzie, in reply, claimed to have attempted to make clear his own conviction that Canadian education has, among its many roots, a rich debt to France, and that the system of education in French Canada has affected all Canadian education, and is itself enriched still from France. He defended his use of "progressive", claiming that, since life does not stand still, educational methods must change. He agreed with Dr. Jeanneret that administrators should teach. To Dr. Lortie's emphasis on discipline he would add the need for self-discipline, since pupils eventually leave the classrooms of their masters. With Dr. Masters' philosophy he fully agreed, but reminded him that translation of philosophy into action presents difficulties.

CULTURAL EVOLUTION

JEAN-C. FALARDEAU (Chairman, Department of Sociology, Laval University) entitled his remarks "The Artist as Dramatic Creator", agreeing to regard "culture" not as the total way of life in any society but as the creation and enjoyment of the finer things of life. Art is an individual activity, and the artist a dissatisfied person who, as Rainer Rilke stated, "starts where God, feeling tired, has stopped", and who strives to resolve or overcome the tension of the drama involved in the very fact of human existence. Like Jacob, he fights a "terrible angel". Until recently, Canadian art has been too largely of a descriptive nature. He continued:

"It has been so in painting, in music, in sculpture and in literature, as seen in the sociological character of the best Canadian novels, such as those of Gwethalyn Graham and Hugh MacLennan, in English; of Ringuet and Gabrielle Roy in French. Dramatic production has inevitably tended towards tragi-comedy or pure tragedy, like Gélinas' *Tit-Coq*. Yet, no future history of the arts in Canada will be complete without an analysis of the extent to which such institutions as the Canadian Broadcasting Corporation and the National Film Board have, both in English Canada and in French Canada, congregated, stimulated and even generated creative talents.

"Up to 1953 there have been in Canada a comforting number of works of art which stand by the exacting criterion which I have just set forth. I have already mentioned some plays. I refer once more to the novels of Hugh MacLennan and the works of great poets like A. M. Klein, Saint-Denys Garneau and Anne Hébert. If the volume of such works has not been what we would like it to be, one must frankly delve into the social factors that may account for such a paucity. The most potent prohibiting factor, in my opinion, has been, in English-speaking Canada, the puritanical mentality that has strait-jacketed the free expression of imagination and of boldness; in French Canada, its equivalent, the strong sanctions of a jansenistic mentality—although in the latter case rampant Jansenism has been swiftly counter-balanced by *joie de vivre* and incidental rabelaisian exuberance.

"An event of tremendous importance has happened last year in the course of our social and literary evolution. With the novel of André Langevin, *Evadé de la nuit,* suicide has appeared on the scene of French-Canadian literature. For the first time, a novelist has hemmed in his characters to the point where they have to face ultimate options, without support from the religious and social norms that hitherto gave meaning to their existence. Great art must have that frankness, and Langevin's novel is undoubtedly the first dramatic, truly 'universal' French-Canadian novel.

"The artist of the age of the atom bomb, of the age of imperial totalitarianism and of the age of emerging fascisms in many areas of North America—including our own house—this contemporary artist cannot feed on the fatness of 'material encouragement', nor on the idealized memories of a Victorian childhood, nor on Proustian psychological niceties. He must wrestle *alone* with Fate, through Hell and Purgatory. If he can, he must also remember that Paradise can be conquered only by spiritual violence."

W. P. PERCIVAL (Deputy Minister and Director of Protestant Education, Province of Quebec) expressed the conviction that "if we can find the means for the encouragement of the arts, letters and sciences, we shall never lack artists, philosophers and scholars." The universities may be the chief guardians of Canadian intellectual life, but the first line of defence is in schools and homes. These schools now carry people to Grade IX, as compared with Grade VII in 1914 and Grade III in the late eighteenth century. He made the further comment:

"This morning much was said concerning that school movement which is called 'Progressive'. This was defined for Canada by Dr. MacKenzie. It should be stated plainly that, though Canada has profited greatly from the Dewey philosophy, and though a few teachers may have carried his philosophy to extremes, the school systems of the Canadian provincial governments have never been too greatly influenced by the doctrines of Dewey's more rabid followers. Naturally, when a good idea is launched, the pendulum is apt to swing too far. The fact is, however, that the character of the school has improved greatly during the present century so that it has turned from one to which many children hated to go to one from which few desire to stay away. The quality of its teaching has also improved greatly and will continue to do so.

"Far from being too liberal in policy, the schools of the English people of Canada have maintained very conservative standards. In this they have been influenced by the schools of Great Britain, which they follow in no small degree, and by those of French-speaking Quebec, which maintains its conservative traditions. The problem is how to blend all these influences into a more mature whole."

MISS FREDA WALDON (Hamilton Public Library) thought that Miss Neatby's admirable paper erred on the side of pessimism, especially as regards libraries. The improvement of libraries is encouraging, because "although the contributions of industry are tremendously important, our civilization is largely based on print. This development in the last five to ten years has had the effect of putting a floor under all our other efforts to make this a more civilized country." More attention should be given to gifted individuals, and national assistance is imperative if genius is not to be wasted.

Hugh MacLennan (Montreal), as a writer, hesitated to tangle with the critics, stating that, like the fox who is the centre of the hunting scene, the author may have to suffer for his prominence. The Canadian author has the disadvantage that what he writes is usually published in New York or London, but Canada can take its place in the world. South Africa is doing well: Canada is improving. At any rate, "there is probably some very good business here, if we can only stop being so self-conscious about all this."

Miss Hilda Neatby, in summing up, claimed that the entire Conference was on the subject of Canadian culture. She came to the defence of the Puritans, stating that we need more of them, not fewer, citing Milton as an example and saying, "I do not agree that a puritanical mentality has curbed free expression of imagination, and I have read many critics who say that this cult of evil is overdone." As to Dr. Falardeau's point of view, she was in thorough sympathy with it, as she was with Dr. Percival's plea for the schools. Miss Waldon's optimism, however, must be balanced by a Canadian journalist's opinion that Canada is the hardest nation in which to sell a book, and a Canadian book merchant's assertion that Canadians simply do not buy books.

Trevor Moore (Vice-President, Imperial Oil Limited, Toronto) later added this comment on Miss Neatby's statement that wealthy patrons of the arts are less numerous than formerly:
    "In the past such patrons have been able to support art galleries, orchestras and individual artists. Taxation, both in-

come and succession duties, has reduced these numbers. I believe that business must take an increasing personal and financial interest in the growth and promotion of artistic appreciation, not only contributing from its own resources, but interesting many individuals in the community to do likewise. I do feel strongly that one of the responsibilities which business has to the community is the promotion of useful and artistic leisure, first, for the community, secondly, for the employees and thirdly, for those who are retired and will retire. The reasons are quite selfish. It seems obvious that workers in business and industry will be happier if their interests are widened and their cultural pleasures looked after."

Canada in the World

Miss Gwendolyn Carter (Professor of Government, Smith College, Northampton, Mass.) confined her comments to Dr. Creighton's assertion that the most significant new factor in recent history has been the emergence of Asia and the fact that India, Pakistan and Ceylon have remained in the Commonwealth. The Commonwealth in turn has become the responsibility of all its members, and Canada has a serious concern with these three successor states. Our opportunity to bridge civilization demands from us more than our present participation in the Colombo Plan, in training programmes of industry for Indians and Pakistanis, and the attendance of Asiatic students in our universities. Said Miss Carter:

"I have been in India since the war, and I realize there has been a wealth of good feeling toward Canada. No one doubts the good feeling toward India in this country, but what are we doing to spread public information and promote a real awareness of the problems of that country? Is there a place in our universities for learning about these countries, their civilization, their contributions, their problems? Are we building enough on the very real interest of our labour and farm groups? I know something is being done there but I wonder whether it is not just a start. I wonder, too, whether

$25,000,000, impressive as it may seem, is enough to be contributing to the monumental task of which Mr. Ambridge spoke yesterday?

"There is another area to which we must turn more attention. Mr. Creighton has said that it is not likely that either South America or Africa will produce important states of the future type of India, and that is quite true. But I think anybody who goes into the East today and moves among peoples of colour, knows that they have an intense feeling one for another; and they know, too, that Africa today is going through many developmental stages such as those which happened in Asia at the end of the war. In Africa a large portion of aid is required for those sections which are moving forward toward Commonwealth status.

"Just over three years ago I was on the Gold Coast where there is an African Prime Minister and virtually a full African Cabinet and the talk is very much of Commonwealth status. As you know, no doubt, Canada already is considering an agreement on aluminium. But I wonder again how much we really know about the problems of that country and whether there is not a great deal more that we could be doing ahead of the time when it arrives at Commonwealth status.

"The Central African Federation is a new experiment, federating Southern Rhodesia, Northern Rhodesia and Nyasaland, an extremely complex plural society. Could not we contribute something special there, because of our federal experience?

"I throw these out as suggestions of ways and means in which we can use what seems to me a highly creative relationship. It seems to me the relationship between this country and the United States can gain in prestige by developing a really creative partnership with Africa and thereby aid in the building up of a responsible, imaginative middle power in the world in the coming generation. And then I think also we should look abroad to our contacts with Asia and develop them."

K. W. TAYLOR (Deputy Minister of Finance, Ottawa) desired that, for the record, Miss Carter's reference to $25,000,000 as Canada's Colombo Plan contribution be understood as meaning that much per year ($75,000,000 up to 1953-54), with the remembrance that Canada has also contributed several millions through UN for technical assistance to less developed countries, and several tens of millions through the International Bank for Reconstruction and Development.

GEORGE V. FERGUSON (Editor, *Montreal Daily Star*) doubted whether events in fifty years would justify the picture outlined by Dr. Creighton and Dr. Carter, and felt that "the world, having rejected not unexpectedly the idea of the rule of law in disagreements, can look forward with some confidence to a war between now and 2003". For this he claimed support from an opinion expressed by Anthony Eden in 1944 that a "durable peace" meant one that would last twenty years, i.e., until 1964. "Before 2003 the pattern of events, of politics, may have taken a crude shift." The prolongation of present tensions would create increased pressures, and our freedom of choice in forming policies may be less than we hope.

"Besides that, it is visible now that a movement may be beginning to gather weight on this continent to discuss the problems of continental defence. We are no longer a distant country. We are a frontier country and we lie between the United States and its principal enemy. Through most of the next half-century we shall have to work out policies along with Asia, work on our policy of developing farm resources and energy, and develop policies with the United States for the defence of this continent. This last may mean the resurgence of the old isolationism that afflicted us over the last century."

EDGAR W. McINNIS (President, Canadian Institute of International Affairs) admitted the possibility of wars, since the past fifty years had seen two major conflicts, in which case there may not be any picture to project or, if there is one, it does not bear contemplation.

"Short of such major catastrophes, the patterns may not

change quite so rapidly as one might expect. We know the factors that are going to make for very great change with the rise of Asian nationalism and the emergence of atomic power. In the next ten, fifteen or twenty years there may be a major shock; but the things that determine Canada's foreign policy will be basically like those which determine it now. We are still going to be a trading nation, needing to find outlets for our growing and more diversified products. Our trade will grow in volume and probably will be more diversified in its outlets, but I doubt whether anything is going to arise so big and drastic in the economic picture of the world at large that it will change our basic relations with the United States or our economic connections on this continent.

"Integration will also grow with the changes in the world, especially those on the political side. The rise of Japan in the last fifty years indicates what may take place elsewhere in Asia. This new major power factor may supply a kind of balance with which we will have to deal.

"Mr. Creighton shared a hankering that comes over most of us at times for a more distinctive foreign policy, but we must reckon with the limitations placed upon us. Even if we set our goal high and evolve for our own purposes that kind of foreign policy which best suits our interests, we are likely to find that it is one which shares its common purposes and ideas with our great partners in the Western World with whom we have been hitherto associated. A foreign policy individually and independently evolved by Canada will, in the nature of things, approximate in its broad outline the kind of foreign policy suited to Great Britain and the United States. It may differ in some things, especially its economic factor. In the future we are likely to exercise an independent voice and outlook in the economic field where our growing power will lead to an individual characteristic of structure and interest that may allow us to make a real and distinctive contribution to the world of the future."

DONALD G. CREIGHTON agreed with Dr. Carter regarding Commonwealth responsibilities, and pleaded limitations of space as the reason for failing to bring out fully the points emphasized by Messrs. Ferguson and McInnis in connection with his anticipation of "a slightly greater independence or autonomy for Canada with respect to foreign policy". The point of view of the United States will be strongly influential in our conduct of foreign policy, but is likely to continue to be "fundamentally in accordance with what we really cherish". Our relationship with our neighbour, however, should be expressed not by silence or by fulsome compliments, but by showing what is in our hearts, modestly, it is true, and "with some appreciation of our ignorance, as a member of what we are proud to call a free world". If the Cold War should explode into a hot war instead of thawing out into a real peace, any prophecy here would be useless.

This concluded the discussion from the floor. The Chairman, after thanking the audience for its sustained interest and its ability to discuss important issues without recourse to jargon, recognized W. E. WILLIAMS (President and General Manager, The Procter & Gamble Co. of Canada, Limited, Hamilton) who expressed the thanks of the entire group to the Canadian Westinghouse Company Limited and Dr. Rogge for the conception that had inspired the Conference and for the hospitality afforded to the guests, and to the Chairman for what he regarded as a skilful handling of the sessions. This motion was seconded in French by LÉON LORTIE, and carried by a rising vote.

At the formal dinner in the evening, no discussion was planned. The dinner address by D. W. BROGAN, on the subject "An Outsider Looking In", was followed by a vote of thanks, proposed by R. C. WALLACE of Kingston, Ontario, to the guest speaker and to the Company. H. H. ROGGE, in acknowledging the thanks of his Company's guests, expressed his pleasure that the Conference had been so lively and profitable, and included the Conference Committee, the special committee on arrangements, the speakers, discussants and the Chairman in his thanks. The Chairman assured Dr. Rogge that the generosity of the Company and the unfailing labour of the Secretary and other Company officials were the real foundation of the Conference's success, and expressed his thanks to the group for their willingness to be guided from the chair in such matters as prompt attendance and the observance of a rigid time-schedule.

DATE DUE

APR 2 0 1981		
MAR 2 9 1981 REC'D		